Hospitality Success Strategies

HOSPITALITY SUCCESS STRATEGIES

Mahesh Chandra Singh

CENTRUM PRESS
NEW DELHI-110002 (INDIA)

CENTRUM PRESS

H.O.: 4360/4, Ansari Road, Daryaganj,
New Delhi-110002 (India)
Tel: 23278000, 23261597, 23255577, 23286875

B.O.: No. 1015, Ist Main Road, BSK IIIrd Stage,
IIIrd Phase, IIIrd Block, Bengaluru-560085 (INDIA)
Tel: 080-41723429

Email: centrumpress@gmail.com
Visit us at: www.centrumpress.com

Hospitality Success Strategies

First Edition, 2013

ISBN 978-93-81460-23-8

PRINTED IN INDIA

Printed at Balaji Offset, Delhi.

Contents

Preface (*vii*)

1. Strategy and Management of Hospitality Sector 1
2. Second Home Tourism: Impact, Planning and Strategy 40
3. Reducing Poverty Through Hospitality Business 84
4. Tourism as a Development Strategy 147
5. Financial Strategies for Hospitality Sector 203
6. Cooperation Strategies in Tourism Industry 229

Bibliography 253

Index 255

Preface

Starting a hotel requires careful choice of a location and strategy, a business plan, access to considerable financial resources, and a customer service mindset. The location for your hotel is highly linked with the opportunity that you feel there is for your hotel. In the right location, where competitors are not fulfilling all customer needs, a hotel can thrive. However, in a beautiful neighbourhood that happens to have heavy competition from existing hotels, success may not be so forthcoming. Likewise, if the neighbourhood leaves too much to be desired, you may not be able to price the rooms low enough to encourage travelers to stay at your hotel, even if you are within walking distance of key attractions. The next step is to know how customers will answer the question "why my hotel?" How will you tailor your services to the customers you want to attract, whether they are families with kids, couples on romantic vacations, businesspeople, or international tourists? Consider the combination of amenities, atmosphere, location, and services that will be right for your customers. Always keep in mind that strategy means making tradeoffs - it is almost impossible to be everything to everyone and succeed. You might have to forgo certain customer target markets in order to make your service offering perfect for your most desired customers. A simple, clear, but persuasive hotel business plan will be necessary not only for you to think through how you will take on the opportunity, but for you to convince any investor or lender that you have the ability to do so. No savvy investor will be attracted by a lack of planning. There is no excuse to not create a plan with the wealth of information available on writing business plans and even business plan templates tailored to the hotel business sector.

Whether you buy an existing hotel, build one from scratch, or renovate a building into a hotel, you will need millions of dollars to invest. Assuming you do not have this money, you will need to seek bank loans and/or angel investment in your hotel. As you will be working with considerable assets, dependable and experienced legal and accounting help is a must as you create deals with investors.

Finally, you must have an ingrained sense of how you want your guests to be treated so that you can instill this mindset in your top management and they can, in turn, teach this to the staff. Staying at a hotel can be stressful and uncomfortable, and guests demand the highest attention to their needs or they will have no problem complaining loudly and publicly. If employees sense you have higher motives than customer satisfaction, customer service may fall by the wayside and your hotel business may fail or never take off in the first place.

It is an approachable and readable text for students at all levels, from undergraduates to professionals retraining.

—Author

1

Strategy and Management of Hospitality Sector

Introduction: Recent and Future Trends in Tourism

Tourism can be considered one of the most remarkable socioeconomic phenomena of the twentieth century. From an activity "enjoyed by only a small group of relatively well-off people" during the first half of the last century, it gradually became a mass phenomenon during the post-World War II period, particularly from the 1970s onwards. It now reaches larger and larger numbers of people throughout the world, and is a source of employment for a significant segment of the labour force.

Although domestic tourism currently accounts for approximately 80 per cent of all tourist activity, many countries tend to give priority to international tourism because, while the former basically involves a regional redistribution of national income, the latter has now become the world's largest source of foreign exchange receipts. According to the latest figures compiled by the World Tourism Organization (WTO), foreign exchange earnings from international tourism reached a peak of US$ 476 billion in 2000, which was larger than the export value of petroleum products, motor vehicles, telecommunications equipment or any other single category of product or service.

International tourist arrivals grew at an annual average rate of 4.3 per cent during the 1990s, despite major international political and economic crises, such as the Gulf War and the Asian financial crisis. According to the latest WTO figures, compiled with data received up to August 2001, the turn of the millennium recorded one of the most impressive annual growth rates in international tourism. The September 2001 terrorist attacks in the United States, however, appear to have had a more serious impact on the tourist sector than any other major international crisis in recent decades. The attacks had a particularly severe impact on air transport, business travel and long-haul travel.

Worldwide travel reservations were estimated to have dropped by 15 per cent at the end of October 2001, although not every destination nor every part of the tourism sector was badly affected. For example, while air transport and luxury hotels have suffered from considerable fall in demand, travel within the same country or region, as well as travel by rail and road, appear to have weathered the worst effects of the crisis, or even benefited from it.

Nevertheless, initial forecasts of 3-4 per cent rise in international tourist arrivals for 2001, made before the September 2001 attacks, were subsequently revised downwards to around a 1 per cent increase over the 2000 figures. The latest data, released by WTO in January 2002, show that there was a sharp decline of 1.3 per cent in international arrivals, to a total of less than 690 million, in 2001.7 Given that the northern hemisphere summer holiday season was coming to end by the time the attacks took place, this significant drop confirms that the short-term impacts of the attacks were devastating to international tourism as a whole. The last four months of 2001, in fact, recorded a drop of almost 11 per cent in arrivals worldwide and substantial decreases in all regions of theworld.

It is worth noting, however, that this considerable fall in international arrivals was caused not only by a widespread fear of traveling generated by the attacks – particularly in airplanes and to certain destinations – but also by a downturn in the world economy. The economic downturn that began in the United States during the first half of 2001 had already been affecting the tourism sector before the terrorist attacks were carried out. The attacks merely aggravated the economic slowdown already under way.

According to the most recent United Nations economic forecasts, growth of only 1.5 per cent in gross world product

(GWP) is expected in 2002, as compared to 1.3 per cent last year. Such a modest improvement is linked to a number of economic uncertainties, notably the high dependency of the global economy on the recovery of the United States. Higher rates of population growth would thus make 2002 the second consecutive year with no real growth in per capita GWP. This, in turn, is also likely to undermine the short-term prospects for a recovery in international tourism, at least until mid-2002, when the summer holiday season begins in the northern hemisphere, and probably until the end of the year. Although much will depend on the evolution of the world economy during this year, it is also likely that some destinations will experience a prolonged decline in tourism revenues regardless of any world economic improvements.

In the medium and long term, however, international tourism is expected to resume its rapid growth, in view of rising living standards and discretionary incomes, falling real costs of travel, expansion and improvement of various transport modes, increasing amounts of free time and other factors. The World Tourism Organization has recently reiterated its long-term forecasts, made before the September 2001 attacks, of an average annual growth rate in international arrivals of over 4 per cent in the period up to 2020.10 The number of international arrivals is thus expected to reach the striking mark of 1 billion by 2010 and 1.6 billion by 2020.

Main Economic Benefits of Tourism

Tourism, as a sector that comprises an extensive range of economic activities, can be considered the largest industry in the world. International tourism is also one of the fastest growing and most ramified sectors of the global economy, covering a broad range of enterprises, sectors and stakeholders. During the 1990s, when the globalization of tourism reached unprecedented proportions, international tourism receipts had a much higher average annual growth rate (7.3 per cent) than that of gross world product. By 1999, international tourism receipts accounted for more than 8 per cent of the worldwide export value of goods and services, overtaking the export value of other leading world industries such as automotive products, chemicals, and computer and office equipment.

Tourism is also the only major service sector in which developing countries have consistently recorded trade surpluses relative to the rest of the world. Between 1980 and 1996, for instance, their travel account surplus increased from $4.6 billion to $65.9 billion, due primarily to the impressive growth of inbound tourism to countries in Africa, the Caribbean, and the Asia and Pacific regions. The 1990s also experienced a significant growth of international tourism receipts in the 49 poorest developing countries: total tourism receipts in these countries more than doubled from US$ 1 billion in 1992 to over US$ 2.2 billion in 1998.15 Tourism is now the second largest source of foreign exchange earnings in the 49 least developed countries (LDCs) as a whole, after the oil industry, which is concentrated in only three of these countries.

Tourism has become the main source of income for the economies of an increasing number of small island developing States (SIDS) – as well as less developed regions of large countries – with a natural environment appealing to tourists. Foreign exchange earnings can, however, vary significantly among these tourism-driven economies because of 'leakages' arising from imports of equipment for construction and consumer goods required by tourists, repatriation of profits earned by foreign investors and amortization of foreign debt incurred in tourist development.

Besides export earnings, international tourism also generates an increasingly significant share of government (national and local) tax revenues throughout the world. In addition, the development of tourism as a whole is usually accompanied by considerable investments in infrastructure, such as airports, roads, water and sewerage facilities, telecommunications and other public utilities. Such infrastructural improvements not only generate benefits to tourists but can also contribute to improving the living conditions of local populations. This increase in social overhead capital can also help attract other industries to a disadvantaged area and thus be crucial to regional economic development.

The tourism sector is an increasingly important source of employment – including in tourism-related sectors, such as construction and agriculture – primarily for unskilled labour, migrants from poor rural areas, people who prefer to work part-time, and notably women. Because the sector is relatively labour-intensive, investments in tourism tend to generate a larger and more rapid increase in employment than equal investment in other economic activities. Furthermore, given that the sector provides a considerable amount of jobs for women and unskilled workers, tourism can significantly contribute to empowering women and alleviating poverty. At the same time, available data suggests that most workers in the tourism sector, notably in hotels and catering, tend to earn less than workers in socially comparable occupations in both developed and developing countries. In addition, the differential tends to be larger in less developed countries and regions, particularly those with high rates of unemployment amongst unskilled labour. Informal employment relations in small and medium-sized enterprises, which employ about half of the labour force in the hotel and catering sub-sectors worldwide, also contribute to a relatively high proportion of child labour and non-remunerated employment in these sub-sectors in many countries.

The increasing reliance of less diversified economies on tourism also increases their vulnerability to international shocks, such as, natural disasters, regional wars and other unexpected events. The recent crisis generated by fear of international terrorism, for example, caused devastating immediate effects on tourism-dependent economies, including regional economies in large countries. In addition, sudden changes in consumer tastes and sharp economic downturns pose significant risks to such economies, given that demand for mass tourism tends to be relatively income-elastic and can produce drastic negative responses to economic recession in source markets. Nonetheless, it is now generally recognized that tourism can make a vital contribution to employment, export receipts and national income in most countries and regions. Furthermore, tourism is often identified as the most promising driving force for the economic development of less developed countries and regions endowed with areas of natural beauty – including small island developing States – because it offers them a valuable opportunity for economic diversification.

Environmental Impacts of Tourism

While tourism provides considerable economic benefits for many countries, regions and communities, its rapid expansion can also be responsible for adverse environmental (and sociocultural) impacts. Natural resource depletion and environmental degradation associated with tourism activities are sometimes serious problems in tourism-rich regions. The management of natural resources to reverse this trend is thus one of the most difficult challenges for governments at different levels. The fact that most tourists chose to maintain their relatively high patterns of consumption (and waste generation) when they reach their destinations can be a particularly serious problem for developing countries and regions without the appropriate means for protecting their natural resources and local ecosystems from the pressures of mass tourism. The main environmental impacts of tourism are (a) pressure on natural resources, (b) pollution and waste generation and (c) damage to ecosystems. Furthermore, it is now widely recognized that not only uncontrolled tourism expansion is likely to lead to environmental degradation, but also that environmental degradation, in turn, poses a serious threat to tourism.

Pressure on Natural Resources

In addition to pressure on the availability and prices of resources consumed by local residents – such as energy, food and basic raw materials – the main natural resources at risk from tourism development are land, freshwater and marine resources. Without careful land-use planning, for instance, rapid tourism development can intensify competition for land resources with other uses and lead to rising land prices and increased pressure to build on agricultural land. Intensive tourism development can also threaten natural landscapes, notably though deforestation, loss of wetlands and soil erosion. Tourism development in coastal areas – including hotel, airport and road construction – is a matter for increasing concern worldwide as it can lead to sand mining, beach erosion and land degradation.

Freshwater availability for competing agricultural, industrial, household and other uses is rapidly becoming one of the most critical natural resource issues in many countries and regions.

Rapid expansion of the tourism industry, which tends to be extremely water-intensive, can exacerbate this problem by placing considerable pressure on scarce water supply in many destinations. Water scarcity can pose a serious limitation to future tourism development in many low-lying coastal areas and small islands that have limited possibility for surface water use and storage, and whose groundwater may be contaminated by saltwater intrusion. Over-consumption by many tourist facilities – notably large hotel resorts and golf courses – can limit current supplies available to farmers and local populations in water-scarce regions and thus lead to serious shortages and price rises. In addition, pollution of available freshwater sources, some of which may be associated with tourism-related activities, can exacerbate local shortages. Rapid expansion of coastal and ocean tourism activities, such as snorkelling, scuba diving and sport fishing, can threaten coral reefs and other marine resources. Disturbance to marine aquatic life can also be caused by the intensive use of thrill craft, such as jet skis, frequent boat tours and boat anchors. Anchor damage is now regarded as one of the most serious threats to coral reefs in the Caribbean Sea, in view of the growing number of both small boats and large cruise ships sailing in the region. Severe damage to coral reefs and other marine resources may, in turn, not only discourage further tourism and threaten the future of local tourist industries, but also damage local fisheries.

Pollution and Waste Generation

Besides the consumption of large amounts of natural and other local resources, the tourism industry also generates considerable waste and pollution. Improper disposal of liquid and solid waste generated by the tourism industry has become a particular problem for many developing countries and regions that lack the capacity to treat these waste materials properly. Disposal of such untreated waste has, in turn, contributed to reducing availability of the above-mentioned resources at the local level. Apart from the contamination of freshwater from pollution by untreated sewage, tourist activities can also lead to land contamination from solid waste and the contamination of marine waters and coastal areas from pollution generated by hotels and marinas, as well as cruise ships. It is estimated that cruise ships in the Caribbean Sea alone produced more than 70,000 tons of liquid and solid waste a year during the mid-1990s. The fast growth of the cruise sector in the region may have exacerbated this problem in recent years. Furthermore, a particular cause of concern for coastal areas and small islands is the illegal disposal of sewage, solid waste and cargo residues by merchant ships, which cause marine and beach pollution.

In addition, relatively high levels of energy consumption in hotels – including energy for airconditioning, heating and cooking– as well as fuel used by tourism-related transportation can also contribute significantly to local air pollution in many host countries and regions. Local air and noise pollution linked to exhaustive tourism development or urban congestion can sometimes even discourage tourists from visiting some destinations.

Damage to Ecosystems

Intensive tourism activity in natural areas can interfere with fragile vegetation and wildlife and cause irreversible damage to ecosystems, particularly if the infrastructure in those areas is not adequately prepared to absorb mass tourism.

Uncontrolled tourism activities can lead to the severe disruption of wildlife habitats and increased pressure on endangered species. As it has been widely documented, it can also disrupt wildlife behaviour, such as, tourist vehicles in Africa's national parks that approach wild cats and thus distract them from hunting and breeding; tour boat operators in the Caribbean Sea that feed sharks to ensure that they remain in tourist areas; and whale-watching boat crews around the world that pursue whales and dolphins and even encourage petting, which tends to alter the animals' feeding and behaviour.

Tourism can also lead to the indiscriminate clearance of native vegetation for the development of new facilities, increased demand for fuelwood and even forest fires. Ecologically fragile areas, such as rain forests, wetlands and mangroves, are also threatened by intensive or irresponsible tourist activity. Moreover, as will be discussed below, it is increasingly recognized that, the rapid expansion of nature tourism (or 'Eco-tourism') may also pose a threat to ecologically fragile areas, including natural world heritage sites, if not properly managed and monitored. In many countries, coastlines are becoming overbuilt due to tourism development until the damage caused by environmental degradation – and the eventual loss of revenues arising from a collapse in tourism arrivals – becomes irreversible. As mentioned above, intensive tourism development and recreational activities in coastal areas can not only lead to beach destruction and coastal degradation, but can also threaten coral reefs and other marine ecosystems. The delicate ecosystems of most small islands, together with their increasing reliance on tourism as a main tool of socioeconomic development, means that these environmental impacts can be particularly damaging since the success of the sector in these islands often depends on the quality of their natural environment. In addition, pollution of coastal waters – in particular by sewage, solid waste, sediments and untreated chemicals – often leads to the deterioration of coastal ecosystems, notably coral reefs, and thus harms their value for tourism.

The equally fragile ecosystems of mountain regions are also threatened by increasing popular tourist activities such as skiing, snowboarding and trekking. One of the most serious environmental problems in mountainous developing countries without appropriate energy supply is deforestation arising from increasing consumption of fuelwood by the tourism industry. This often results not only in the destruction of local habitats and ecosystems, but also in accelerating processes of erosion and landslides. Other major problems arising from tourist activities in mountain regions include disruption of animal migration by road and tourist facilities, sewage pollution of rivers, excessive water withdrawals from streams to supply resorts and accumulation of solid waste on trails.

Environmental Threats to Tourism

In many mountain regions, small islands, coastal areas and other ecologically fragile places visited by tourists, there is an increasing concern that the negative impacts of tourism on the natural environment can ultimately hurt the tourism industry itself. There is now plenty of evidence of the 'life-cycle' of a tourist destination, that is, "its evolution from discovery, to development, to eventual decline, ... attributed to a site's overuse and the subsequent deterioration of key attractions or facilities." In other words, the negative impacts of intensive tourism activities on the environmental quality of beaches, mountains, rivers, forests and other ecosystems also compromise the viability of the tourism industry in these places.

In addition, tourism in many destinations could be particularly threatened by global environmental problems, notably the potential threat of 'global warming'. There is increasing scientific evidence that human activity has begun to change the average temperature on the Earth's surface. According to the authoritative United Nations Intergovernmental Panel on Climate Change (IPCC), this process of global warming has been caused by several factors associated with the intensification of economic activities, including the emissions of 'greenhouse gases', such as carbon dioxide produced by burning fossil fuels and forests.

Sustainable Tourism: The Way Forward

Countries and regions where the economy is driven by the tourism industry are becoming increasingly concerned with the environmental, as well as the socio-cultural problems associated with unsustainable tourism. As a result, there is now increasing agreement on the need to promote sustainable tourism development to minimize its environmental impacts and to ensure more sustainable management of natural resources. The concept of sustainable tourism, as developed in the United Nations sustainable development process, refers to tourist activities "leading to management of all resources in such a way that economic, social and aesthetic needs can be fulfilled while maintaining cultural integrity, essential ecological processes, biological diversity and life support systems."

These sustainability concerns are, therefore, beginning to be addressed by governments at national, regional and local, as well as international, levels. In addition, given the leading role of the private sector in the tourism industry in most countries, many initiatives have also been taken by this sector. Broadly speaking, the main policy areas regarding sustainable tourism are: (a) the promotion of national strategies for sustainable tourism development, including the decentralization of environmental management to regional and local levels, (b) the use of both regulatory mechanisms and economic instruments, (c) the support for voluntary initiatives by the industry itself, and (d) the promotion of sustainable tourism at the international level.

National and Regional Strategies for Sustainable Tourism Development

Generally speaking, the main priority for national and regional governments is to incorporate tourism planning and development effectively into overall sustainable development strategies. For example, regional development strategies for areas containing water resources that an integrated manner that considers all potential water users. Government policies to promote the domestic tourism industry and to attract foreign direct investment should also ensure that tourism is properly planned and managed so as to minimize adverse environmental impacts and its use of natural resources.

Since the environmental impacts of tourism development are primarily felt at the local and regional levels, national Governments need to promote decentralization of public environment management to the regional and municipal levels. Given that in many countries, local and regional governments already have important responsibilities for tourism development, central Governments should also support capacity building programmes at lower levels in order to enable local and regional authorities to better respond to the challenges of sustainable tourism development in the areas under their jurisdiction. National and local governments also need to develop clear strategies to monitor progress towards sustainable tourism.

Last but far from least, governments at all levels can greatly benefit from working in partnership with all major stakeholders, including local communities, to ensure their active participation in tourism planning, development and management, as well as in the sharing of benefits. Participation of local communities in decision-making and sharing of benefits also helps to generate better awareness of the environmental costs of tourism and thus provides strong incentives to conserve natural resources and protect local environmental assets. Governments, together with the tourism industry and other stakeholders, should also promote or support various efforts to raise public awareness about the impact of tourists on destinations, to promote respect for local communities and their cultures and to protect the environment. Such public awareness campaigns often succeed in promoting positive behavioural changes not only in tourists, but also in tourism workers and host communities as a whole.

Regulatory Mechanisms and Economic Instruments

Sustainable tourism can also be promoted by a careful mix of government policies comprising both direct regulation and market-based instruments, although financial incentives that encourage environmentally damaging activities, such as energy subsidies, should be reduced or removed. The major challenge for governments is, therefore, to formulate and effectively apply an appropriate mix of regulatory and economic instruments for both sustainable natural resources management and environmental protection.

The most direct tool for promoting sustainable tourism involves the use of regulatory mechanisms, such as, integrated land-use planning and coastal zone management. In many cases, it may be necessary to protect coastlines through rigid building restrictions, such as, existing with externalities is thus to internalize them through taxes so that the full costs of production are reflected in prices.

One well-known example of charging user fees to support environmental conservation is the Bonaire protected marine areas in the Netherlands Antilles. This was one of the first protected marine parks in the Caribbean to become entirely self-financing through the levying of admission fees on scuba divers. The (private) diving industry in Bonaire was initially opposed to the levy because of its potential negative impacts on future demand and revenues, against the background of intense competition offered by many Caribbean diving destinations.

The system, however, has been an unqualified success since it was introduced in January 1992 because many divers (and an increasing number of tourists in general) are willing and able to pay higher prices to support environmental protection. Fees from this scheme also support the active management of the park's coral reef and mangrove ecosystems, as well as educational activities and orientation sessions for divers.

Voluntary Industry Initiatives

As noted above, tourism services in most countries are provided primarily by the private sector, which tends to oppose greater government regulation and taxation of the industry on the grounds that they are ultimately detrimental to efficiency, competitiveness and profits. The predominantly private tourism industry has thus developed several self-regulation and voluntary initiatives to promote greater environmental sustainability. These include waste and pollution reduction schemes, voluntary codes of conduct, industry awards and eco-labels for sustainable tourism. In addition, environmental management schemes to encourage responsible practices have been promoted in various sub-sectors, including hotel and catering, recreation and entertainment, transportation, travel agencies and tour operators.

For example, the World Travel and Tourism Council (WTTC), the main international industry association, has developed an environmental management programme (Green Globe), for both travel and tourism companies and tourism destinations, aimed to raise the level of environmental awareness and to provide a low-cost practical means for improving the environmental performance of the industry. It is also responsible for ECoNETT, an internet-based tool that provides an extensive information resource on all tourism and environmental issues. Another innovative global programme is the International Hotel Environment Initiative (IHEI), led by a council of leading international hotel chains, aimed to promote environmental management in the hotel industry, which is one of the main consumers of resources and sources of waste. Such initiatives are particularly important not only because they can lead to significant reductions of water and energy consumption, as well as liquid and solid waste, but also because they promote positive behavioural changes in both tourists and employees. In addition, they can lead to improved economic efficiency and increased profitability.

At the regional level, it is worth noting the successful implementation of the Blue Flag Programme, which now extends to 18 countries in Europe, in providing an incentive to protect and improve the quality of beaches and coasts. Under this programme, environmental standards at individual beaches in Europe are assessed by measuring compliance with acceptable concentrations of a range of pollutants to ensure clean bathing water. Beaches are also judged by their compliance with guidelines dealing with litter management, the availability of sanitary and beach safety facilities, and environmental education. Beaches that meet these stringent criteria receive Blue Flag awards, which also serve as a marketing tool to attract tourists.

Despite these helpful initiatives of the tourism industry to improve its standards of environmental management and protection, the very proliferation of such voluntary codes of conduct and eco-label awards at global, regional and local levels – which are not, in any case, adopted or recognized by all industry enterprises – can sometimes lead to confusion and difficulty to evaluate and compare them. While national and regional governments should fully support these voluntary initiatives and encourage the dissemination of the best practices in the private tourism industry, there is also a role for independent supervision, monitoring and comparative assessment by relevant government agencies.

In addition, trustworthy codes of conduct, transparent eco-label awards and internationally agreed programmes of action for sustainable tourism are required at the international level. The international community has a particularly crucial role to play in developing a set of internationally recognized accreditation and monitoring systems for assessing the sustainability of tourism services around the world.

International Activities in Support of Sustainable Tourism

Although tourism was not specifically addressed in Agenda 21 – the international programme of action on sustainable development agreed on at the 1992 Earth Summit in Rio de Janeiro (Brazil) – its growing economic importance, significant use of natural resources and environmental impact all contributed to its gradual introduction into the international sustainable development agenda over the past ten years.

One of the first concrete sectoral programmes of action arising from the increasing cooperation between the tourism industry and inter-governmental agencies was 'Agenda 21 for the Travel and Tourism Industry,' an action plan for sustainable tourism development jointly launched by the World Tourism Organization, the above-mentioned WTTC and the Earth Council in 1996. Among its innovative key objectives are the estimation of the economic value for resources, such as wildlife, natural areas and cultural heritage, "whose conservation would otherwise be seen as having no financial value," and the establishment of "essential infrastructure, such as water treatment plants, for residents as well as visitors ... (in order to) stimulate other economic activities." Many tourism-based communities and regions have also formulated their own 'Agenda 21s' at the local and regional levels.

In 1997, the United Nations General Assembly, at its special session to review the five-year implementation of Agenda 21, decided that there was a need to consider the importance of tourism in the context of Agenda 21 and to "develop an action-oriented international programme of work on sustainable tourism." This request was followed up during the seventh annual session of the United Nations Commission for Sustainable Development (CSD), held in New York in 1999, which discussed tourism as an economic sector and held a multi-stakeholder dialogue on the topic.

The Commission adopted an international work programme on sustainable tourism development, which is due to be reviewed during the forthcoming World Summit for Sustainable Development in Johannesburg (South Africa) later this year, as part of the ten-year review of progress achieved since the Earth Summit. The CSD also invited the World Tourism Organization to seek further input from the private sector, non-governmental organizations and other stakeholders in the further development of its proposed global code of ethics that had been drafted in consultation with the industry over the previous two years.

The final 'Global Code of Ethics for Tourism,' introduced by the World Tourism Organization in late 1999, sets a frame of reference for the responsible and sustainable development of international tourism. It includes nine articles outlining the basic rules for governments, tour operators, developers, travel agents, workers, as well as host communities and the tourists themselves. The tenth article deals with implementation and includes a proposed mechanism for conciliation, through the creation of a World Committee on Tourism Ethics made up of representatives of each region of the world and representatives of each group of stakeholders in the tourism sector, governments, the private sector, and labour and non-governmental organizations. The United Nations General Assembly adopted the Global Code of Ethics for Tourism at the end of 2001.

Although progress has been achieved over the past ten years, one of the key remaining challenges for the international community is to devise ways and means to assist developing countries to ensure that their tourism industries become more internationally competitive without damaging their natural resources and environmental assets base. This will require, amongst other things, greater technical and financial assistance, including human resources development, institutional capacity building and the transfer of environmentally sound technologies to many developing countries. The international community could also support the wider use of 'debt-fornature swaps', through which a portion of the foreign debt of developing countries is purchased at a discount by various international partners in exchange for the debtor's country investment of an agreed sum of local currency in environmental protection projects.

Economic Impacts, Economic Values, and Market Segmentation

An important factor in Eco-tourism development is the amount of revenue that remains within local economies (Seidl 1994). For example, economic benefits derived from Eco-tourism can contribute to residents having positive attitudes toward local natural areas (Lindberg and others 1996) and serve as economic incentives for natural resource conservation (Wunder 2000). Alternatively, if local residents bear the costs of tourism without receiving any benefits, they may be unsupportive of not only tourism but also the conservation of natural areas on which tourism is based. Sustainable tourism development must meet the needs of the host population in terms of improved living standards while satisfying the demands of tourism and protecting the natural environment (Seidl 1994). The costs and benefits of protection may not be distributed equally among tourism providers and local residents (Dixon and Sherman 1990).

Measuring the economic impacts of tourism and outdoor recreation has received considerable attention in academic literature. Economic impacts generally are examined within a costbenefit framework with the benefits measured by using expenditure surveys combined with input-output analysis. Travel cost or contingent valuation methods also are commonly used to place dollar values on natural areas or marginal changes in their characteristics. The trend toward greater reliance on user fees in the financial management of public lands also has led to many studies examining fees and pricing policies.

Measuring economic impacts or values derived from tourism necessitates differentiating between the economic benefits derived from the various forms of tourism. One of the problems in determining the economic impact of Eco-tourism, for example, is knowing what is meant by the term (Tisdell 1996). Differentiating between economic benefits derived from Eco-tourism and those derived from general tourism can depend on how each is defined.

When Eco-tourism is defined less restrictively, as simply tourism derived from nature preserves, parks, or refuges, researchers tend to assume that all economic impacts derived from those natural areas are Eco-tourism-derived impacts. Economic impacts are measured by using expenditure surveys of tourists visiting those areas. Tourism expenditures assumed to be generated by a particular natural area may be reported for a well-defined geographic area or combined with input-output analysis to describe secondary impacts. An alternative to surveying tourists is surveying local businesses and residents.

When Eco-tourism is defined more restrictively and confined to particular types of tourism activity or particular types of tourists, researchers attempt to segment tourists into the categories of ecotourist and general tourist. One approach identifies ecotourists as those individuals pursuing recreational activities that are assumed to characterize Eco-tourism. Economic impacts might then be based on the economic value of specific outdoor recreation activities. For example, studies have estimated the economic value of wildlife viewing (Navrud and Mungatana 1994), birdwatching, and whitewater recreation (Johnson and Moore 1993), among other activities.

Another approach confines Eco-tourism to tourists possessing certain attitudes or motives. Attitude or motive-based segmentation combines surveys of tourists with factor and cluster analysis to segment tourists according to their trip motives or socioeconomic characteristics. This method has been used to segment ecotourists from general tourists and ecotour operators from nonecotour operators (Bottrill and Pearce 1995). Segmentation can be used to disaggregate expenditure, travel cost, or contingent valuation survey results into Eco-tourism and general tourism economic impacts. Segmentation also can be used to evaluate how preferences for site management differ among ecotourists and general tourists.

Selecting an appropriate method for segmenting different types of tourism and tourists depends on the location and situation of interest. Focusing on specific natural areas may be appropriate in some cases, whereas focusing on different types of tourists may be appropriate in others. Some tourists may visit one location to escape commercial development, whereas others may expect typical tourist services offered by national franchises. Different tourists may differ in their spending and rates of visitation. Individual trips might take on characteristics of Eco-tourism at some times and characteristics of general tourism at others (Lindberg 1991). Recognition of different types of tourism and tourists, the economic impacts different tourists generate, and the use and nonuse values they hold with respect to their tourism experience can have important implications for how tourism economics research is conducted.

Planning and Development Case Studies

Perhaps the greatest proportion of published Eco-tourism literature presents case studies examining political, social, economic, and environmental issues related to tourism development in specific locations. Some studies focus more directly on difficulties associated with Eco-tourism planning and development. For example, Eco-tourism development can be adversely impacted by inadequate protection of natural areas on which Eco-tourism is based (Wells 1993). National political and economic priorities can dominate regional or local priorities, thereby leading to national policies that are incompatible with sustainable tourism development (Tosun 1998). In other locations, prodevelopment and proprotection roles might be reversed. Disagreement may exist between national protection interests and the economic development aspirations of local communities (Prunier and others 1993).

Sustainable tourism advocates may not always agree with local residents. What sustainable tourism advocates may see as potential conflicts between tourism development and natural resource protection, local residents may see as desirable economic development. Failure to involve communities in tourism development decisions along with an inability of policymakers to form an integrated regional vision can be obstacles to sustainable development (Ioannides 1995). Progress toward sustainability most likely occurs in communities that recognize the potential costs and benefits of tourism and are willing to take a proactive approach in its planning and management (Godfrey 1998).

Collaboration is a common theme advocated for successful Eco-tourism development. Cooperation and coordination between public and private sectors are important. Several case studies describe integrated roles of natural resources management agencies, tourism service industries, government agencies, and local communities as important factors leading to successful Eco-tourism development. Many studies advocate the need for community involvement and outline community-based tourism development strategies.

Community involvement can be impeded by disagreement over the level or type of tourism development desired (Wyllie 1998). It can be difficult to discern whether tourism development is an appropriate alternative to other types of economic development in different locations (Joppe 1996). A potential problem of basing a local economy on tourism is that tourism injects money into the economy without producing more goods for people to consume. This can result in local price inflation, which is worsened by the presence of tourists who increase demand (Seidl 1994). For many communities, tourism will have a limited growth potential. Economic activity based on tourism and recreation can suffer significant seasonal variability (Keith and others 1996). Eco-tourism is subject to fluctuations owing to ups and downs in the trendiness of given destinations and modes of travel (Seidl 1994). Local residents also may face significant opportunity costs associated with restrictions on local resource use, whereas the benefits of protection may not be readily apparent. Tourism should be viewed as part of an overall economic and environmental plan that includes other industries (Anderson 1994).

Researchers argue that overdeveloped or unsustainable tourism results from the openaccess nature of natural resources on which tourism is based. Overdevelopment can result in damage to natural resources and reduced enjoyment by tourists because of congestion and site degradation.

Steele (1995) argues that problems derived from open access can be remedied if control over the resource is assigned to governments, local communities, or private entities who can restrict access. Assigning control to one entity, however, can lead to other problems. For example, governments may feel compelled to maintain open access as a service to the public (Lindberg 1991). Development of seemingly sustainable tourism also can lead to unsustainable tourism development if tourism businesses are unable to resist the temptation to increase visitors (Weaver 1995). Economic incentives often run counter to preservation and favour development (Backman and others 1994). Tourism development also potentially can spark desired or undesired growth in nontourism sectors.

Establishing Criteria for Success

Several studies propose specific principles, criteria, or guidelines by which to judge Eco-tourism development success. Some attempts at sustainable tourism development also have relied on the implementation of charters or codes of ethics designed to guide the activities of tourists and the tourism industry. Dowling (1993) proposes an environmentally based tourism development planning model as one way to implement environmentally compatible sustainable tourism. The usefulness of such prescriptions for Eco-tourism likely are dependent on specific circumstances of specific locations.

Tourism Research and the USDA Forest Service

National forests and other public lands undoubtedly have played a role in attracting tourism in many communities located near them, by providing significant outdoor recreation opportunities in relatively undeveloped settings. Much of this tourism fits within new nature-based tourism, Eco-tourism, and sustainable tourism concepts.

Many of the issues and concerns that motivate interest in new forms of tourism are consistent with the traditional conservation-oriented multiple-use objectives that have characterized national forest management. Although outdoor recreation historically has been an important component of research conducted by the USDA Forest Service, tourism research has not. Although recreation and tourism research address many similar concepts and issues, little integration exists between the two. Increasing recognition of the role of national forests as tourism destinations may imply a need to expand traditional outdoor recreation planning to include inquiry into the economic, social, and ecological impacts of tourism.

Evaluating National Forests as Tourism Resources

An important factor in tourism development is whether natural or cultural resources exist on which to base a tourism industry. New tourism concepts, such as Eco-tourism, may require natural areas or cultures that are relatively unique or pristine. Economic feasibility depends on a site having a marketable product (Seidl 1994). Not all locations are sufficiently unique to draw tourists. If a location is a less popular or highly specialized destination, there can be risks involved in developing a reliance on tourism (Anderson 1991).

Poor accessibility owing to remoteness or inadequate transportation systems can constrain tourism growth. Some communities may be unable to provide or develop necessary complementary tourist services.

Different scales and types of tourism development may be appropriate in different locations. Some communities located near national forests or other public lands likely possess comparative advantages in offering relatively undeveloped natural areas potentially of interest to tourists seeking outdoor recreation opportunities. Whether their comparative advantages in tourism exceed those in other natural resource-based industries is not always clear. Evaluating the existing and potential role national forests can play in attracting local and regional tourism likely would aid national forest managers in natural resource planning.

Forest Management Impacts on Tourism

In addition to the natural resource endowments provided by national forests, how those endowments are managed will significantly impact the numbers and types of tourists that will be attracted. Traditional multiple-use objectives of national forests may be incompatible with certain types of tourism. For example, it is plausible that certain types of tourists may be unwilling to accept any signs of intensive forest management for commercial timber production. Locations that can enhance or maintain their relative environmental quality will improve their comparative advantage over other destinations. Also, certain recreational activities may be incompatible with others, thereby resulting in conflicts between different tourists seeking different forms of recreation. Hikers may be at odds with off-road vehicle users, hunters may be at odds with birdwatchers, and motorized boaters may be at odds with nonmotorized boaters. Accommodating every type of tourist may be infeasible in every location. Tourism planning may require aligning forest management with the preferences of tourists in specific locations. User surveys could assist in identifying specific outdoor amenities and forest management activities that attract or repell different types of tourists and aid in developing appropriate forest management prescriptions in specific locations.

Evaluating Economic, Social, and Ecological Tradeoffs

Recent literature on tourism tends to differentiate between mass tourism, which is viewed as environmentally and culturally destructive, and alternative forms of tourism developed on a smaller scale so as to minimize adverse impacts to local environments and cultures. These alternative forms of tourism, it is argued, provide local residents greater employment opportunities, maintain a greater share of economic benefits within the local area, and result in less negative impacts (Hampton 1998). In contrast, mass tourism is associated with large-scale, high-density accommodations, contrived attractions, seasonal markets, and limited benefits to the local economy with minimal concern for carrying capacity and a lack of local involvement (Weaver 1995). One advantage of tourism development on a larger scale, however, is the ability for local government agencies to control accommodation standards and recoup tax revenues through licensing, which is more difficult with more fragmented and small-scale tourism development (Carey and others 1997). Different types and scales of tourism development imply economic, social, and ecological tradeoffs.

Virtually any kind of tourism activity will result in some impact to natural resources somewhere (Cater 1993, Hunter 1997). Despite strong ethical and environmental motives, ecotourists still are seeking primarily pleasure and entertainment (McKercher 1993a). As Prunier and others suggest, a person who wishes to be a "green" holidaymaker should remain at home. Wildlife biologists are concerned that even Eco-tourism can adversely affect wildlife (Jacobson and Lopez 1994). Moscardo and others (1996) suggest that rather than embracing a simplified dichotomy between "good" and "bad" tourism, a more useful analytical framework may be to examine the dimensions underlying the different manifestations of tourism. A successful tourism industry in one area may not fit in another.

In their discussion of recreation carrying capacity, Stankey and McCool (1984) suggest that the question of "how much is too much?" may focus on the wrong issue. Rather, the focus should be on identifying what kinds of resource and social conditions are appropriate and acceptable in different settings. In considering if tourism development is appropriate in a given location, the comparative advantages of different types and scales of tourism development need to be evaluated. Social, economic, and ecological constraints need to be identified. Successful tourism development will depend less on how tourism is labeled than on the natural endowments in given locations and the existing infrastructure, local expertise, and community support necessary to complement those endowments. Studies could address what types and scales of tourism development are appropriate in certain locations from economic, social, and ecological perspectives.

National Forest Fees and Local Economic Impacts

In recent years, there has been increasing interest in charging user fees for access to public lands. Revenue can be made both by entrance fees charged to tourists and by use permits charged to businesses offering tourist services such as guided tours on public lands. Fees can help public agencies recoup the costs of natural resource management and reduce congestion at certain sites by creating economic disincentives to visit. Entrance fees to parks and natural areas frequently are set below amounts visitors are willing to pay and below amounts required to finance park budgets (Laarman and Gregersen 1996). Low fees often persist because of a lack of information regarding site demand, and potential impacts of charging higher fees often are unknown (Lindberg and Johnson 1994). Pricing potentially can lead to greater efficiency, fairness, and environmentally sustainable nature-based tourism (Laarman and Gregersen 1996). For national forests, this may imply setting user fees that are sufficient to capture positive unpriced benefits derived from forest resources.

For local communities, however, a significant socioeconomic factor in tourism development is the proportion of tourism income that can be captured by the local economy. Such income is generated through employment in tourism-related services such as food and lodging, gasoline, local tour guiding, and sale of souvenir and outdoor recreation equipment. Charging access fees to public lands potentially reduces visitation and can result in adverse economic impacts to local communities where access to public lands is a primary attraction. User surveys incorporating contingent valuation, travel cost, or other methods could be used to provide information about the impact of fees on rates of visitation. Such studies could be combined with economic impact assessments within local communities to describe different fee levels in terms of potential local economic impacts. The fiscal benefits of access fees on public lands could be evaluated within a broader context to include the tourism industry in which public lands are a part.

Defining the Role of the Forest Service in Tourism

National forests likely will have an increasingly significant impact on tourism in communities located near them. As the U.S. population continues to grow and become more urban, so do ever-increasing demands for outdoor recreation opportunities. Such increased demands will place growing pressure on National Forests and other public lands to provide the types of nontimber amenities desired by many recreationists. These changes will lead to increasingly difficult decisions about national forest management as managers try to balance traditional multiple-use objectives. The role the USDA Forest Service intends to play in tourism development in local communities is not clearly defined. Should the agency be more actively involved in local tourism development planning? Are there types of tourism the agency should encourage or discourage? How would the role of the agency differ depending on local economic, social, and ecological conditions, and in relation to economic diversification, community resiliency, and economic dependence on public lands? These likely will be some of the questions confronting researchers and policymakers in the future.

Key Strategies of Eco-tourism Development

To ensure that tourism at a protected area is sustainable, it is necessary to implement a strong and effective management program that involves all stakeholders in dynamic, creative ways.

Zoning for Visitor Use

The appropriate zoning of an Eco-tourism site is fundamental to all other management strategies. Zoning is the division of a site into a number of different sectors, or zones, for the purpose of distributing different types of use or non-use (i.e., protection) in the most appropriate places. The number and types of zones depend upon:

a) the management objectives and priorities of the site;

b) the quality and variety of the natural and cultural resources and the degree of alteration they have suffered; and

c) the types of use that have been planned (many types of use conflict with one another an d thus must be separated geographically). Each zone is managed to maintain or achieve a particular natural setting within which Eco-tourism and other activities take place, and thus, each zone has its own set of rules and regulations for activities carried out within its boundaries.

Typically, a site or a protected area within it, has one or two zones dedicated primarily for public use (such as Eco-tourism) and two or three other zones where public use is of secondary consideration.

Visitor Site Planning and Design

At most Eco-tourism sites, visitor use is concentrated in only a few locations, or "visitor sites," both to facilitate its management and to limit its impact upon the natural environment. Because of the concentration of people and infrastructure, it is important that these visitor sites be well planned.

The main goals in good visitor site planning are:

- efficient use of the space by locating infrastructure in places where it will be most easily, safely and effectively used by the visitors, employees (e.g., guides, cooks) and site managers;
- minimal impact of visitor use and infrastructure development upon the surrounding environment; and
- planning infrastructure in accordance with the determined capacity of the natural area to receive a defined number of visitors (e.g., building a fixed number of cabins for the maximum allowable number of guests).

Site planning requires the preparation of an actual plan and topographic map on which all existing and planned Eco-tourism infrastructure is placed, be it an ecolodge, a trail, a campsite or a latrine. All infrastructure should be located to establish the geographical relationship with the significant natural and cultural features before any construction begins. Site planning also means that "best practices" for Eco-tourism activities and infrastructure must be followed.

A good site plan requires the professional services of a topographer and a landscape architect that are experienced in Eco-tourism development, or similarly experienced specialists.

Sustainable Infrastructure Design

Eco-tourism implementation requires infrastructure different from that of a conventional tourism setting, particularly if visitor lodging or food service is involved. In natural areas, Eco-tourism infrastructure must blend in with the surroundings, use predominantly renewable energy sources and manage sewage and food waste without damaging the surrounding environment. In the last 20 years or so, significant advances have been made that allow infrastructure planners and designers to minimize these impacts.

Several organizations have developed effective "best practice" guidelines for Eco-tourism architectural design and development.

Revenue-Generating Mechanisms

As we all know, money makes the world go 'round. The major goals of Eco-tourism are to generate income for conservation and to benefit local communities and other stakeholders that are also participating in the Eco-tourism program in or near a protected area. The degree to which a visitor site produces income depends in large part upon its importance as a tourism destination and, secondarily, upon its management and marketing capabilities.

In order to generate revenue, the following questions must be answered:

- Which mechanisms are needed to generate revenues?
- How should revenues be managed?
- How should income be spent?

It is important to recognize that income generation should never become an end in itself. The ultimate goal is site conservation. If adding another Eco-tourism activity to increase funding for a site is going to interfere with effective long-term site conservation, then it should probably not be carried out.

There are many ways to generate income in an Eco-tourism site, some of which may not apply to all situations.

Visitor Impact Monitoring and Management

Every time a visitor sets foot in an Eco-tourism site, he/she causes a negative impact. This is an unavoidable fact. The job of

Eco-tourism managers is to minimize those impacts and ensure that, via Eco-tourism management strategies, the positive impacts outweigh the negative ones. Monitoring and managing visitor impacts are fundamental Eco-tourism management strategies; unfortunately, they are also ones most frequently left unattended. If the effects of Eco-tourism activities on the site's natural environment and on the surrounding communities are unclear or unknown, then there can be no certainty of success.

Careful monitoring of impacts, both positive and negative, needs to be a primary activity of a site's overall management plan. This costs money and requires trained personnel and the assistance of interested stakeholders.

Naturalist Guides – The Heart of Eco-tourism

Most Eco-tourism takes place in remote natural areas where it is typically not feasible for visitors to fully experience the attractions without the accompaniment of trained, knowledgeable guides. Even in more easily accessible areas, the success of Eco-tourism depends in large part on the abilities of naturalist guides to interpret the environment in ways that inspire and educate visitors. Guides can also help to monitor the impact of tourists when accompanying them.

It is crucial for protected area managers to establish a guide licensing system because naturalist guides can:

- significantly enrich the visitor experience through education and consequently
  a) create new supporters of the site's conservation goals and
  b) generate additional demand for tourism in the area;
- ensure that the negative impacts of visitation are minimized and that positive impacts are maximized;
- generate income for themselves and for others in local communities;
- strengthen links between conservation and community development goals;
- increase the safety of visitors; and

- be additional eyes and ears for protected area administrations and proxies for protected area management.

Because the role of naturalist guides is so very important to an Eco-tourism program, a site's administrators need to effectively manage guides' involvement with the site to ensure that their activities conform to Eco-tourism standards. There are two basic mechanisms to accomplish this:

i) provide mandatory training of all naturalist guides who work within a site; and
ii) license all naturalist guides who work in the site, thus maintaining control over their activity.

Through implementation of each of these Eco-tourism management strategies, a protected area will be well positioned to harness the potential of Eco-tourism as a force for conservation and sustainable community development.

Eco-tourism in Mountain Areas

Mountains are one of the world's most important tourist destinations. Their soaring peaks and beautiful landscapes are becoming increasingly attractive as a place of escape in a stressful, urbanized world. But tourism presents both opportunities and dangers for mountain regions. Tourism revenues have become a primary source of income for many mountain communities. Yet, the influx of visitors into mountain regions poses a threat to these unique and often pristine environments. Mountain people are the stewards of mountain ecosystems, so any decision to develop tourism must be made with their involvement and agreement. Most of all, tourism must be sustainable, planned to ensure that the beauty of mountains can be enjoyed by present and future generations.

The Call of the Wild

More than 50 million people visit mountains each year. They are drawn to these areas by the physical beauty of alpine environments, the many forms of recreation available in mountainous terrain and the opportunities for experiencing cultural heritage in the communities found there. The clean, cool air and awe-inspiring scenery of mountain areas, combined with the unique customs, arts, crafts and culinary traditions of the communities that live there, make trips to the mountains attractive holiday options.

Sport-based tourism in particular has boomed in mountain regions over the past 30 years. It has expanded from the traditional areas of North America and the European Alps to largely untouched mountain regions, including parts of Central Asia, the Himalaya, Karakorum, Caucasus, Andes and even Antarctica.

Typical mountain activities include hiking, skiing, snowboarding, climbing and birdwatching. However, extreme sports, such as bungee jumping, hydrospeeding, rafting, paragliding and canyoning are becoming increasingly popular, especially with affluent urban thrill-seekers. Another growth area for alpine tourism focuses on mountains as a source of well-being and health. An ever-increasing number of mountain tours offer opportunities for contemplation and meditation.

The tourism boom has undoubtedly brought benefits to many of the world's mountain regions. Thanks to tourism revenues, mountain people, many of whom are economically disadvantaged, can aspire to greatly improved living standards. Mountain tourism has given young men and women the option of building a future in their home community, instead of becoming part of the rural exodus to cities. The influx of visitors has also created a market for products made by local crafts workers, as well as for produce from the land.

Yet although tourism – and mountain tourism in particular – is one of the fastest growing economic sectors in the world, it is also one of the least regulated. Short-term profits need to be balanced against long-term losses if the industry is to become a lasting source of benefit for mountain people.

A Double-edged Sword

Experience has already shown that mountain tourism can have a range of damaging effects. It can degrade and stress fragile mountain ecosystems, destroying the qualities that make these environments so alluring. Mountains are among the world's most important repositories of biodiversity, yet construction, pollution and noise all threaten this precious asset. In many of the developing world's most beautiful mountain regions, litter and waste have emerged as key problems, as well as trees being felled to supply timber and fuelwood. The mysticism of sacred mountain sites is often diminished by the numbers of people who come from all over the world to make pilgrimages. Tourism means more transportation networks and links, which can blight the mountain environment, disrupt traditional ways of life and threaten the existence of local languages. If mountains become the world's playgrounds, there is a risk that mountain people will lose their own cultural identity.

Counting the Cost of Fun in the Snow

Winter sports are booming, with resorts now operating all over the world. The snow sport business has spawned a large and complex commercial network that includes hotels, shops, restaurants, cable cars and ski schools. For many isolated mountain communities, it has meant a new lease on life. But in some cases, it has also come at a high price. Building ski runs often involves destroying swathes of forest, planting pylons for chairlifts and cable cars and building roads and tunnels. In the Alps, emissions from the millions of vehicles that bring visitors to the slopes threaten the health of trees and worsen the effects of global warming. Paths and ski runs harm sensitive mountain ecosystems and disturb plant and animal life. And constructions that look acceptable under a mantle of snow can become a scar on the landscape once the winter fun is over.

How not to Kill the Golden Goose

Tourism can provide benefits for mountain people and visitors alike if sensitively planned and managed. Often, the development of tourism in mountain areas is concentrated in the hands of outside interests, with little of the profits going to local communities. This is especially true of developing countries and emerging economies, where venture capital is in short supply.

Mountain tourism needs to be developed according to specific local conditions and cultures, an approach that will help communities gain a niche in an increasingly competitive market. Policy-makers could favour activities that build on local knowledge and traditions to ensure that tourists respect the natural and cultural diversity of the places they visit and encourage mountain people to view their home as a source of pride.

Because it is notoriously volatile, and often seasonal, the tourism industry needs to be developed as part of an overall economic development strategy, with diversification to ensure local economies do not become reliant solely on tourism revenue. Governments can help mountain communities by investing profits in programmes to ensure sustainable livelihoods for local people. Non-governnmental organizations and the private sector can also help get the tourism equation right by offering education and training in responsible tourism practices.

Eco-tourism in Mountains

One promising answer to the challenge of developing mountains wisely for recreation is Eco-tourism. As well as being the International Year of Mountains, 2002 was also the International Year of Eco-tourism, and there is a strong and important link between the two. Eco-tourism can help reduce poverty and hunger, a key issue in mountain areas where a high proportion of the world's poor and food-insecure live. It also has considerable potential for strengthening communities and for protecting mountain ecosystems.

Defined by the International Eco-tourism Society as "responsible travel to natural areas which conserves the environment and improves the welfare of local people," Eco-tourism currently accounts for between 2 and 4 percent of global tourism. This form of holidaymaking makes a point of putting something back into the area and culture being visited, in terms of revenue and financial support for conservation projects, but often also in-kind. Some tourism operators plant trees to combat desertification, collect garbage from trekking regions and ensure tourists use biodegradable wrapping on food and drink. During many eco-holidays, tourists help out with projects that protect endangered species and habitats. Handled properly, Eco-tourism can be a valuable tool in advancing tourism, especially for poor mountain communities in the developing world, without destroying natural resources and the environment.

Cultural and Eco-tourism in the Mountainous Regions of Central Asia and in the Himalayas

Tourism is coming to the previously isolated mountainous regions of Central and South Asia. The challenge is to ensure that it is well-managed and that its benefits are shared by all.

The spectacular mountainous regions of Central Asia, the Hindu and the Himalayas, closed for many years to visitors from abroad, now attract growing numbers of foreign tourists attracted by the unique cultures and natural beauty of these hitherto isolated areas.

However, while growing tourist numbers are bringing economic opportunities and employment to local populations, helping to promote these little-known regions of the world, they have also brought challenges with them: How to ensure that local communities fully benefit from the development of tourism and that growth in tourism helps to preserve and sustain the natural and cultural riches of these regions, rather than putting them in danger?

This project, the Development of Cultural and Eco-tourism in the Mountainous Regions of Central Asia and the Himalayas, generously sponsored by the Norwegian Government as well as by UNESCO Regular Programme funds, aims to establish links and promote cooperation between local communities, national and international NGOs, and tour agencies in order to involve local populations fully in the employment opportunities and income-generating activities that tourism can bring.

An interdisciplinary project, drawing on the expertise of international NGOs and tourism professionals in the seven participating countries, the project is making a practical and positive contribution to alleviating poverty by helping local communities to draw the maximum benefit from their region's tourism potential, while protecting the environmental and cultural heritage of the region concerned.

Mountain areas concerned by the project include Ladakh in India, Masouleh in Iran, the Northern Tien Shen Mountains in Kazakhstan, the mountainous region around Lake Issy Kul in Kyrgyzstan, a Biosphere Reserve of the UNESCO Man and the

Biosphere Programme (MAB), Humla in Nepal, Chitral and the Kalash Valleys in Pakistan and the Pamir Mountains in Tajikistan. Local project partners include the Mountain Institute and Snow Leopard Conservancy in Ladakh (India), the Aga Khan Rural Support Programme in Chitral (Pakistan) and the Kazakh Mountaineering Foundation and the Novinomad Eco-tourism Development Company in Kazakhstan and Kyrgyzstan, respectively.

In Tajikistan, UNESCO is working with ACTED, L'Agence d'aide a la cooperation technique et au development, in the Pamir Mountains, and in Nepal with the Nepal Trust in Humla, one of the poorest and most isolated regions of the country. Project activities include training local tour guides, producing high-quality craft items and promoting home-stays and bed-and-breakfast type accommodation, while fully involving local communities in these income-generating activities. Recommendations on best practices, Web resources and a database on community profiles, including maps, research data and regional attractions and resources, are all included in the project.

The aim is to promote these unspoilt regions of the world for foreign tourists and researchers, while helping local communities to benefit fully from the economic opportunities that their environments can bring.

Hill & Mountain Cosystems

Importance of Hill &Mountain Areas

* Home to most indigenous populations
* Provider of essential resources
* Major source of water supply
* Centres of culture and indigenous knowledge systems
* Repositories of unique forms of biodiversity & ecosystems.

Hill & Mountain Tourism

* Nature and adventure tourism (trekking, rock climbing, mountaineering, rafting)
* Winter sports (alpine skiing, cross-country skiing)

* Summer holidays in warmer countries (accommodations in holiday cottages, less activity-oriented)
* Pilgrimages (traditional tourism, particularly in the Himalayan).

Impacts of Tourism on Hills & Mountains

* Basic infrastructure – electricity, water, waste disposal, transport and transportation related, development and securing of infrastructure, utilities
* ccommodation infrastructure for lodges/resorts/ restaurants/cafes/bars
* Additional services – e.g., shops and other commercial establishments
* Recreational activities – main and complementary activities
* Recreation infrastructure – paths/trails, sports facilities, golf courses, cable cars etc.
* Directly and indirectly induced developments – regional migration, urbanisation, changing values etc.

Environmental Impacts

* Establishment of protected or conserved areas to meet tourist demand
* Defining new uses of marginal or unproductive lands
* Programmes to protect the attractiveness of locations
* Assist refurbishment and reuse of heritage buildings & abandoned properties
* Pollution
* Visual impact
* Degradation / alteration of ecosystems
* Construction activities & infrastructure development
* Depletion of and Access to Natural Resources –land, water.

Eco-tourism ...Sustainable Enough?

Tourism & Environmental Issues

* Exploitative trends of mainstream tourism

* Contribution as a million dollar industry
* Towards conservation of the destination.

Reasons for Growth

* Environmental awareness
* Aroused interest among middle class
* Promotion of nature through print and electronic media.

Tourism & Environment

The stress is on niche tourism products;

- Wildlife Tourism
- Nature-based Tourism
- Eco-tourism
- Sustainable Tourism.

Tracing History of Eco-tourism

- 1st coined by tour operator in Costa Rica – 70s
- Defined by IUCN –1996
- Became popular with industry
- Lucrative option
- Cover up for bad practices
- Boost after IYE 2002.

Fall Out

- Tourism in ecologically sensitive regions is being qualified as Eco-tourism
- Opening up more and newer areas
- New forms added – rural, adventure etc.
- Entry of new players – Forest Dept.
- Tourism industry claims on a few eco-friendly practices.

Critical Areas Being Targeted

Andaman Islands, North East, Numerous PA's, Other ecologically rich & sensitive areas.

Components

- Contribute to conservation of biodiversity
- Benefit indigenous / local communities
- Minimum consumption of resources
- Address site specific issues
- Stress upon local participation, ownership and business opportunities
- Cater to small groups by small-scale businesses
- Include an interpretation / awareness experience
- Involve responsible behaviour on the part of tourists and tourism industry.

Case Study: Andamans

- Low volume high end tourism
- High-end tourism infrastructure
- Private sector investment
- Reduction of no development zone from 200m / 500m to 50m from HTL
- 40 islands to be opened by Forest
- Dept. for Eco-tourism
- 7 studies & master plans-MoT-WTOUNDP master plan (1996-97) selected by tourism vision.

MoT-WTO-UNDP Master Plan (96-97)

- Linking with other SE Asian destinations ! resulted in twinning Port Blair & Phuket
- Targets to be achieved: growth, marketing & high quality international tourism
- Relaxation of development norms & regulations (draconian CRZ!)
- No environmental sustainability, livelihood generation for local community.

Impacts

Impacts of Eco-tourism on Indian Coast;

- Habitat fragmentation from infrastructure
- Denial of access to coastal communities
- Competition over natural resources
- Ecosystem degradation:
- Leveling of sand dunes
- Destruction of mangroves
- Disturbance to wildlife – e.g. turtle nesting sites
- Destruction of coral reefs.

Community Based Tourism Projects

- Management Plan for Community based conservation and Eco-tourism in the Nanda Devi Biosphere Reserve
- Initiation and complete management of tourism activity in the area by the Village Council
- Abiding with regional, national and international guidelines on sustainable tourism
- Declaration on Nanda Devi Biodiversity Conversation and Eco-tourism, 2001 onwards.

Khonoma, Nagaland

- Tourism is seen as a vehicle for bringing development
- Needs of community are prioritized over tourism needs
- Impacts of tourism are identified beforehand and adequate systems and mechanisms put in place to minimize impacts
- Eco-tourism, as a set of values, would mean-
    * no disturbance to natural areas or areas under traditional land use like agriculture;
    * low infrastructure that blends with the local setting & architecture;
    * an enriching and learning experience for tourists, which becomes the unique selling proposition and hence brings benefits to the local community.

Planned and well managed tourism with regular monitoring strengthened by research;

- Need for alternative technologies
- Training of local people for implementation
- Value addition to intrinsic properties of the village
- Planning for better utilisation of energy within the village
- Bringing in community managed Eco-tourism to Khonoma
- The Khonoma Village Council to drive the process.

2

Second Home Tourism: Impact, Planning and Strategy

Urbanization and Second-home Tourism

Definitions of Second-home Tourism and Residential Tourism

Second-home tourism deserves special attention from researchers, in revealing what sort of reasons lead someone from elsewhere to decide to spend long periods of time in a particular place, and to constantly return to that place. There are also issues related to the impacts of second-home tourism, and planning implications.

The definition of second-home tourism is based on two main aspects:

1. The type of tourist dwelling where tourists stay, which may be privately owned, rented or cost-free (visiting relatives or friends)
2. Frequent return to the same holiday place.

Generally, second-home tourists live in privately owned or rented dwellings, and have particular characteristics. They return to the same place for leisure time, and thus demonstrate great knowledge of, loyalty towards and appreciation of the destination. They often make friends or have relatives in the location, establish close links with the destination and are committed to the sustainability of the place. Second-home tourists spend long periods of time at the destination where they purchase their house. Such periods of time are long compared to the other forms of tourism, but are obviously less than a year at a time – otherwise the individuals concerned would not be considered tourists.

It is useful here to highlight the difference between second-home tourism and residential tourism, which is based on the period of time travellers stay at the destination.

In the case of residential tourism, the length of stay may be longer than a year – that is, people change their place of residence and in some cases can even get a job at the destination. According to the WTO definition, if that happens the travellers cannot be classified as tourists. This can be the case with aged people living in rest homes. There is, however, an important difference between such travellers and local residents, since the former consume income at the destination whilst their money is generated at their usual place of residence. Distinction between second-home tourism and residential tourism involves consideration of the reasons why second-home tourists become residential tourists. There are certain socio-economic determinants or jobs that might facilitate the change of place of residence. According to recent research, climatic conditions, price, political and social stability, cultural factors, etc. are amongst the factors that influence the demand for second homes.

Time sharing is another form of second-home tourism, but in this case tourists do not spend long periods of time at the same destination. It could be considered a particular form of second-home tourism, depending on the way the participants use their tourism dwelling.

The final consideration demonstrates the third characteristic of second-home tourism, which is related to the relationship established between the tourist dwelling and the visitor. Often tourists stay in private dwellings that can be owned, rented, owned just for a period of time (timesharing), or free (the visiting friends and relatives (VFR) market).

Second-home tourism has a considerable impact on the local economy through the economics of the building industry. However, the impact is different from that of the 'classic' tourism industry, as these tourists tend to cook their own meals and often organize their own trips and entertainment. Hence hotels, restaurants, travel agencies and tour operators may not be used, whilst the building industry, agriculture and retail may gain more benefits from second-home tourism demand.

When researching second-home tourism, four main aspects should be considered:

1. The second-home tourists, who are very often characterized by a strong affiliation with and loyalty to the destination.
2. Businesses that provide products and services to this market, including the building industry, which is responsible for the construction of private tourist dwellings and a wide range of decorative and household services.
3. The government and local authorities, whose responsibility is geared towards the provision of adequate levels of services and infrastructure. If second-home tourism is a dominant sector at the destination, there are special needs and services that must be provided by the planning and governmental services. For example, the process of urbanization, generally depending on local government, requires planning and the provision of land and infrastructure.
4. The host community, which often looks on the sector as being responsible for creating employment. It is also important to consider the social and cultural consequences of the interaction between the local communities and secondhome owners.

As second-home tourism implies long-term commitment from visitors, it is only when all the stakeholders have compatible aims and objectives that coexistence can be peaceful and mutually beneficial. The local authorities therefore need to provide a planning framework that ensures coordination of the activities and the optimization of impacts.

The Socio-economic and Environmental Impacts of Second Home Tourism: The South Pacific Coast of Nicaragua

Attractive coastal regions of Central and South America have recently experienced a rapid growth of second home developments. Informed by the experiences of Europe and the Americas, this study examines the socio-economic and environmental impacts of second homes on the South Pacific Coast of Nicaragua. An extensive review of Spanish, French and English academic literature as well as secondary data from the Rivas region were examined. Nicaraguan press releases from the two main national papers, La Prensa and El Nuevo Diario, were scanned to add congruence to the local debates and opinions collected. In-depth, semi-structured interviews and participant observation were used to collect additional qualitative data. Twenty-one decision makers and tourism officials were interviewed in the months of January and February 2007. The interviewees were representatives from the local government, Ministry of Tourism and the local tourism industry. The main impacts include conflicts with local and indigenous communities over land use and ownership, seasonal and low-income employment generation, an increased burden of municipal budget to provide public infrastructure, and environmental degradation.

It is argued that the second home tourism sector, strongly driven by private real estate investors, fails to generate tourism activities which are expected to sustain community development. This study further indicates that municipalities concentrating on the second home tourism segment may deprive access to resources to other forms of tourism activities.

Urbanization and Second-Home Tourism

Over the last few years second-home tourism has become more popular, emerging as an important part of the tourism sector in a number of countries. In most cases second homes are located near attractive locations, such as the sea, lakes, mountains or rural areas, whilst often they have a connection to their owners' origins and may be inherited properties. They offer a peaceful and environmentally friendly holiday home for city dwellers. The USA is considered to be the country in the world with the largest proportion of tourism second homes. In the European Union the demand for second homes is increasing, notably in southern European countries, and such homes are very often purchased by northern Europeans.

Although initially the demand for second homes was driven

predominantly by nationals seeking regions with better climatic conditions, recently there has been an important growth in the sector from foreigners. In Spain the foreign investment in second homes reached 5.7 billion Euros in 2002, which represents a total of 90 000 houses and an average growth rate of 10 per cent. Studies conducted demonstrate that the highest levels of demand come from Great Britain (35 per cent), Germany (31 per cent), France (7 per cent), Italy (5 per cent) and The Netherlands (3.1 per cent). A number of factors have contributed in the growth of second-home demand in Europe, namely:

- greater confidence in the European Union
- experience of destinations through frequent visitation
- the internationalization of the building

"Tourism & Second Homes Reality Check South of the Border"

By Mitch Creekmore, Stewart International

Wall Street is mired in a downward spiral due to oil and financial stress. On Friday, Washington announced concerns over Ginnie Mae and Freddie Mac with possible government intervention. The two mortgage giants have taken $11 billion in write-downs over the last nine months and their stock fell by 30 percent and 45 percent, respectively, for the week ending July 11. Where are Americans going to invest? Where can we safely put our money to work in a reliable investment atmosphere? Housing had always been one such "safe" venue.

We all wish our domestic financial and residential real estate woes would improve over the next six months. Unfortunately, that is unlikely. They probably won't get much better until we have a new president in the White House and well after the first of the year. News out of Washington and the U.S. Commerce Department in April said new home sales plummeted by 8.5 percent to a 17 year low in the month of March. The report gives little hope the housing market is near the bottom.

The economy expanded at an annual rate of one percent in the first quarter, the Commerce Department said last week. That caps the weakest six months of growth in the last five years.

The world's biggest financial institutions have taken about $400 billion in writedowns and credit losses tied to the U.S. housing slump, according to data compiled by Bloomberg. Eli Broad, founder of homebuilder KB Homes, said in an interview with Bloomberg that with homes sales and prices declining and consumer confidence at a 28 year low, "I don't see it turning around very quickly. This is worse than any recession we've had since World War II." Selling off vacant, unsold homes could take "several years," he said. REALTOR® Magazine reported in a survey in the May issue of *Business Week* that cities like Los Angeles, San Diego, Las Vegas and Phoenix saw sellers reduce asking prices on their residences by more than an average of 20 percent in the last 12 months. The number of Americans in danger of losing their homes to foreclosure rose to the highest level in three decades during the first quarter of 2008, according to data from the Mortgage Bankers Association. "I think housing is going to continue to have a corrosive effect on consumer psychology and the economy in general to a far greater extent than people think, or even far greater than I thought about a month or two ago," Broad said in his interview.

These are stark and worrisome headlines, to say the least, about the challenging plight we'll all face in the coming months. Interestingly, on the same day as the REALTOR® survey, *USA Today* had a front page headline in their Money section entitled "Foreign Buyers Snap Up U.S.

Real Estate." With the continuing decrease of the dollar against the Euro and Pound Sterling, coupled with the reduction in home prices in popular destinations, the U.S. has become a "great buy" for international purchasers that have stronger currencies and greater disposable incomes.

The question now, though on a very cautious and 'wait and see basis,' is: where will *Americans* invest? Where will they look for real estate opportunities, whether it is a second home or a retirement destination? There seems to be no sense of urgency in today's market like there had been in the years from 2000 – 2005. Annualized appreciation in the "big four" second home markets was staggering at over 100 percent in residential values during that same time period, according to the National Association of

Realtors. Today, Americans are concerned about rising oil prices, the cost of gasoline, healthcare issues, the pending presidential election and the overall credit crunch that has crippled the mortgage industry and led to widespread mortgage foreclosures. The subsequent impact all of these factors create on American buying mentality is being felt throughout the U.S., as well as in Mexico and virtually all of Central America. With that said, many U.S. citizens will still look south of the border for second home purchases due to its close proximity, increased airlift capacity, access and affordability (even with higher fuel costs), and a lower cost of living that cannot be attained anywhere in the U.S. – especially on a fixed income!

The biggest unanswered question is, "When?" Like Mexico, the countries of Costa Rica, Panama and the Dominican Republic (DR) have seen dramatic increases in tourism and real estate activity over the past seven years. Mexico is the most important tourist destination in Latin America. According to the InterAmerican Development Bank (IDB), the country receives about 30 percent of its total income from international tourism in the region. Eight percent of Mexico's GDP comes from the tourist sector and accounts for six percent of their nation's employment. Mexican tourism is heavily dependent on North American visitors, and at the same time, it is extremely vulnerable to U.S. economic fluctuations. A major advantage that Mexico has in the region is FONATUR, the National Trust Fund for Tourism Development.

Since it's inception in 1974, FONATUR has been the public trust and part state-owned entity that has been responsible for the development of Cancun, Los Cabos, Ixtapa, Huatulco and Loreto. The mission statement of FONATUR is, "To be the institution responsible for the planning and development of sustainable tourism projects of national impact. To be an instrument of promotion for investment and training of the tourism sector; thus being the national entity that lends its experience to regions, states, and municipalities, along with small and medium businesses." Today, FONATUR has additional new master planned projects like the Nautical Ladder in the Sea of Cortez, the Riveria Maya and Costa Maya developments in the State of Quintana Roo, Litibu in the State of Nayarit, and Palenque in the state of Chiapas.

During the six-year presidential term of Vicente Fox Quesada, FONATUR realized more than six billion dollars in foreign direct investment. For these many reasons, Mexico has continually retained its reputation as the "big enchilada" in tourism and real estate development within the Latin American region.

When the U.S. economy began to show signs of weakness, many speculated as to whether American tourism in Costa Rica, Panama, the Dominican Republic and the rest of the Central American countries also would begin to decline. So far, this has not been the case. In fact, Costa Rica saw one million visitors in the first five months of 2008, according to the Costa Rican Tourism Board (ICT). This represents a 16 percent increase of approximately 133,000 visitors when compared to the same time period in 2007. The Dominican Republic enjoys about 4.5 million visitors each year. Even though Americans have less discretionary income, meaning fewer dollars to spend on vacations both domestically and internationally, they're still willing to travel to these countries. Close proximity to our border makes airline tickets and hotel accommodations more palatable even in the face of rising fuel costs. Tourism will remain one of the biggest generators of GDP for most of these countries. All of these so called "banana republics" of old have tourism boards that are aggressively and strategically marketing to North Americans. Eco tourism and sustainable developments are no longer exclusive to Costa Rica.

Each country has something different to offer with its own rich culture and history, archeological presence and special natural amenities that make the experience unique. Some of the biggest names in the development world from countries like Spain, England, Canada, Mexico and the U.S., to name a few, have world class resorts and master planned projects established or under construction in these nations. It's worth mentioning that the professionalism and integrity of the real estate agent community in most of these countries has improved as well. It's not as much about "my commission" and a general lack of disclosure as in years past, but instead about creating a greater level of comfort and security for buyers. Title insurance and escrow services have helped push real estate agents to adopt higher standards of service and ethics for the benefit of their customers. As a result, one only needs to determine where they want to be, what geographical amenities they like, and whether they are beach people, rain forest or colonial aficionados.

Guatemala, El Salvador, Nicaragua, Honduras and Belize have something for everyone. Why? Because it's simply the truth! All of these markets will attract a particular buyer based on their personal preference and their price point. The latter criteria will become an increasingly more important component in the selection of where to buy and where to invest in the coming years.

With the tremendous appreciation that Mexico's residential sector has experienced, coupled with that of Costa Rica and Panama, many North Americans will be "priced out" of some international markets. Where a two-bedroom condominium sold for $180K five years ago in a given destination, and was affordable then, that same unit today sells for $400K or more. As a result of this dynamic value appreciation, foreign purchasers will seek a geographic location suitable for their given means and disposable income that will still provide them with acceptable amenities, healthcare, infrastructure, enjoyment and upside investment potential. A lot has been written about the vast inheritance the "boomers" will realize over the next decade.

Many, many North Americans will have, and have now, a lot of money that can be invested in something or somewhere. Why not second homes in any of these countries? Our neighbors to the south are keenly aware of the investment impact this unprecedented group of inheritors can make on their country. Not to mention the impact they'll have on improving the quality of life with new infrastructure, tax revenue and development wherever they invest. Today, that total is over two million purchasers from North America.

The perception and viability of owning a home in these wonderful countries has changed a great deal. Foreign buyers now understand and recognize the safeguards that can be provided for real property acquisitions outside the U.S. There is a greater sense of comfort and security with North American buyers. Given the dire second home landscape in America over the next 18 months, and maybe longer, Mexico and Central America will be the places to be, the places to invest, the places to own that second home!

Planning Laws Could Restrict Second Home Ownership

The Government is considering measures that will deter second-home owners from buying properties in desirable rural locations. Around 240,000 people own a second home in England and the detrimental effect of this on rural communities has long been recognised. In some areas property prices have risen beyond the reach of local people and village schools shops and pubs are threatened with closure because properties remain empty for large parts of the year.

Prime Minister Gordon Brown has now commissioned an enquiry that will look at whether local councils should have the power to prevent homes being sold to buyers who will not use them as their main residence.

In such cases, planning permission would be needed to convert a property from a full-time home into a second home.

Any scheme recommended by the enquiry is likely to be piloted in the areas facing serious difficulties from second-home ownership, such as the Isles of Scilly, South Hams in South Devon, North Cornwall and North Norfolk.

In April of this year, Capital Gains Tax liability on the sale of second homes will be reduced to 18%, a move that is being strongly opposed by the Government's Rural Advocate, Stuart Burgess.

Assetsure News 21st September 2007

The Impact of Second Homes and UK Holiday Homes on Communities

The growth in the amount of disposable income over the last 20 years, achieved by homeowners in the UK has been considerable. As a result many people have purchased second homes to act as a uk holiday homes both here in Britain and in other European popular destinations like Spain and France and Portugal. Britain has fantastic countryside and traditional seaside resorts and scenery that have attracted hundreds of thousands of a people to purchase second properties using the equity they have amassed in their own homes and their disposable income, as the economy has strengthened during the last 10 to 20 years. This has led to house price growth... The amount of land available for new building holiday properties is under immense pressure and at the same time the number of traditional cottages is finite.

Here in the UK, the continued rise in property prices has had some negative effect on local villages and communities popular holiday destinations such as Devon, Cornwall, the Lake District and the New Forest. Residents of these largely rural communities (which rely heavily on tourism from holiday makers) are finding it increasingly difficult to get onto the property ladder because of huge demand for holiday homes pushing up the overall price of property out of their reach. In some extreme areas this has created resentment and bitterness as locals cannot afford to buy property in their own village and they have been indirectly forced out of their own area to look for cheaper property elsewhere.

The problem is widely recognised among local communities, councils and housing authorities. Some local councils have actively sought to intervene to stop holiday home usage. For instance, they have sought to restrict the usage of the property in its local planning guidelines for people that have not lived in the area for a fixed time as well as influence local planning guidelines. Recent proposals by new forest district council to increase the level of council tax above the standard 90 per cent rate for second homes left unoccupied, is currently being considered. The government has also signalled that it may change the law to give councils more flexibility to adjust its own council tax rates to reflect the needs to balance the local economy with the volume of holiday homes in its area. In addition, major new national housing reform is being introduced to bring three million new affordable homes to the UK by 2020, particularly for key workers and first time buyers.

The wider economic impacts on local people migrating from their local town has knock on effects for the economy. Without affordable accommodation key workers have a to migrate away from the local area. Businesses and local services are also on the decline us local people who run these small businesses also cannot afford can to purchase property. The huge decline in some villages in South Wales is a notable example where areas have been left unoccupied as holiday homeowners have left them for the winter. The fact they are left empty for most of the year means spoilt the traditional community feeling and spirit between the old villages that used to rely on coal and industry with strong history and bonds, is now dependant upon tourism from people who do not live there or only visit a few weeks a year. Another obvious example is the Lake District where an amazing 50% of homes in the village of Berwick are empty throughout the year.

The problem looks set to continue as more and more of us seek second homes to escape the pressure of a modern lifestyle.

The Impact of Empty, Second and Holiday Homes

Executive Summary

In response to the increasing requirement for public policy to be evidence-based, the Economic and Social Science Research Council (ESRC) has funded a programme of research projects to examine how evidence can be generated in a number of social policy areas. Beyond developing the evidence base in a number of topic areas, the programme aims to develop the methods of systematic reviewing. Systematic reviews are considered to be a key tool for the identification, comprehensive assessment and synthesis of research evidence.

A systematic review aims to provide a comprehensive and unbiased summary of available evidence on a given topic. This is achieved by the use of a clearly defined search strategy to ensure that an extensive range of potential sources of evidence is explored. In addition the use of explicit criteria to appraise the quality of the evidence retrieved ensures that only robust evidence is synthesised in the production of the final review.

This review addresses two questions:

- What are the impacts of privately owned empty or irregularly occupied properties on the sustainability of rural communities?
- To what extent have the policy interventions addressed the effects of empty of irregularly occupied properties on the sustainability of rural communities?

These questions address key national and local policy concerns, notably sustainable communities and housing demand. Furthermore the social and economic impacts of second homes in particular on rural communities are contested, and have been the focus of considerable and often emotive debate over the last three decades.

Methods

An essential first step was to ensure there was no ambiguity around the questions being addressed by the review. The review was concerned with vacant property, second homes and holiday homes (i.e. properties rented out on a series of short term lets) in the private sector located in settlements with populations of less than 10,000. We adopted the ten dimensions of sustainability proposed by Long (2001) as a framework for organising the evidence.

A review protocol was drawn up at the outset of the review, detailing *a priori* decisions about the selection and appraisal of studies, the search strategy, and data synthesis methods. Ten electronic databases and many internet sites were searched. The process produced 1060 references. Of these 273 were relevant to the review. Once the specified inclusion criteria were applied, 30 references remained. Of these, 23 met our quality criteria and finally entered the review. Information was extracted from each study in a uniform manner, and data synthesised to provide a narrative account of the findings.

Evidence-Base

Seventeen of the review studies addressed second home ownership. The studies included in the review were undertaken in various locations across the UK over a period of more than 30 years, using a variety of methods, and various definitions of second or empty homes. The definition of what constitutes a second home has been a perennial problem. Another fundamental difficulty has been the accurate identification of the number of properties that are empty or used as second homes. Different studies have focused on different aspects of empty and irregularly occupied properties. The political problematisation of second homes has led much of the research to have a relatively narrow focus, and second homes have (with some notable exceptions) been studied in isolation from other expressions of external housing demand in local areas, such as retirement and commuting.

The impacts of privately owned empty or irregularly occupied properties on the sustainability of rural communities: key findings

The evidence was organised thematically around four of the ten dimensions of sustainability proposed by Long (2001). The evidence only addressed the impact of empty or irregularly occupied properties on one of these dimensions – demand for housing/access to affordable housing – in any great depth. There was a smaller literature that addressed impacts of second homes on community cohesion and viability, and the built environment. There is as yet no evidence that addresses the impact of empty or irregularly occupied property on a number of dimensions of community sustainability, notably: reputation or image of the community; crime and anti-social behaviour; social exclusion and poverty; and accessibility of facilities, services and employment.

Rural Housing Markets

- The issue of empty or irregularly occupied properties cannot be considered in isolation from the other processes of change within rural housing, including the undersupply of alternative forms of housing, changes to local economies, loss of industries and transport.
- Although it is widely believed that rural depopulation is a consequence of local residents' inability to compete with incomers in rural housing markets, many studies conclude that outward migration is more closely allied to a lack of employment, education, and leisure opportunities than to a lack of housing.
- Low wage economies, restrictions on the supply of new housing and external demands combine to raise house prices and disadvantage many local people in rural housing markets.
- Second homes remain a localised phenomenon. Certainly their national significance in Wales, at least, has declined over the last decade.
- Second homes are not the sole source of external demand; however they have been subjected to more attention than other external demands such as commuting and retirement.

- Ageing and retirement are the key factors likely to impact on housing markets in the next 25 years.

Community Cohesion

- Early studies indicate that second home ownership was seen by host communities to be part of a wider process of social change rather than a cause of outward migration.
- Attitudes towards second home ownership vary between locations; areas where tourism and recreation have been dominant appear to be more tolerant of second home ownership.
- There is little evidence of conflict between second homeowners and local residents.
- Profiles of second home owners indicate that they are generally middle aged or retired, and wealthier than the national average, however much of the profile data is more than 20 years old.
- It is difficult to compare 'incomers' with 'locals' as few studies profile host communities.
- More recent studies report concerns that the age profile of rural communities is unbalanced, as younger people migrate away and are replaced by older incomers.
- Demand for housing from commuters, the retired and second home owners has changed the profile of rural communities.

Community Viability

- Second home ownership was seen to make a useful contribution to local economies as part of the tourist industry, but differences in levels of contribution between different localities make generalisations regarding the impact of second home ownership problematic.
- Spending on renovation and modernisation of second homes has in the past bought new income into local economies, however these are one-off spends.
- Through payment of local taxes, second home owners support public services in their host communities without creating additional demands.

- There is little evidence regarding the contemporary spending of second home owners on local services such as retail and leisure.
- Early studies suggested that employment related to renovation was created by second home ownership; however, more recent evidence suggests that any additional jobs are low skilled and seasonal.

Built Environment

- Early studies suggested that second home ownership had a positive impact on the built environment particularly with regard to conservation and renovation of previously derelict properties.
- No studies address broader environmental concerns.

The Impact and Effectiveness of Policy Interventions

We identified few studies that had evaluated policy interventions, and these were mainly concerned with empty properties as opposed to second homes. There was, however, a larger literature that investigated the type of local policies that were in place to control second home ownership, and various policy recommendations were presented.

Second Homes – Policies, Policy Evaluations, and Policy Recommendations

- Only a minority of local authorities and National Parks in England and Wales report having a specific policy towards second homes. Where these policies do exist, they usually relate to occupancy controls on new dwellings.
- Recent research in England suggests strong support from authorities for greater powers in respect of second homes, although fiscal measures are preferred over planning controls.
- Evaluations of specific policy interventions towards second homes have been very limited and have focused upon the use of restrictions on occupancy on new development.
- Very little work has been undertaken to assess the impact of local occupancy on rural housing markets; instead

research has focused on mechanisms for delivering affordable housing in the countryside.

- Authors' policy recommendations reflected the period in which their research was conducted. Most recently authors suggest planning and policy tools should be used in a focused way and targeted on those communities with the greatest housing pressures, with greater partnership working between local government and rural communities.

Empty Properties: Outcomes of Policy Evaluations

- Policy intervention directed at bringing empty property back into use in rural Scotland appear to offer a way of addressing housing need, especially in remoter rural locations where development of new affordable housing by housing association may prove problematic.

Conclusions

Part of the rationale for undertaking this report was to reflect on the specific benefits that the methods of systematic reviewing can bring to social policy, using the example of an investigation of the impact of empty and irregularly occupied dwellings on the sustainability of rural communities.

Given the often emotive nature of the view of second home ownership as a key driver causing dwellings in rural areas to be empty or irregularly occupied, the approach of 'going back to basics', rigorously searching for material, and considering only empirical evidence (rather than opinion or observations), allows reflection on the topic in a more neutral way. This is not to say that the study can claim objectivity or transparency, but allows the reader to see how and why decisions have been made through the process of this review, and how the available evidence has been handled. In this respect systematic reviewing offers a valuable set of methods in approaching the secondary analyses of existing evidence. However, whether a systematic review is perceived to be more rigorous and valuable in terms of output and findings than a traditional literature review conducted by experts in their field remains an empirical question.

Further, in looking afresh at the empirical evidence contained in existing studies, a systematic review attempts to draw out answers to questions which the original research may not have been designed or set up to answer. This represented a challenge but it is important to note that the difficulty relates to the process of asking research studies to answer questions which are not their primary focus rather than xii to any fault in the original studies. Nevertheless, a defining feature of much of the evidence in relation to empty or irregularly occupied property is its age. A considerable body of work investigating second homes, particularly, relates to UK society over twenty years ago. The value of more recent evidence on second homes lies in highlighting the scale of the issue and the efficacy of possible policy responses. However, in relation to providing a succinct answer to the two questions regarding the impact of empty or irregularly occupied dwellings on the sustainability of rural communities and the effectiveness of policy interventions, the available empirical evidence is limited, and this in itself is useful to know.

Introduction

This introductory chapter describes the background to the development of this ESRC-funded review of the evidence regarding the effects of privately owned empty or irregularly occupied properties on the sustainability of rural communities, and the extent to which policy interventions have mitigated these effects. The chapter explains why a systematic review of this area of public policy is important, and introduces the relevant policy context.

Introducing the Study: Developing Evidence-based Policy

There is a growing requirement for public policy to be evidence-based. A key tool in the formulation of evidence-based policy is the systematic review which seeks to provide a comprehensive assessment of existing knowledge in a given area through extensive searching and critical appraisal of available evidence. The methods of systematic reviewing are commonly used in the fields of health, and education, and are increasingly being adopted to consider social and public policy topics. The ESRC has funded a programme of research projects that aim to develop and refine the methodologies required for the identification, appraisal and synthesis of evidence in the social policy context, and examine how evidence-based policy can be generated in a number of social policy areas.

As part of this ESRC programme, the University of York has established an 'evidence node' in health and social policy, focusing upon the methodology of reviews in social policy and social care. The first review undertaken by the node examined the evidence related to the effectiveness of current public and private safety nets available to mortgagors in unforeseen financial difficulties, attempting to link policy responses or 'interventions' with specific outcomes, notably mortgage arrears and repossessions. Other reviews undertaken by the York node have addressed how carers access health care and the effectiveness of respite services for carers of people with dementia-type illnesses. A number of other reviews have also been generated by the ESRC programme at other academic centres in the UK. As intended, this growing body of work has helped to stimulate methodological debate and development regarding how systematic reviews can be undertaken in complex policy areas. This review therefore adds to the growing body of work undertaken at the University of York and elsewhere and has two purposes: to provide a rigorous and authoritative account of the evidence in the topic area; and to take forward some of the methodological debates related to undertaking reviews in complex policy areas raised by Croucher *et al.* (2003).

Why Undertake a Review in This Topic Area?

A review in this area of interest is timely. The topic addresses key national and local policy concerns, notably sustainable communities and housing demand. The complexities of the policy context also present particular methodological challenges. Furthermore, the social and economic impacts of second homes, in particular, on rural communities are contested, and have been the focus of considerable, often emotive debate over the last few decades[1].

Policy Context

As part of its publication *Sustainable Communities: Building for the Future* (Office of the Deputy Prime Minister [ODPM], 2003) the Government has developed the themes that were identified in the Rural White Paper to tackle social exclusion. The policy agenda has set out its intentions with respect to sustainable and inclusive communities principally through the development of affordable housing. Housing is not only the major contributor to the experience of disadvantage in rural areas, but has been described as the principal engine of social change in rural England. At the same time, these policy developments are linked with sustaining and developing rural economies, particularly in relation to tourism, alongside the maintenance of environmental quality.

Vacant or Empty Properties

A fundamental issue in relation to the maintenance of sustainable communities in the countryside is the extent to which the stock of residential dwellings in any community is fully occupied. The government have drawn attention to the issue of stock under-utilisation. Dwellings may be empty or irregularly occupied for a variety of reasons. Research has drawn attention to the need to distinguish between two types of vacant dwellings. The first, *transactional vacants,* are an inherent function of the housing market and represent properties vacant whilst being sold or let. Included in this type are properties undergoing renovation or improvement and which are intended to be re-occupied relatively quickly. In contrast, the second type can be described as *problematic vacants,* and are unoccupied for substantial periods of time and are often in poor condition. There are many reasons for dwellings remaining vacant for considerable periods of time. The consultation paper on empty homes issued by the ODPM (2003) identified factors such as dilapidated dwellings, requiring substantial investment to bring up them to a habitable standard; in extreme cases buildings that have been abandoned by their owners; cases where ownership is unresolved, say if an occupant died intestate; properties held as speculative assets; property held as an investment, say for retirement; and property held by two home owners who begin co-habiting, leaving the other property vacant. The consultation paper noted that the latter two examples are often viewed as second homes. A significant additional factor in the rural context is that vacant properties may arise as a result of the rationalisation of agricultural labour on farm holdings and estates, which has led to a consi lerable number of dwellings becoming redundant as tied acco modation, although owners have often been reluctant to sell or let these dwellings on the open market.

Second and Holiday Homes

Cutting across these policy areas are the factors of production and consumption in relation to leisure and housing. Increased leisure time and cultural and lifestyle choices can be expressed in the free market through the consumption of property and can act as one component of the drivers of social change in rural areas that the Government is seeking to mediate. A further variable is the use of property for leisure purposes that also coincides with individual strategies in relation to retirement planning and investment. Such dynamics have contributed to an increase in second home ownership and an influx of households into the countryside. An essential feature of such migration, alongside other migration flows resulting from commuting or retirement, is that it is differentiated by income and wealth and throws into sharp relief the unequal capacities within the general population to attain owner occupation in the countryside. As part of these phenomena, second homes have a localised impact in rural localities leading to micro-crises in local housing markets.

Policy Responses

Policy responses to second and holiday homes are centred around attempts to mitigate the impact of demand-led pressures on the rural housing stock. In contrast, policies aimed at tackling vacant dwellings in the private sector are focused upon supply-led considerations encouraging, or compelling, owners to bring properties back into use. The issue of empty homes was the subject of recent policy attention in England in the form of the consultation paper *Empty Homes: Temporary Management, Lasting Solutions* (ODPM, 2003). This paper set out a range of approaches for tackling empty homes, including the potential for new statutory powers for local authorities to take over the management of some private sector empty homes.

A rationale for policies aimed at bringing empty properties back into use in rural areas is that they enable more households to live in these communities. This has a knock-on effect on the viability of local services and facilities such as shops and schools.

Further, such schemes often ensure that such properties are targeted on households that need affordable housing. There are a number of examples of schemes at national level, such as the rural empty property initiative in Scotland, or at local level, the farm cottage scheme, run by Kennet District Council, Wiltshire.

Second and holiday homes occupy the interface between the two policy areas of leisure and housing. Tensions between these policy areas were highlighted by the operation of the controversial policy in the Yorkshire Dales National Park whereby a redundant barn could be converted into accommodation for a holiday home, but could not be converted into a permanent dwelling to meet a local housing need. This policy was subsequently revised, and indeed, Yorkshire Dales National Park recently adopted a policy whereby the sale of new homes or barn conversions will be restricted to buyers who qualify under the scheme as 'local'.

At the same time, the subject of second homes has been increasingly the focus of policy attention at the national level. The Government legislated to reduce the discount on second homes in England with respect to council tax from 50 per cent to ten per cent and Part 6 (Council Tax Provisions) of the Local Government Bill came into force in 2003.

Local authorities can spend any additional funds thus raised on improving public services such as transport, affordable housing or policing. However, it is significant that the discount will not be removed entirely, and will be set at a minimum of ten per cent. It is hoped that this retained discount will provide an incentive for individuals to continue to register their second homes to enable local authorities to monitor the scale and impact of second home ownership within their areas.

This step marks the view that from a policy perspective it is deemed necessary to separate out the impact of second home ownership from other influences upon local housing markets. Similarly, local authorities in Scotland have the new power to reduce the discount on second homes from 50 per cent to ten per cent. It will come into effect at the start of the financial year 2005-06. Any additional income generated by cutting the discount will be retained locally and used to provide new-built affordable social housing Unitary authorities in Wales have had the discretion to charge full council tax on second homes since 1998. The research by Tewdwr-Jones *et al.* (2002) noted that by 2001, all but two of 22 authorities had done this.

Policy attention at local level has also focused upon the issue of second homes. A review of planning authorities in other parts of the UK has noted that a number of authorities are proposing specific second homes policies for their areas. For example, the Draft Unitary Development Plan for Gwynedd Council sets out that any proposal for developments that would lead to an increase in second homes will be refused in communities where the level of second homes has reached ten per cent.

Whilst policy documents in particular note that such use of dwellings on an irregular basis in rural areas may have both positive and negative impacts, the costs and benefits of second and holiday homes have not been elaborated in a systematic way. Further, it is necessary to understand the diverse impacts that vacant, second and holiday homes have upon rural housing markets and economies in the context of sustainable communities.

Methodological Challenges

In addition to the policy relevance, the context for the review is complex and presents particular methodological challenges. A clearly defined question is the essential first step in undertaking a systematic review; the question frames the review, generates the consequent search strategies and study selection criteria. In addressing review questions in complex policy areas, however, it is necessary to resolve the tension between the defined question (and seeking the material to address that question), and the requirement to provide a 'contextual map' in order to understand the question and make the conclusions of a review meaningful.

Croucher *et al.* (2003) recognised that although the focus of their review was on the various safety nets available to mortgagors, the findings of the review had to be seen in the wider context of a complex interaction of factors-economic cycles, interest rates, housing prices, financial regulation and lenders' practices-that impact on sustainable home ownership. The context for this review is similarly complex.

Various factors, such as the growth of home ownership and the 'Right-to-Buy' legislation, changing patterns of employment, and the so-called 'flight from the cities', have resulted in growing housing demands in rural areas from both local people and new residents, high house prices, and a lack of social rented housing. Evidence gathered in the Countryside Agency's annual 'state of the countryside' reports indicate growing housing demand from local people and new residents, high house prices, low incomes, and a lack of social rented housing in many rural areas.

However, demand for housing and the operation of housing markets must be seen against a broader background of on-going socio-economic and environmental changes occurring in the countryside. A review of the impact of empty or irregularly occupied properties, particularly second homes, must therefore be located in this complex context.

In preparing this review we have not sought to provide a 'contextual map' as time and resources did not allow for the examination of the wider contextual literature. Fortunately the Countryside Agency has recently published a review of countryside issues in England, drawing on the evidence collated between 1999-2003 for the preparation of the annual 'state of the countryside' reports. It provides a valuable portrait of emerging trends across a number of key themes, including: rural demography; health and social care provision; education; transport; environment and recreation; and the rural economy. It provides a valuable background to our review.

A further methodological challenge relates to the difficulties of defining key concepts such as 'rural', 'second home', and 'sustainability'. In Chapter Two we present the definitions we have adopted for the purpose of the review. It is important to note latthis point that our thinking regarding sustainability has been shaped by the work of Long (2001).

Indeed the dimensions of sustainability outlined by Long provided a framework for organising the evidence we retrieved. Long presents a series of headings relating to different aspects of sustainability including: housing demand; quality and design of housing; crime and anti-social behaviour; social exclusion and poverty; accessibility and viability of facilities; and community cohesion. We have sought to present the evidence against these headings, in an attempt to distinguish the different ways in which empty and irregularly occupied properties impact on rural host communities.

As noted above the social and economic impacts of second homes, in particular, on rural communities are contested. There are about 100,000 second homes in rural England representing less than 1% of the total stock; nevertheless second homes are widely perceived to be a manifestation of social inequality, and a main cause of rural housing shortages. A review in a contested area such as this may be particularly useful in moving the debate forward.

Report Structure

This report is presented in seven chapters. Chapter Two presents a detailed account of the methods and definitions employed in the review. Chapter Three presents a commentary on the research methods adopted by the studies – highlighting some of the difficulties regarding different definitions particularly of 'second homes', and the range of methods used in the studies that entered the review. Chapter Four presents the substantive findings of the review examining the impact of empty, second and holiday homes upon the sustainability of rural communities.

The nature of policy interventions on empty, second and holiday homes, examining studies that have evaluated policy mechanisms, and also drawing together recommendations for policy, which have been set out by various studies in the review. Chapter Six addresses the particular methodological challenges encountered during the review process. Finally Chapter Seven provides the conclusions from the review, highlighting possible avenues for future research. Substantial appendices are attached for reference, providing more detail on the search strategies, data abstraction methods and studies included and excluded from the review. 7

Methods

Introduction-What is a Systematic Review?

A systematic review aims to provide a comprehensive and unbiased summary of available evidence on a given topic. This is achieved by: the use of a clearly defined search strategy to ensure that an extensive range of potential sources of evidence is explored; and the use of explicit criteria to appraise the quality of the evidence to ensure that only robust evidence is synthesised in the production of the final review.

The review process is guided by a protocol in which the approach to be taken by the review team is explained in some detail, making transparent the basis on which decisions will be made, the source of studies, the reasons why studies will be included or excluded from the review, how quality will be assessed, and on what basis the data will be synthesised. Once a review is underway a greater understanding of the content and type of literature may develop. If it is found that changes to parts of the protocol are necessary, these are documented and justified within the final report of the review.

Systematic reviews are complex (and often costly) studies, but they offer an invaluable means for policy makers and practitioners to make sense of large volumes of evidence that may be difficult and time consuming to locate and of variable quality. In addition they can be used to direct future research towards that which is poorly understood or under-researched. The six stages of the review process are set out in Table 1.

Table 1 Review process

1. Formulate the review question/s
2. Develop review protocol
    - Define appropriate study design
    - Define quality assessment criteria
    - Devise search strategy
    - Devise data abstraction method
    - Decide data synthesis method
3. Document identification and retrieval
4. Application of study selection criteria
5. Extraction and synthesis of data from studies entered into the review
6. Presentation of review findings.

Location and Timing of Studies

Study inclusion was limited to material in English published in the UK. It was beyond the scope of this review to examine literature from other countries as interpretation of any studies retrieved would require a comprehensive understanding of that country's cultural norms regarding housing markets, finance systems and perhaps leisure trends. It is unknown whether restricting the search in this way omitted any research that included empirical data relating to the UK that was not published in the UK, although this seems unlikely. The resources available to the review did not allow the additional effort required to locate, retrieve and filter literature from outside the UK. 13

In setting the boundaries of a review, it is usually necessary to decide a 'cut-off' point, where evidence from before a given time is considered to be less useful as it addresses concerns or interventions that are too far removed from current context and practice to be meaningful. There was no obvious date that would provide a logical cut-off point for research in this field. There were no major policy changes that would suggest any prior research was inappropriate (with the possible exception of the 1980 Housing Act that introduced the 'Right-to-Buy' council homes which had significant implications for rural areas) or notable housing market events that would suggest major changes in the field. Gallent *et al.* (2002) note that the theme of second homes flourished in academic literature in the 1970s. Moreover many of these early studies continue to be frequently cited in more recent reports and publications. Initial scoping searches showed that we would not be overwhelmed with potentially relevant studies and so a decision was taken not to restrict studies on date. Studies were therefore included regardless of when they were published, which produced substantial debate within the review team surrounding the applicability of older research in this field to contemporary policy making, especially when examining dynamically changing housing markets. We return to this issue in Chapter Six.

Study Design

One of the challenges for a review addressing policy is deciding on the type of 'evidence' that will provide the most trustworthy answers to the review question/s, and this was a central concern for this review. We are aware there are lively debates about what constitutes 'good' or 'good enough' evidence when promoting evidence-based or evidence-informed policy and practice. For the purpose of this review we took evidence to mean any contribution that is based upon primary empirical material as part of the study – be that qualitative or quantitative. Any study setting out views or opinions that could not be substantiated by its own empirical data was not included in the review. We recognise that there may be other types of 'evidence' that could have informed this review, however given that second home ownership is a highly politicised and emotive subject, we were keen to ensure that the evidence we included could be grounded directly in empirical research. We also recognise the use of hierarchies of evidence in many systematic reviews – particularly in the health care field-that privilege experimental over other types of study design, as they are deemed to provide the most robust internally valid results when assessing the effectiveness and outcomes of health care inventions. For reviews in complex policy areas however, such hierarchies are less useful, in part due to the (almost complete) lack of experimental studies, but also because 'evidence' is more broadly defined and drawn from a range of research paradigms.

Study Selection Criteria-Quality Appraisal

One strength of systematic reviewing is the consistent critical appraisal of the evidence-base. It examines what is known about a subject and how confident we can be in this knowledge. It also ensures that the conclusions and recommendations derived from a review are based on evidence in which the research design and its conduct can be assumed to offer a reasonable level of confidence in the results. Studies of poor quality are therefore excluded. A quality criteria tool developed by Croucher *et al.* (2003) was chosen to establish whether a study met the quality threshold. Although there is little consensus over the use of appraisal tools in reviews, this tool has been successfully adopted by other reviewers since its development. It was also utilised in this review as reviewer and readers alike can readily understand it; it includes guidance on its practical application; it offers prompts to aid reflection on the study and is not resource intensive. These criteria were applied to each study that met the initial inclusion criteria. As noted by

Croucher *et al.* (2003), those criteria marked as essential are those with the potential to alter the findings of the research, and the reviewers had to be confident that studies going forward to the review had addressed these criteria satisfactorily. Those criteria marked as desirable aid interpretation of results and may help explain variance in findings.[2]

Devising the Search Strategy

The aim of a search is to identify as comprehensive a list as possible of studies that relate to the review questions, reducing the potential for bias that may arise from too narrow a consideration of the field of investigation. A search strategy should therefore aim to be as inclusive as possible of the range of sources of primary studies, within the confines of resource constraints of the review. This section details how our search was conducted.

The subject of vacant and irregularly occupied property has relevance to a variety of different policy areas such as housing, planning, recreation and environmental health. Further, in an academic context, both housing and rural studies can be characterised as having a strong inter-disciplinary focus. These features suggest that the search strategy needed to have a very broad focus. Research evidence was identified using a number of channels.

Table 2: Identifying Research

- Searches of appropriate electronic databases
- Reference checking of all articles received
- Checking relevant internet sites
- Hand searching of journals
- Contact with a sample of local authorities with high concentrations of second homes

The review team included an Information Scientist from the NHS Centre for Reviews and Dissemination (NHS CRD) who developed and conducted the electronic search strategy working with the research team to establish key search terms, and potential sources of studies. The search terms included in the search strategy are set out in Appendix One. Recognising that many social science databases do not allow for sophisticated searching, the aim was to develop a strategy that would be highly sensitive, and facilitate identification of the greatest number of potentially relevant studies in the subject area.

Electronic Databases

Electronic databases represent a powerful source of references for a review. However different databases are constructed in different ways, and tend to specialise in certain types of data sources, or particular topics or disciplines. In addition, some are better indexed and contain more detailed abstracts than others. It is therefore important to utilise a range of databases within any one review. The requirement to search a range of databases is increased in a complex area of study, where different disciplines may have been involved and a range of approaches may have been taken to addressing research questions. As noted by Croucher *et al.* (2003), electronic databases do not appear to be as valuable a source of references for social policy reviews as for reviews on social care or health topics. Very few of the studies retrieved from electronic databases entered this review, nevertheless the studies provided a valuable source of additional references from which a number of included studies were drawn.

A full list of the databases searched is presented in Appendix One. A total of 10 were searched including the key social science databases (e.g. Social Science Citation Index and ASSIA), as well as the databases for related disciplines like economics (EconLit) and planning (Planex), and those covering grey literature (SIGLE). The inclusion of databases covering grey literature was thought to be particularly important as a significant number of the studies eventually included in the review conducted by Croucher *et al.* (2003) were retrieved from indexes of grey literature. Hansard was also searched for evidence cited in government sources.

The majority of databases were searched for no cost, as they are available through the University of York resources, or access to them at the British Library has been financially supported through the ESRC Evidence Network.

Only some databases were sophisticated enough to run a complex search. Those where this was possible include: Sociological Abstracts, SIGLE, ASSIA, Econlit, PAIS, SCCI and SSHICP. The remaining databases were searched using a simplified version of the search strategy. To ensure consistency in searching procedures, the search strategies were designed and undertaken by a specialist Information Officer from the NHS Centre for Reviews and Dissemination. The search strategies are presented in Appendix Two.

Internet Web Sites

Internet web sites can prove a valuable source of up-to-date material and grey literature. A number of websites were browsed for relevant documents. The websites searched in this review cover a range of national and local government sites, academic research institutes, professional organisations, and research funders.

A list of these websites is presented in Appendix Three. As noted by Croucher *et al.* (2003), not all websites incorporate search engines or allow easy navigation. Although a number of potentially relevant references were found on the web (n=11), only one went forward for inclusion in the review.

Hand Searching

Electronic databases may be incomplete or not up to date in their coverage of the field so some hand searching was included in the search. Croucher *et al.* (2003) noted that in their review on safety nets for home owners that hand searching proved a fruitful source of studies for their review. Appendix Four includes a range of journals from policy and academic fields with a remit in the housing and rural 17 studies area that were hand searched for papers that may not have been catalogued on databases or cited elsewhere.

Reference Checking

The reviewers checked the reference lists of all retrieved literature for additional references, including unpublished material. Each new reference identified in this way was also searched in turn for new references until this process was exhausted.

Citations in retrieved studies were an important way of tracing older studies. In this particular review, reference checking provided more that half of the studies that were finally included.

Local Authority Contacts

Local authorities are charged with undertaking comprehensive assessments of their local housing markets, although until recently this has primarily concentrated on the needs and requirements for social housing. Nevertheless, it was thought that certain local authorities may have undertaken research into empty or irregularly occupied dwellings, given the reported level of interest in this issue and recent policy changes concerning the council tax reductions for second homes.

It was thought too onerous to canvas each rural local authority in the UK; therefore, a sample of authorities in England and Wales, identified by FPD Savills (2004) as having in excess of three per cent of dwelling stock used as second homes, were contacted and asked about research in their area. A list of the authorities contacted is presented in Appendix Five. If more time had been available the comprehensiveness of the review would have been improved by contacting authorities in similar positions in Scotland and Northern Ireland. One Welsh county council provided major reports by key researchers that had not been identified elsewhere, however other local authorities did not appear to possess significant unpublished research.

Document Identification and Retrieval

The search process produced 1060 references. Once duplicate references were removed, a total of 963 remained. All references were entered into Reference Manager, an essential tool to ensure that that the progress of each reference at each stage of the review is tracked and recorded. The number of studies retrieved at each stage of the review, broken down by source of reference. If studies were unavailable within the research unit or University of York's library then they were obtained from the British Library Documents Supply Centre or other university libraries and inter-loans arranged. We were unable to obtain some studies and these are detailed in Appendix Six.

Applying the Selection Criteria

The initial reference set of 1060 reports and studies became the 23 included in this review. After the lead reviewer scanned each reference, 273 were identified as being potentially relevant and copies of the reports retrieved. If the relevance was uncertain because of the absence, or quality, of the abstracts then the report was retrieved anyway. The reports were then examined in more detail and checked against the inclusion criteria. Studies that looked likely to pass the inclusion criteria were then subjected to the data extraction process using the form in Appendix Seven, which was created with Microsoft Access. At least two reviewers checked the decisions made regarding the application of the inclusion criteria and quality appraisal, with disagreements decided by consensus within the whole review team. This left 30 studies that met the inclusion criteria but 7 of these did not meet the quality threshold, meaning a total of 23 studies went forward to the final reDetails of the seven studies that did not meet the quality threshold are included in Appendix Eight. Three of these were conducted for Masters or Diplomas in Town Planning, and, although they demonstrated sufficient understanding of the topic and research methods, were not adequately robust to meet the quality threshold of this review. One other study did not use methods that were sensitive enough to capture data relating to second homes, or other empty or irregularly occupied properties, as acknowledged by the authors. Two further studies did not contain enough information about the methods used in the study to convey any confidence in the findings reported. Although this may have been due to poor reporting rather than poor research, it was nevertheless problematic. Finally one study mainly reported an unsystematic literature review; although there was some new research reported in addition to secondary data, again this was not reported in sufficient detail.

Wallace *et al.* (2004) report how some authors express concern at the reduction of such large initial reference sets to the small numbers of studies that go forward for review, suggesting that a large quantity of relevant evidence is being lost in the process. The two most common reasons for studies not passing the inclusion criteria were that they did not address the issues of empty or irregularly occupied property or were not based upon empirical research. Many studies did not pass the inclusion criteria in the review of assistance for mortgagors in financial difficulties for very similar reasons, either they did not pass the inclusions criteria or were not empirical studies.

As reported in Arksey *et al.* (2004) the table should be treated with some caution when assessing the utility of different databases for the review. Once the initial references were received the duplicate entries from different databases were removed according to a hierarchy of databases relevant to this review. The less sophisticated databases, such as Planex or IBSS, were deduplicated against the more specific ones, such as SSCI, SSHI, SocAbs, SIGLE, Econlit or ASSIA. Nevertheless, it is interesting to note the dominance of grey literature databases and reference checking as sources of studies for this systematic review. As in Croucher *et al.* (2003), the academic peer-reviewed databases were less helpful as a supply of studies that were worth consideration for the review. It is apparent that journal articles are not the prime publication source of primary research in housing. Those journal papers that were retrieved were usually excluded in favour of the main report to the commissioners, as they included more detail about the substantive topic and the research methods.

Document Retrieval

Most retrieval was conducted through the British Library Document Supply Centre (BLDSC), which generally worked very well. However, 35 reports were found to be potentially relevant but were unavailable through the BLDSC, the research commissioners or other libraries. These studies are listed in Appendix Six. They were mostly from the 1970s and generally evenly split between those focussing on second homes and those focussing on general rural housing issues. One of the reports dated from the 1960s, 14 from the 1970s, 5 from the 1980s, 10 from the 1990s and 1 from 2000 onwards. The 1970s reports were more concerned with second homes, and the 1990s reports with general rural housing issues. Many of these studies were produced at the local authority level, and not deposited within the public domain which may account for the difficulties in locating them. Emails and letters were sent to the rural authorities with the most concentrations of second homes, but apart from one authority where a particularly interested information officer was employed, this resulted in few studies being identified, despite local authorities being charged with conducting local housing market area analysis. The information officer with whom the review team was in contact actually supplied some key studies that were not identified through any databases but that were included in the final review. It is also of concern that fifteen studies conducted in the 1990s and 2000s were also unavailable. One of these was produced for a private client who would not agree to the full report being released, but others were requested from libraries and commissioning organisations with no success.

From the patterns of decisions made as the other reports went through the review process, it may be surmised that many of the reports would not have met the inclusion criteria for the review because they were not based upon empirical research. In addition many of the reports that focussed on general rural housing issues may not have included work on empty or irregularly occupied properties, as it is likely that they may have only have addressed the supply of social housing or planning concerns, for example. It is likely, however, that the earlier studies on second homes would have been the most rewarding to have found, albeit that they are several decades old.

Data Abstraction and Synthesis

An electronic data extraction form was designed: to ensure a uniform and structured set of data was extracted from each study; to record the reasons for including or excluding studies from the review; and to aid comparison between the studies. Reviewers completed a form for each of the studies that passed the relevance criteria for the review. An Access database was used to manage data extraction forms. Over and above the bibliographic and descriptive data extracted from each study, these forms were used to record the different strands of evidence relating to the impacts of empty and irregularly occupied properties on the different dimensions of sustainability set out. In regard to policy initiatives data were abstracted regarding the structure, process, and outcome of policy.

Two matrices were developed. The first matrix charted the evidence from each study concerned with the impacts of empty and irregularly occupied properties on rural communities onto the different dimensions of sustainability. We drew on raw data from the studies and the interpretations of the authors of the studies. The second matrix charted different types of policy interventions – planning, fiscal, housing market, environmental – and evidence relating to their structure, process and outcomes. These matrices enabled us to organise the evidence around particular themes, and compare findings across different studies.

Achieving an actual synthesis of the findings has been problematic. In particular it has been a challenge to draw conclusions from evidence on housing markets. Housing markets are dynamic systems and change considerably across both time and location. In addition, the disparate nature of the studies, in terms of case study areas, time when research was conducted, various methods adopted, and inconsistent definition across studies means the review relies heavily on a descriptive account of study findings. The review team are aware of the debates surrounding methods in narrative synthesis but recognise that more empirical testing of various approaches is required to develop these methods further.

Conclusion

The review has presented particular methodological challenges. These are further explored in Chapter Six. We are confident however that the rigour of the search ensures that very little evidence has been overlooked, and that through the application of study selection criteria only robust evidence has been synthesised and presented in the findings of this review. view. Definitions of empty, second and holiday homes

The definition of what constitutes a second home or holiday home has been a perennial problem. This is an issue in all aspects of the research as it impedes comparison between studies and has the potential to cause confusion. Although individual studies may provide a clear definition of the types of accommodation that were included or excluded, it is unclear whether studies that compared evidence from other research findings to each other or to the Census material were talking about the same phenomena. For example, a study that reported the growth in second home ownership in local areas may have recorded the growth in purpose built holiday villages, rather than existing dwellings in villages, smaller settlements or dwellings that stand alone in remote countryside.

A degree of permanence relating to the dwelling physical structure was often included in definitions of second homes. However, other studies included chalets, log cabins and static caravans. Their inclusion could be problematic as the analysis did not always disaggregate the findings for these distinct parts of the second homes market. It was therefore capable of overestimating the number of second homes in a locality with potential as permanent first homes for local people. Local demand for residence in holiday parks, with chalets, log cabins or static caravans, appears to be generated by lack of other housing opportunities rather than housing preferences, although residency in Park Homes may be more long term. Exploring these differences would have added some clarity to any analysis of the degree of competition in the local housing market between locals and second home owners.

Several studies were careful to draw a distinction in principle between second homes and holiday homes, Tewdwr-Jones *et al.*(2000), Pyne 1973, South West Economic Planning Council, 1975, Bennett, 1979, Davies and O'Farrell, 1981, Capstick, 1987). However, difficulties with differentiating between a second and holiday home were readily acknowledged by a number of the studies. Bielckus also noted that where households owned two properties, it was not always clear which could be defined as the first home or second home, since the way in which such properties were used, and also length of occupancy in the different residences were not always clear cut.

Distinctions were also blurred between the dwellings used as holiday homes and second homes, as second homes were sometimes let to defray costs associated with ownership. One study defined holiday homes as a reduction in supply and conceptualised them as part of the tourist stock of accommodation, such as hotels. This may also be problematic if looking comprehensively at demand in local housing markets as they remain dwellings unavailable for use as permanent residence for local people but have been removed in the analysis of total dwelling stocks.

Some definitions emphasised the use made of the dwelling for leisure or recreation. As there are changing patterns of employment for some, with home-working, tele-working and dual income households, the distinction may today be less clear. One partner may use the 'other' dwelling to work from whilst the other does not, as household and working arrangements become more diverse. This pattern of changing housing consumption has yet to be explored in research concerning second or holiday homes.

Identifying Empty and Irregularly Occupied Property

A fundamental difficulty that studies have sought to address is the identification of an accurate figure of the number of empty, second homes and holiday homes, either nationally, or in case study areas. As has been noted above, this difficulty relates in part to the definition of the types of dwelling that constitute empty, second and holiday homes. A further difficulty stems from the way that empty, second and holiday homes are identified in sources of data, and potential confusion over the precise use to which dwellings are put. Subsequently, these factors have implications for the comparison of the number of empty, second and holiday homes between studies and over time.

The Census provides a readily accessible source, in that it attempts to measure the number of empty, second and holiday homes. The Census has provided data on second and holiday homes every ten years since 1981 – prior to this, second homes were not recorded in the Census. However, whilst the 1981 and 1991 Censuses differentiated between second homes and holiday homes, the 2001 Census only included an aggregate figure including both second and holiday homes. Furthermore, studies have highlighted that it is likely that the Census undercounts the actual number of second homes. Second/holiday homes were identified in the 2001 Census as being distinct from vacant dwellings either by the enumerator or from a household completing a Census form for an address that was not their principal residence. Households that returned a form where all household members are visitors are classed as second or holiday home. Unoccupied dwellings are classified as a second or holiday home if at least one of the household spaces within it (or the single household space if the dwelling is unshared) is a second or holiday home. However, as Gallent *et al.* (2002) point out, enumerators exclude properties that are not known to be secondary residences or holiday homes, and this is where an undercount may occur. These authors also noted that it is not known to what extent second homes are enumerated as occupied accommodation on Census night.

Difficulties in accurately distinguishing between empty, second or holiday homes was also noted by Murie *et al.* (1995) who described problems in the way in which properties are recorded as empty by surveyors as part of surveys of empty properties in Scotland. A number of properties recorded as empty were in fact second or holiday homes, which casts doubt on the way these are recorded.

For example, the Post Census Survey of Vacant Properties (PCSVP) was conducted in 1991 by the General Register Office for Scotland as a follow up survey of properties classified by Census enumerators as being vacant on Census night. It did not include households spaces identified in the Census as not used as main residence or occupied household spaces where the household was absent on Census night. The qualitative research conducted by Murie *et al.* (1995) noted problems with the classification between these two categories and the truly vacant category and suggested that it was probable that some vacants were student housing or were second or holiday homes. Other research on empty properties in Scotland has reinforced this finding. The evaluation of the Scottish Empty Homes Initiative found that many properties identified as empty were in fact being used as holiday homes.

A further concern about the Census is that it only provides data every ten years, and thus the figures soon date. Studies subsequently need to have recourse to other sources to obtain current numbers between Censuses. Historically, rating registers have provided an important source of data for studies of second homes. The majority of the studies undertaken in the 1970s drew upon rating registers for this purpose. However, the registers did not identify second home owners directly, and instead noted which owners had an address outside of the county. Thus they only indicated the possibility of dwellings used as second homes. Surveys were then required to identify which properties were actually used as second homes. However, in line with the identified drawbacks of the Census, a number of studies recognised that such methods might lead to an undercount of the actual number of second homes. As highlighted by the De Vane (1975) study, the work by Tuck (1973) and Pyne (1973) estimated that the rating register undercounted second homes by about ten per cent.

To attempt to mitigate this undercount, a number of studies used alternative sources to identify second homes to complement the figures drawn from the rating registers. Thus Coleman (1982), Bennett (1976), Bollom (1975), De Vane (1975), the South West Economic Planning Council (1975), Tuck (1973) used a case study approach to draw on alternative sources to corroborate the figures identified from the rating register.

These studies used the local knowledge of local residents to try and identify second homes in their respective settlements. Bollom (1975) and the South West Economic Planning Council (1975) also used the electoral register as a method of identifying possible second homes. Other studies used field surveys such as Davies and O'Farrell (1981) – an approach which may offer the potential for additional accuracy, but which would be a costly method to reproduce in future research.

Recent research such as Gallent *et al.* (2002) identifies council tax returns as the most promising source of data on second homes, although these authors also highlighted drawbacks. To a certain extent confusion arises from the way that properties may, or may not, be registered by owners for council tax. At the time that the research by Gallant *et al.* (2002) was undertaken, a 50% discount for properties used as second homes was available, and the authors point out that, individuals may not necessarily have claimed the discount of 50%, even though they may have been eligible, thereby removing themselves from any count. Murie *et al.* (1995) also noted that in Scotland, although the majority of dwellings that qualified for two discounts for council tax were second homes, this number was not wholly accurate as a count for second homes specifically. Greater clarity over second home numbers may develop as local authorities in Scotland develop their monitoring and identification of second home owners as part of the billing process.

Which Methods Have Studies Used?

The authors of the various studies had employed a mixture of methods, primarily surveys, interviews and discussion groups with various key respondents. Some also utilised secondary data sources such as previous research or market surveys. The summary table in Appendix Nine includes a brief description of the methods employed by each study.

Surveys

Many of the earlier studies undertook large-scale postal surveys of second home owners. Second home owners were usually identified through rating registers. Two smaller studies also surveyed much smaller samples of second home owners. Questions posed to second home owners addressed a variety of topics across the different studies; for example, location of primary residence and distances travelled to second homes, seasonal use of property, frequency and length of visits, amenities used, average expenditure, age and socio-economic status of second home owners, as well as questions about the location, age and state of repair, and amenities in the properties used as second homes. Other studies surveyed rural officers in local authorities, and local estate agents.

Case Studies

Nearly all the studies investigated second homes in different case study areas although the location and connection between the case studies varied. Only one study considered case study areas across the UK. Others used case studies in particular nations or other 31 defined geographic areas such as a National Park. These multi-area case studies were very useful to illustrate the diversity in the experiences of the same phenomena displayed in different local housing markets. Only two studies considered second homes in a single location.

Key Informants

A key feature of this body of research was collating the views, experiences and judgements of key informants on various aspects of empty, second and holiday homes through surveys or interviews and discussions. However there was some variation across the studies regarding the type of respondents that were considered as key informants, reflected to some extent the shifting focus of the research.

As noted above, a feature of studies investigating second homes in rural areas in the 1970s and 1980s was a focus on assessing impacts by surveying second home owners themselves. With the exception of one study, all the studies also presented local residents' views regarding second home owners and, sometimes, local housing demand, usually via interviews/discussion groups with local residents, although an alternative approach used by many of the studies was to examine impacts of second homes by contacting local key informants. In some instances, these informants included local contacts, such as police, local businesses, members of the clergy. Some studies reflected methods of gauging local feelings that would now be considered inappropriate for research. Examples include using village gatekeepers such as the clergy, police officers, postmasters or teachers. With greater commuting and turnover in employment, the ability of such professions to talk on behalf of a community may be more limited today. Moreover, it may be more acceptable to actually the hear the voices of those who are the subjects of that part of the study, for example, holding focus groups of villagers.

On a similar theme, no studies interviewed or surveyed first time buyers in rural areas, and yet their ability to enter owner occupation underpinned many assumptions about the problems second homes may be causing. One study held a focus group of young people, but they were not engaged in the process of registering or searching for property to rent or own at that time. Although, one study did make the point that the ability of households to trade up as household circumstances change is also vital for sustainable communities and so retaining existing homeowners is a problem in areas of high house price rises. Inclusion of data from those making house searches in case study areas would be beneficial for comprehensive analysis, to highlight similarities or differences between the type and price of property they are seeking to buy.

A considerable proportion of the studies also interviewed professionals in the public and/or private sectors. Many studies used the knowledge of housing and planning officials or staff from housing associations to gauge knowledge about local housing markets. However, many local authorities did not have housing needs assessments and some were out of date. Few had conducted comprehensive housing market analysis and so the ability of these people to comment on the local housing market was drawn mainly from their local knowledge and experience of the areas where they worked. Government and regulatory pressure has recently been exerted on local authorities to conduct more comprehensive analyses of local, sub-regional and regional housing markets, and so it is hoped that local policymakers will have a more robust evidence-base on which to draw in the future. There are already richer sources of contemporary data available now relating to house prices and neighbourhoods. These data are available at small output levels, such as the Census and other official statistics and market research tools such as Mosaic.

Some studies presented data based on interviews with estate agents; however, it was unclear whether a range of local agents had been sampled and the how the data were analysed. Greater use could have been made of key players – estate agents, lenders and solicitors – in the private market to provide more information about market processes and gauge levels of inward and outward migration.

Other studies interviewed key informants such as local tradesmen, planners and local residents to gauge the impact of second home ownership on local economies. These interviews were rarely supported with financial information.

Secondary Data

Some studies also drew on secondary data such as government report and market research data, Census, employment and labour market statistics, statistics on vacant properties, and Local Plans in Wales, Scotland and England.

Limitations of the Studies

The political problematisation of second homes has, in effect, led to the focus of the initial questions posed and research commissioned perhaps being too narrowly defined. The issue of second homes has been, with notable exceptions, studied in isolation from other expressions of external demand in local areas, such as retirement and commuting.

The study of second homes in isolation from other drivers of housing demand meant that it was difficult to separate impacts attributed to second homes from other factors, although authors continued to attribute shortages of affordable housing for local people and external competition in housing markets to second homes. One author did, however, decide to abandon the aim of assessing the impact of second homes on house prices as it was not possible to identify contrasting areas with high and low levels of second homes where direct comparison between housing markets could be achieved.

Where the issue of second homes was set within a wider economic and social context, authors drew on data from multiple case studies and examined other sources of external demand. For example, Gallent *et al.* (2002) noted that assessments of the economic impact of second homes in rural areas need to consider broader impacts such as e-shopping and the role of supermarkets in changing shopping habits of residents in rural areas. The multitude of factors from which housing market imbalances emerge should be included in any future analysis of rural housing markets.

The issue of second homes would be interesting to explore in the context, not only of the impacts on local housing markets, but as part of changing patterns of housing consumption, housing wealth and subsequent housing inequalities. The point of how home is interpreted was raised briefly in the evidence, but exploring this further in relation to use of second homes would be interesting, given changing patterns of work and residence.

Measures that have been taken to intervene in local markets have been poorly evaluated, such as those to restrict occupancy in National Parks, for example. Greater evaluation might shed light on the directions in which policy should develop in this respect.

3

Reducing Poverty Through Hospitality Business

Tourism is an economic tool which, when planted in a community expresses its positive presence through the jobs that spring from it. It then also contributes to the particular place's exposure to its external world drawing attention to it and with its visits that create the establishment of the logistics to address the needs of the visitors while they are there; food, drinks, transportation, communication, friendship, souvenirs.

Tourism is therefore a tool for poverty alleviation and social cohesion. The abject poverty in our rural areas could be reduced if tourism is developed. This is because most of our attraction sites are dotted in the rural areas where poverty is prevalent. Tourists spend on accommodation, food, souvenirs and so on at places visited. However, the fact that tourists embark on return visits and sleep in the urban areas after visiting the sites does not augur well for poverty reduction. The provision of social amenities in such areas will therefore go a long way to open up these areas to entice tourists to spend days at the attraction areas.

Tourism also orientates the community towards new introductions which may be positive or negative or both. Tourism never leaves a place without planting its footprints in there. It also makes a people conscious of their environmental cleanliness, and good conservation practices in a very sustainable way, because so long as the community area is acceptable to the visitors, they will continue to arrive and drop some benefits to the host community. It addresses the social and cultural issues of the community in a very positive way. In Ghana, tourism as a tool for poverty alleviation is not in doubt. What is in doubt is the understanding of the industry because not much by way of education as to what it is and is not is brought home to the Ghanaian society. Tourism enjoys a lot of global attention due to its economic power to generate huge incomes to nations and its massive job creation base. The potential of tourism to transform developing economies and leapfrog them into middle income economies within record times has never been doubted both by economists and politicians.

The advanced countries commit so much budgetary allocations to the tourism industry and they receive the biggest chunk of business travellers who have all the money to spend. In recent times, developing countries especially those in Africa have taken to tourism as one of the possible panaceas for their economic challenges. Notable among nations that have given priority to tourism on their developmental agenda are Malaysia, Morocco, Mauritius, Kenya, Egypt and Singapore. These countries invested so much into developing tourism and are making gains.

We are told that Ghana's tourism makes almost $1.1bn USD in foreign exchange earnings, contributing four percent to the national Gross Domestic Product and creates about 220,000 direct formal employments across the country.

Tourism Development

Tourism has become a major global economic activity. In many countries it has overtake agriculture and manufacturing. The diversification of Ghana's economy in 1985 and the need to shift focus from the over- reliance of the economy on the traditional commodities brought the tourism sector into the front line as a major economic activity that has the potential of resuscitating the ailing economy. Ghana offers a wide range of unique and exciting natural, cultural and historical resources which are highly undeveloped but must be developed. As a traditional export, tourism has the potential to become a powerful tool in pro-poor development strategies. It has the ability to create jobs and wealth. This potential can be realized if sound economic and social development strength of tourism is effectively mobilized to create wealth and fight poverty in the communities in particular and the country at large. The positive impact of tourism can be assessed in terms of foreign exchange earnings, employment and income as well as a conservation of the biodiversity and also a catalytic tool for the growth of other businesses. Indeed, the tourism sector in Ghana is experiencing some significant growth since 1996 with tremendous positive impact from the year 2000. The growth experienced re-emphases the government's commitment to the development of the tourism sector. This statement has been re-echoed by President John Agyekum Kufuor in his 2005 sectional address to parliament when he said, "tourism is a gold mine that must be tapped." Tourism in Ghana is indeed the untapped gold mine of the economy.

Even though about 80 percent of the tourism potentials of the country remains untapped it is the fourth foreign exchange earner of the country after remittances from abroad, Cocoa and Gold. However, the Ministry of Tourism and Diasporan Relations is the least resourced. This has led to little publicity, poor marketing, sites are not properly developed, no promotional materials, and hence, tourism is relegated to the background. Looking at the fact that tourism is the fourth foreign exchange earner in Ghana's economy without any efforts, imagine what will happen if it is given little push with funding and support.

Though the country is blessed with pristine beaches stretching over 500 kilometers, these beaches are left undeveloped while portions have been turned into places of conveniences. Our habitual littering is also anathema to tourism development. How do we expect tourists to repeat their visits if we are misusing our tourism assets? We are renowned for our hospitality but when it comes to providing services we are not up and doing. Tourism is a very competitive business as people demand value for money if we wish to make the requisite gains then we should put our house in order.

Tourism Development and Poverty Aliviation

The Tourism Ministry in Ghana recently adopted a new approach to tourism development that maximizes the net benefit of tourism to the poor. This concept "Pro-poor Tourism" enhances the linkage between tourism businesses and poor-people so that tourism's contribution to poverty reduction is increased through the active participation of the local people in the development of the tourism product. The travel and tourism industry is itself human-resource intensive due to the service nature of the industry. Additional, one job in the core tourism business creates about two additional jobs (indirect) in the tourism-related economy.

Available statistics indicate that in the area of employment, between year 2000-2003, total employment in the tourism sector in Ghana increased from 90,000 (direct- 26,000; indirect- 64,000) to 127,645(direct – 37,283; indirect-90,362) representing 42 percent increase. Of those employed 56 percent were males and 44 percent females. It is projected that by the year 2009, tourism will employ about 300, 000 people. The gender dimension here is very important: according to the United Nations Development Programme empirical evidence which suggests developing countries with less gender inequality tend to have lower poverty rate. The implication for us is that gender equality through creating opportunities for women, as is typical of the tourism industry, has much stronger effect on poverty and the national economy.

Ghana is certainly endowed with a wide range of unique and exciting natural, cultural, historical and heritage resources, majority of which are located in the rural areas of where poverty is endemic. These resources are however, underdeveloped to harness the fullest potentials for the benefit of the communities within which they are located. City, district, municipal and traditional authorities who make efforts at developing the tourism resources within their localities are making gains from their investment.

This effort offers a wide range of service providers in the community economic and social benefits. It enriches members of the community, thereby enhancing their social life since they could afford the very basic necessities of life through descent work. Tourism is said to have a multiplier effect, once it is well developed and promoted. A case study is the Hohoe Municipal Assembly that declared its highest revenue coming from their investment in tourism. About 19 eco-tourism sites around the country are not exceptions.

Tourism is also a catalytic tool that boosts growth in the other sectors of the economy which equally employs a good number of people. The agricultural sector employs about 60 percent of the country's total labour force. The tourism sector provides ready market for farmers at the restaurants and traditional/indigenous restaurants thereby helping to sustaining farmers in their trade. It is an undeniable fact that, tourism also sustains the industrial sector by patronizing their product likewise the manufacturing sector. Producers of local textiles, that is, tie-dye and batik fabrics have their products highly patronize by tourists as unique identification of "been to" a destination.

The vision of the Tourism Ministry to support and promote the achievement of the overall vision of the Government of Ghana aims at achieving a per capita income of USD$1,000 by 2015 through the realization of the sector's full potential in contributing to economic wealth creation, employment generation, poverty reduction, environment conservation, as well as national and international cohesion.

To achieve this vision, the Ministry seeks to attract about a million tourists which imply a corresponding growth in the expansion of tourism plants across the country including restaurants, pubs, night clubs, tourist receptacles, and the like.. With the current incentives available to attract investors L.I. 1817 when effectively implemented there is the likelihood to realize the continued and fast growth in the expansion of tourism plants that create more descent jobs for the citizens.

Challenges Facing the Tourism Industry

The tourism industry is beset with scores of challenges. These include; poor marketing of Ghana as a destination; lack of Ghana Tourism Brand; low awareness of the potential of tourism as a viable economic sector; poor infrastructure especially poor condition of access roads to tourist sites; inadequate funding from government for the sector; and inadequate skilled manpower as well as lack of professionalism to enhance service delivery. Paucity budgetary allocation, lack of logistics, poor human resource base, lack of domestic awareness and patronage, waste management, lack of corporate support, lack of favourable credit facilities, the perception of tourism as a high risk sector, quality products and services, lack of branding, marketing and a respectable attractive tourism image abroad, rampant road accidents among others are myriad of problems that the Ghanaian tourism sector has to contend with.

Other challenges include poor institutional commitment, collaboration and support for tourism development at the District level; slow private sector investment in the sector; limited capacity and access to credit especially women entrepreneurs such as caterers and local fast food vendors; poor waste management and sanitation especially in the major cities; Ghana perceived as a high cost destination in the sub- region due to relatively high air fares and hotel tariffs; and low budget allocation

Justification for Government Support to the Tourism Sector

The vision of Government is aimed at achieving a per capita income of USD$1,000 by 2015. This implies that all sectors of economy must ensure growth to aggregated meet this target. The tourism sector has the magic to attain the overall vision of the country. A simple statistical calculation as follows proves this magic. Considering the fact that, the average spending of a tourist as at 2006 is US$1,985 and average length of stay is 10-days. Ghana attracted 497,129 tourists. Mathematically, revenue accrued in 2006 total US$986,801,065. This imply that tourism per capita in Ghana is US$41.12 with the assumption that the population at then stood as 22 million.

However, the ratio of international tourists to domestic tourist generated is 1:7, meaning each international tourist arrival has a complimentary seven domestic tourists. Conventionally, both tourists have the same expenditure pattern, it signifies that total receipts from the tourism sector is approximately US$ 6,907,607,455.00 and holding constant the total population, it's very convenient to conclude that the per capital income of tourism is say US$ 314.

Given that the Ministry is adequately resourced and all other factors favouring growth of the sector are conducive and we attract a million tourists as targeted it is very comfortable to say that the tourism sector could drive the growth Ghana needs to become a middle level income country. Therefore, we need a tourism fund, and serious talk on this is very important factor for tourism development. Financing and management are the most critical factors for tourism development.

Everything including product development, training and human resource development as well as marketing and promotions are directly dependent on financing and management. The financing factor or lack of it has had the most debilitating effect on our tourism development: the terms of banks for long-term financing are quite prohibitive and tourism projects tend to have long gestation periods. The solution to this palpable situation is the National Tourism Fund, whether it takes the form of a special bank or a revolving fund for the private sector tourism service and plant operators.

Tourism marketing starts with the product that we are promoting. Financing will determine how well we add value to our tourism resources. Financing will also determine how accessible our tourist products become to both our domestic and international markets. We need money to develop our attractions where value-adding is necessary. The Metropolitan, Municipal and District Assemblies need to invest in tourism and support tourism investments. Financing is necessary for reaching the markets that we find lucrative to tap and exploit. Marketing and promotions has become a complex, competitive and highly technology-based activity, not aided at all by the facts that tourism is highly competitive and has a highly elastic demand. The industry needs soft financing to support facility development, to provide infrastructure at our tourism hot spots, to do good maintenance on existing facilities and amenities, and to start new projects in an expanding industry.

We need to use the opportunity to as a matter of urgency review outdated and archaic legislation and regulation that regulate our tourism industry, since the sector is very robust and dynamic. Sadly the Ghanaian sector is being regulated by laws as old as thirty years and above. The Ghanaian sector deserves better attention, since each and every hamlet, village, town, city, district or region in Ghana has one unique tourism plant or facility that are scattered around the country, whose potential is crying for exploration and development, which has the potential to ensure an even development of the country to above all stop the rural-urban drift, in search of non-existing white collar jobs. Tourism thrives on good roads, portable water. Electricity and effective telecommunications apart from the attraction itself. Unfortunately, most, if not all, of our attraction sites are in their raw state and the only way to exploit this gold is to develop them to meet international standards. If the Ministry of Tourism and Diasporan Relations target of attracting one million tourists annually is attained, tourism will rake in $1.5 billion with the corresponding 300,000 employees in the sector.

Indeed, Ghana is endowed with a lot of natural resources, and there is enough we can do to compete with the International Community in terms of development. What we have, no country has, as far as Tourism is concerned. The industry is the only area that brings in foreign exchange earning without export It is an indisputable fact that Ghana has today emerged as a special African tourist destination, drawing people and visitors to experience not only its fascinating cultural diversity, history and natural endowments, but all that there is to go with peace, stability, good governance and a hospitable people.

It plays a central and decisive role in promoting the development of responsible, ?sustainable and universally accessible tourism, paying particular attention to the ?interests of developing countries.? Ghana's opportunity to use tourism as a major pillar for its economic growth is realistic. Globally, Tourism today, is the second largest industry, which employs the most people and it is still growing. It is the major foreign exchange earner of more than 60 countries. It creates jobs at all levels. From shoe shine boys and porters, through receptionists, tour guides, accountants, managers, and the like, tourism also creates micro and small enterprises. Tourism will create jobs, jobs, jobs-attractive jobs; productive jobs and for that matter reduce poverty.

Customer-Driven «Green» Tourism

In its efforts to diversify the nation's economy, the Government of Trinidad & Tobago has identified tourism as an area of potential growth. In this respect, we may consider ourselves fortunate that several of our Caribbean neighbours have many years experience in the Tourism Industry. Barbados and Jamaica, for example, have been established tourist destinations for many decades. Even in the relatively new eco-tourism thrust, Belize and Dominica have more experience than we do. Thus, the opportunity presents itself for us to learn from the experience of our neighbours. In particular, we can identify problems which they have experienced, and study how they sought to solve those problems.

This paper discusses the issue of Customer-driven Green Tourism, which is increasingly becoming an issue in neighbouring Caribbean islands. There are those who would consider Green Tourism to be a benefit to our countries, but anecdotal evidence suggests that the demands of the Green Movement are posing significant problems to the owners and operators of tourist plant. Specifically, questions have been raised about:

* the criteria applied by the «Greens»,
* the sources of data used to evaluate individual facilities,
* the transparency of the process, and
* the lack of recourse by facility owners/operators.

Each of these issues will be addressed in this paper, but first there is a brief introduction of the concept of «Green Tourism».

Green Tourism

Customer Discretion

Of all industries, Tourism is the one in which the customer has absolute discretion. The tourist may choose one destination or another, or none at all; applying any criteria he sees fit. Destinations and individual facilities must therefore seek to provide a product which will satisfy the requirements of a suitably large number of customers, or they will face financial ruin. After all, in this industry the Customer is Always Right!

Environmental Concerns

There has been a growing trend of environmental consciousness among tourists, particularly those from Europe. This has led to two trends:

* Eco-tourism, and
* Green Tourism.

The Eco-tourist is one who has a keen interest in nature, and seeks a vacation which will maximize the naturalist experience. Eco-tourism is the fastest-growing segment of the tourist industry, and Eco-tourists tend to spend more at their destination (per person, per day) than other types of tourist (Final Report on the Feasibility Study for the Bloody Nature Project, Tobago, prepared by Eco-engineering-Eco-logistics, 1997). In addition, many facets of nature can be used as the basis for an Eco-tourism industry: mainland rain forests, island rain forests, coral reefs, marine turtle nesting, etc. It is therefore not surprising that many Caribbean countries (Belize, Dominica, Guyana and Trinidad & Tobago, to name a few) have opted to develop a strong Eco-tourism component to their overall tourism product.

Green Tourists, in contrast, may not have as strong an interest in nature as Eco-tourists. However, they consider it important that the facilities which they use are designed and operated in such a way that adverse impacts on the environment are eliminated (or, at least, minimized). This is clearly a laudable approach, so why does it create a problem? Hotel operators in the Organisation of Eastern Caribbean States (OECS) can attest to the fact that enquiries received from European travel agents and tour operators now frequently include the question: «Is your hotel classified as environmentally friendly?». Implicit in this question is the assumption that there are accepted criteria for such classification; whereas in our region such criteria are not readily available. In the absence of ratings within the region, it appears that many potential tourists rely on environmental groups in their own countries to determine which facilities are «green», and which are not.

Green Classification

Criteria

Criteria for rating the «environment-friendliness» of any facility usually relate to:

* Operational Practices at the Facility,
* Services and Products used at the Facility, and
* Waste Disposal.

Operational practices cover a wide range of environmental concerns. External lighting of the facility and the nature and timing of sound emissions can affect neighbouring residents or wildlife in adjacent areas. The frequency of washing linen affects the water demand at the facility, as well as the volume of waste water that is generated. Similarly, the nature of detergents used will influence the type of impact which is experienced in receiving water bodies. In like manner, composting of part of the solid waste would reduce the load being placed on landfills.

In all cases, the diversity of the Caribbean region makes it very difficult to define a universally-applicable «best approach». For example, some facilities may reduce demand on the public electricity supply by the use of solar water heaters or on-site generation via windmills or solar cells. This may not be a practical approach in other locations. Likewise, the use of treated waste water for irrigation of lawns and plants is very effective in dry islands like Barbados or the Bahamas. However, in places like Dominica or Trinidad & Tobago, irrigation during the rainy season has proved unmanageable. In preparing this paper, enquiries were made to determine what criteria were used by international environmental groups in rating the «green» status of tourist facilities in our region. Unfortunately, no definitive answers were received. However, there was a clear suggestion that the criteria are applied uniformly across the region, without considering the diversity of the region.

Rating

Having decided on a set of criteria, the second question relates to the actual process of rating. Simply put, there are concerns about the information being used to rate facilities. These concerns relate to:

* the Accuracy of the Information, and
* the Currentness of the Information.

As with the criteria, we were unable to ascertain the sources of information being used to rate specific facilities. It is doubtful if this information comes from «Official Sources», because few (if any) of our governments collect and publish data on this type. We are also unaware of any International Environmental Groups which actually visit our region to collect such information. This leaves two sources: local environmental groups and surveys/ questionnaires sent directly to owners/operators of tourist facilities. The first concern is that the information used in rating facilities should be accurate. Regardless of whether the source of the information is a local environmental group or a questionnaire/ survey, the information must be validated. It would be foolhardy to assume that neither of these sources of information would bias the information to serve some ulterior purpose. In like manner, it is important that the information be kept up-to-date. Tourist facilities seldom remain in a fixed form over a long period. In the quest to satisfy their customers, frequent changes are made. Some of these changes would affect the «green» rating of the facility.

Transparency of the Process

Several owners/operators have complained that the present system of «green» ratings lacks transparency. Owners/operators of tourist facilities wish to know how the ratings are being done, and by whom. It is a fact that tourists (and by extension, travel agents and tour operators) consider these ratings (among other criteria) in deciding which facilities to use. The owners/operators feel that they should have access to the rating criteria (to make changes which would improve their rating), as well as the information used in rating (to ensure that it is accurate and current). The enquiries made in preparation of this paper suggest that such transparency is lacking.

Lack of Recourse

Because of the lack of transparency, owners/operators of tourist facilities feel that they have no meaningful recourse if they are disadvantaged by the present rating system. If they do not know how the ratings are being arrived at, they cannot correct errors. Even where they learn «through the grape vine» that they have been given an undeserved poor rating, they are unsure where their complaint should be directed.

Environmental Management Systems

Benefits of EMS

The implementation of Environmental Management Systems (EMS) represents one approach to addressing some of the problems indicated above. These tools permit the facility operator to devise an Environmental Policy which recognizes the uniqueness of his facility as well as his country. By their very nature, these systems also address local regulations and standards. Finally, the EMS relies on progressive improvement toward the goals, so that the operator is not faced with a «pass/fail» choice, but rather one of management by objectives.

Cost Implications

Anecdotal evidence suggests that the cost of implementing an EMS, per se, is not necessarily prohibitive. However, the cost of certification can be significant. In the circumstances, the following suggestions are made to bring the EMS within the reach of small and medium operators in the tourism sector:

i. The OECS Region should invest in the preparation of a Handbook on EMS, specifically designed for the needs of the Tourism Industry. This is not intended to «re-invent the wheel», but rather should be tailored to exclude many details which are included in general texts but which are not directly relevant to the Tourism Industry.

ii. The OECS Region should also provide broad-based training to operators in the Tourism Industry to ensure that the nature, objectives and procedures of EMSs are generally understood.

iii. The OECS should support initiatives by regional organizations to become registered as EMS Certifiers. For example, the Trinidad & Tobago Bureau of Standards has indicated that they will shortly seek such registration with the International Standards Organization. Having such a registered organization within Caricom (in contrast to bringing certifiers in from the metropolitan countries) will certainly lower the cost of certification.

iv. The OECS should explore whether economies can be gained by grouping facilities for the purpose of EMS certification. The concept of «grouping» is different from the «generic EMS» which has been discussed in some quarters, in that it would involve the selection of facilities which have features in common, and are similarly located.

Dialogue

In suggesting an approach to solving the problems high-lighted above, several factors were considered:

* Customer-driven Green Tourism can be harnessed to the benefit of our Region. Thus, our thrust should be to improve, not to eliminate.
* International environmental groups tend to be very receptive to meaningful dialogue with local groups. Unfortunately, they have been less co-operative with «official» agencies.

The suggestion, therefore, is that the tourism industry in the Caribbean Region should engage the international environmental groups in a meaningful dialogue on the subject of «green» rating of individual facilities. This dialogue should be aimed at ensuring that ratings are based on criteria which are acceptable in the Caribbean and on data which is accurate and current. It should also seek to build the necessary transparency into the system. It is our opinion that an industry grouping, such as the Caribbean Tourism Organization, would be more likely to succeed in this endeavour than a governmental organization.

Tourism in the Polar Regions: Facts, Trends and Impacts

This section describes how polar tourism grew to become a mature and highly diversified industry in both Polar Regions; the characteristics of its current operations; and prominent factors that will affect its future. This information is essential for understanding tourism's present and future impacts on the Polar Regions.

Evaluating tourism impacts, both beneficial and otherwise, requires knowledge of total numbers as well as where, when, and how tourists cause impacts. For example, the many thousand cruise-ship passengers who passively view the Arctic from offshore, and occasionally disembark to visit land based souvenir shops, affect the region in ways that differ from the smaller numbers actively engaged in Eco-tourism or wilderness recreations activities such as river rafting, mountaineering, and sport fishing. By accurately identifying the full array of tourist activities and their behavioral patterns, then placing that information within the context of their natural and human resource settings, we can begin to understand key relationships.

Nearly Two Centuries of Arctic Tourism

The Arctic has attracted tourists since the early 1800's. The earliest Arctic tourists were individual anglers, hunters, mountaineers, and adventurers attracted to abundant fisheries, exotic wildlife species, and remote regions. Many articles describing their recreational pursuits appeared in the growing genre of recreation, mountaineering, hunting, and fishing periodicals that emerged in the mid-1800's. During the same era, several pioneering travellers to the Arctic published journals that became popular guide books for future Arctic tourists.

Mass tourism in the Arctic has thrived since the mid-1800's when steamships and railroads aggressively expanded their transportation networks providing access to numerous destinations throughout the Arctic. Tourism entrepreneurs, such as Thomas Cook, formed partnerships with railroad and steamship companies and thereby pioneered the popular tourism industry. By the 1880's, the "Land of the Midnight Sun" in the Scandinavia Arctic, Alaska, and the popular excitement of the Klondike Gold Rushes firmly established the Arctic's mass tourism market.

During the past two centuries numerous advances in transport technologies have contributed to the steady growth of Arctic tourism. At the present time, advanced ship technologies together with improved marine charts and navigational aids have allowed cruise ship travel to increase exponentially. Diesel locomotives, four wheel drive and tracked vehicles further opened access to vast regions of the Arctic. And, most importantly, air transport in all of its forms, provides immediate travel to the Arctic. Collectively, these improved transport technologies not only added numbers of tourists, but also expanded the seasonal and geographical reach of Arctic tourism.

Antarctic Tourism

Antarctic tourism began in 1957-59 with four visits by Argentinean and Chilean naval transports, which accommodated tourists whose fares helped to pay costs of servicing the national expeditions. Antarctica received extensive international publicity from the explorations led by Richard Byrd, Vivian Fuchs and Edmund Hillary.

Entrepreneurial tour operators recognized the commercial value of feasible access and positive international publicity. In 1966 Lars Eric Lindblad began expedition cruising to the Antarctic and initiated the use of zodiacs to land passengers at diverse sites. As a result of the success of the Lindblad model, government affiliated voyages were quickly superseded by dedicated cruises in small 'expedition' ships carrying 50-120 passengers. For many years this type of travel dominated the trade. Increasing numbers of expedition ships are transporting larger numbers of passengers, and making more landings at several hundred sites. The first larger cruise ship to enter the field, Ocean Princess in 1990-93, had a capacity of 480 passengers, but carried only 250-400 on its annual Antarctic voyages. The most recent development has been the advent from 2000 of liners carrying between 800 and 3,700 passengers, including crew members.

Over the last decades, tourism activities have expanded tremendously with the number of ship-borne tourists increasing by 430 % in 14 years and land-based tourists by 757 % in 10 years (IAATO 2007). The tremendous increase of ship-borne tourism and its impacts on the Antarctic environment resulted in the members of the Antarctic Treaty adopting a resolution (May 2007) which recommends the Parties of the Treaty to:

1. Discourage or decline to authorize tour operators that use vessels carrying more than 500 passengers from making any landings in Antarctica; and
2. Encourage or require tour operators to:
    a. Coordinate with each other such that not more than one tourist vessel is at a landing site at any one time;
    b. Restrict the number of passengers on shore at any one time to 100 or fewer, unless otherwise specified in applicable ATCM Measures or Resolutions; and
    c. Maintain a minimum 1:20 guide-to-passenger ratio while ashore, unless otherwise specified in applicable ATCM Measures or Resolutions.

Commercial air transport of tourists to the Antarctic includes both small groups travelling to the continent and larger numbers viewing from over flights. Adventure Network International (ANI) has been providing flight services to Patriot Hills in the Heritage Range since 1985 and other charter air companies have provided tourist transport between South Africa and Dronning Maud Land, and between Punta Arenas, Chile and King George Island.

Polar Tourism Today – Diverse and Growing

Polar tourism is now a mature industry providing diverse experiences in both Polar Regions. The polar tourism industry is enticing an increasing clientele with expanding numbers of attractions, recreational activities, international destinations, and visitor accommodations. And now that regularly scheduled excursion travel is provided to both the Arctic and Antarctic, year-round polar tourism has become a reality.Polar Tourism's Diverse Markets

Polar tourism is not a single, monolithic industry, but rather a collection of diverse specialty markets that appeal to an equally diverse clientele. Each of these distinct markets is growing and expanding for an obvious reason – they appeal to tourists who are willing to pay for the unique experiences they offer. The five highly specialized market segments currently dominating the polar tourism economy are best defined in terms of their primary attractions and the ways in which those attractions are experienced. This approach to classifying tourist markets explicitly acknowledges tourist expectations, the service delivery methods used to realize those expectations, and the distinct impacts resulting from those activities. The five markets are:

1. The mass market, comprised of tourists primarily attracted to sightseeing within the pleasurable surroundings of comfortable transport and accommodations.
2. The sport fishing and hunting market, with participants who pursue unique fish and game species within a wilderness setting.
3. The Eco-tourism market, consisting of tourists who seek to observe wildlife species in their natural habitats, and experience the beauty and solitude of natural areas. These

tourists are also concerned with conserving the environment and improving the wellbeing of local people.

4. The adventure tourism market, providing a sense of personal achievement and exhilaration from meeting challenges and potential perils of outdoor sport activities.
5. The culture and heritage tourism market, a very distinct market comprised of tourists who either want to experience personal interaction with the lives and traditions of native people, learn more about a historical topic that interests them, or personally experience historic places and artifacts.

Each market has distinct visitor experiences and economic dimensions, involving different tourists' motivations, expectations, on-site behaviour, and resource uses. Market segmentation provides a useful framework for understanding polar tourism in terms of the use of natural and cultural resources, economic activity, and visitor behaviour. But obviously, tourists themselves are not constrained by this classification: they participate freely in many types of activities.

The enormous geographic scope of the five markets deserves emphasis. All eight Arctic nations, and their seas and oceans host all five markets, while Antarctica hosts most of them with the exception of the sport fishing and hunting and the culture and heritage markets. Most of that geography consists of land masses that are true wilderness and oceans with the world's most severe maritime conditions. The challenge of managing tourism across those vast lands and seas is well known to the Arctic nations and to those concerned about Antarctic tourism.

Environmental, Economic, Social and Cultural Impacts of Polar Tourism

Environmental impacts

There are serious concerns that tourism is promoting environmental degradation in the Polar Regions by putting extra pressures on land, wildlife, water and other basic necessities, and on transportation facilities (GEO 2002 and GEO 2006). According to the Arctic Council Working Group on the Conservation of Arctic Flora and Fauna (CAFF), the main environmental impacts of tourism in the Arctic are the following (CAFF 1997, 1998, 2001):

* The transport of tourists to the Arctic, in itself, increases the volume of ship and airplane traffic. In addition to the impacts on climate by long distance air and water traffic, increased ship traffic in these waters could lead to increased risks of groundings and other accidents, the results of which can include oil spills and other environmental consequences.
* Many visitors want to see areas of great beauty or richness, such as bird colonies, marine mammal haul-outs, and caribou aggregations. Because there are relatively few places where such sights are accessible and reliable, tourist traffic is often concentrated. Arctic vegetation is typically unable to withstand repeated trampling, and paths of bare ground have appeared in some heavily visited spots.
* Helicopters, used sometimes for recreational purposes, are noisy and produce a variety of sounds that are disturbing to seabirds. Helicopters cause panic flights and can lead to egg loss particularly in birds.
* In the forest-tundra areas of the Arctic, tourism, including sport hunting and fishing, attracts moderate though increasing numbers of visitors. This places additional pressure on the region's resources, sometimes leading to conflicts between local and visiting hunters. The forest-tundra in general has a low tolerance for trampling. Even the temporary presence of humans often leaves a lasting impact.
* Visits to Arctic seabird colonies by tourists are rapidly growing. Currently cruise ships visit or sail by colonies in the low and high Arctic of Canada, west Greenland, Iceland, Norwegian coast and Svalbard, eastern Russia, and the US (Alaska). Colonies chosen for visitation tend to be large and spectacular and usually are home to species such as murres, puffins, kittiwakes, and fulmars. During a colony visit, passengers typically board smaller boats from the larger ships, and cruise by colonies observing the seabirds and taking pictures. Occasionally passengers make

landings at suitable colonies and view the seabirds from above or below the cliffs.

* Recreational activities, such as boating and fishing, cause local disturbance at bird colonies in several Arctic countries. In the Russian far-east, coastal and lowland species such as ducks, gulls, terns and Spectacled Guillemots are frequently disturbed by visitors.
* Garbage, waste, and pollution are significant problems for many tourism operations, especially as decomposition is slow and waste remains visible atop the permafrost in many Arctic areas.

In the Antarctic the most important impact of tourism concerns the disturbance of cetaceans. Certain studies have lent increasing strength to concerns that human activities may be influencing the fitness of these animals. Tourism activities in Antarctica present also a risk to the marine environment (pollution resulting from operations or maritime accident (e.g. grounding)) as well as to terrestrial ecosystems as over 80 % of the tourists land one or more times during their journey (introduction of alien species; disturbance of birds colonies; damage to the vegetative cover (e.g. lichen). In addition, high-risk unsupported (adventure) tourism can potentially impact on national research programmes in terms of search and rescue operations.

The main positive impact of polar tourism, if well done, is its educational value. Arctic and Antarctic visitors are fascinated by the sheer beauty, wilderness and natural phenomena of the polar environment. This can be used to make them not only to ambassadors for the protection of the visited regions, but also supporters of conservation activities and organizations worldwide.

Economic impacts

Growing public and private resource commitments to promote and further develop tourism demonstrate strong intentions to strengthen tourism's economic role in the Arctic. Given these circumstances, economic impacts, both positive and negative, include the following:

* Many Arctic people seeking economic security perceive tourism as a positive means for improving economic

stability. From their perspective, reliance on predictably arriving tourists offers a more stable economic outlook than exhausting finite natural resources to meet the boom and bust needs of world markets.

* Arctic communities generally appreciate the economic benefits resulting specifically from the angling, hunting, and nature tourism market because most tourist expenditures remain in the community. Tourists employ local guides, pilots, charter boat captains and crews, outfitters, and suppliers. They use local transport, stay in local accommodations, and eat in local establishments.
* Culture and heritage tourism provides critical support for language preservation, the practice of traditional ceremonies, and the perpetuation of ancient customs and art forms. The presence of appropriate and effective interpretation and education methodologies will dramatically impact effectiveness. Additionally, this form of tourism creates a market for art and other native manufactures and services.
* The cost of building, operating, and maintaining tourism infrastructure is a huge economic burden for Arctic communities and governments. Support facilities and services of all types are built and maintained to serve relatively large numbers of persons that exceed the resident population. Transport facilities, law enforcement, medical services, other emergency services, water and waste water utilities, and waste collection and disposal incur capital and operating costs, require advanced work force skills, spare parts, and need specialized supplies in order to sustain there functions. Tourism normally occurs for a few months of the year, but the infrastructure must be maintained under adverse conditions for the entire year.
* The economic and human costs of providing emergency services deserve special attention. Highly trained personnel, many of whom are volunteers, risk their lives in search and rescue operations. Expensive transport and medical equipment and supplies are required to evacuate victims and treat their injuries. Law enforcement resources

must respond to large populations visiting their communities and need specialized equipment to patrol back country regions. Fire suppression service faces similar challenges.

* The cost of responding to environmental hazards is included in the budgets of all Arctic nations, but may not be sufficient. Oil spill containment and recovery, hazardous materials handling and storage, and hazardous waste disposal all represent substantial costs. Adequate funds and the availability of specialized equipment, trained personnel, and essential supplies may or may not be sufficient to respond to events.
* Finally, the question of who benefits economically from large-scale Arctic tourism is a very sensitive issue. Many of the transport, tour and hotel corporations conducting tourism in the Arctic are head quartered outside the region. Consequently, much of the money paid by polar tourists to those nonresident corporations escapes the Arctic people.

The continent of Antarctica derives absolutely no economic benefits from tourism, but can suffer environmental and heritage resource costs. Unlike most parts of the world, there are no indigenous people to benefit from tourism in Antarctica and thus tourism is not an alternative to local unsustainable economics activities. This blunt fact is a serious consideration for anyone motivated to propose tourism management practices on the southern continent. There is no continuous stream of money devoted to tourism management, environmental monitoring, emergency services, waste collection and disposal, the design and implementation of risk minimization or mitigation programmes, or any other "best practices" normally associated with reasonably managed tourism. Specifically:

* Aside from the fees collected by the Antarctic Historic Places Trust to maintain heroic era huts in the Ross Sea region, no revenues or fees of any sort are collected from either tour operators or the tourists themselves for the management of Antarctica's environmental resources.

Some scientific stations and heritage sites generate revenues from the sale of souvenirs, but these are neither dedicated to resource management nor sufficient to support tourism management programmes.

* As with all who travel to Antarctica, costs are incurred by tour operators for the preparation of environmental impact assessments required by the Protocol on Environmental Protection to the Antarctic Treaty. Scientific stations incur costs for the assistance they provide in emergency situations such as search and rescue or medical support. The true costs of emergency response include not only direct expenses for personnel and equipment, but the risk to additional lives and distraction from scientific missions.
* To the credit of many tourists who learn about Antarctica's economic dilemma, generous personal donations have been given in support of environmental research and heritage preservation projects in Antarctica and the sub-polar islands.

Social impacts

There are serious concerns regarding the negative impacts of a growing tourism industry to the people in the Arctic world. Social norms, values and unique ways of life are all subjected to impacts from polar tourism. Tourism impacts affecting polar communities and their people are presented below.

* The most obvious social impacts result from the number of visitors that temporarily overwhelm the social norms of some Arctic communities during tourist season. Community institutions such as educational, religious, and civic organizations often experience altered roles and functions when the tourists are in town. Based on the attitude of the community, this may or may not be a major disruption, but large numbers of tourists relative to local populations always exerts a dominant presence.
* Social impacts of Arctic tourism can be mitigated by the terms and conditions of collaborative agreements between the tour operators and the local community. In some instances, tax revenues and special fees can offset local

costs. When tourist seasons are expanded there are greater economies of scale and efficiencies result from the extended use of infrastructure and longer duration of employment and income benefits.

Cultural Impacts

The Arctic environment is not merely a setting in which a rich diversity of Native People live, but rather it encompasses the essential resources upon which the lives and culture depend. Consequently, any events that endanger those resources place Native People at grave risk. By their own declarations the most severe threat facing Native People is climate change. The loss of Arctic sea ice with its attendant effects on wildlife habitat, numbers, and migratory behaviour; the transport routes needed to subsist; the duration of seasons; and the condition of fisheries are of critical importance to the cultural and economic wellbeing of Arctic people. According to a statement by Sheila Watt-Cloutier, former International Chair, Inuit Circumpolar Conference:

"What is at stake here is not just the extinction of animals but the extinction of Inuit as a hunting culture. Climate change in the Arctic is a human issue, a family issue, a community issue, and an issue of cultural survival."

The cultural impacts described below must be evaluated from that perspective.

* Large numbers of tourists can produce significant cultural resource impacts. They further stress increasingly scarce natural resources and that results in a variety of pressures on indigenous subsistence practices and value systems.
* Ironically, as traditional indigenous lifestyles succumb to change resulting from climate change, there will be fewer opportunities for tourists to support authentic cultural traditions. This will affect Arctic culture and economies.
* In addition to their numbers, the introduction of technologies and tourist service amenities can impact Native People's desires to maintain traditional lifestyles.
* Intrusive, inappropriate visitor behaviour violates traditional customs. Tours that do not include educational

practices can generate conflicts that damage both Native People's quality of life and the tourist experience. When that happens, both parties lose.

* In summary, the ways in which Arctic communities allow their natural and cultural resources to be used affects the character of those communities. As Arctic communities continue to achieve self determination, they will increasingly decide how their natural and cultural resources will be utilized and this will ultimately determine how those resources are managed. Arctic communities and Native People must determine how tourism will, or will not, occur and how natural and cultural resources should be used and safeguarded. They can be aided by good management practices that are relevant to their objectives. But the final decisions regarding natural and cultural resource uses must be made locally. Any other solution would be yet another example of intrusion from the "outside".

The Outlook for Polar Tourism: Reduced "Barriers to Entry"

Polar tourism expands because of a continuous reduction of what economists call "barriers to entry". The concept suggests that the extent to which these barriers are increased, reduced, altered, or eliminated directly controls the amount, geographic distribution, seasonal duration, and types of tourism likely to occur. Since its inception, the most difficult barriers confronting polar travel include difficulty of access, environmental conditions (both real and perceived), cost of travel, time to travel, and jurisdictional restraints. Both human-induced and natural events are making the Polar Regions increasingly accessible. Vastly improved geographic and hydrographic knowledge; advancements in transport and navigational technologies; more comfortable clothing; more durable recreational equipment; significant reductions in the amount, extent and duration of sea ice; and a relatively more tolerable climate are all contributing to growing access to the Polar Regions. The cumulative impacts of these events are larger numbers of polar tourists spending more time in more locations.

Polar tourism was slow to start, but is now a popular and rapidly-growing industry that is expanding in terms of tourists, tour operators, diverse recreational pursuits, geographic scope, and seasons of use. Arctic economies have seen it evolve from an incidental activity to a vital sector upon which they increasingly rely. This has been particularly true for newly enfranchised indigenous people of the Arctic seeking self-sufficiency, and for gateway cities in the southern hemisphere eager to realize the economic benefits of Antarctic tourism.

Sustainable Tourism in the Polar Regions: Setting an Agenda

The conservation and sustainable management of polar environments and cultures including by means of good tourism practices will require both mutually accepted goals and a solid commitment to implement appropriate management techniques. Fortunately, the first of those tasks has been carefully deliberated by the international community. As previously stated, the United Nations Environment Programme and the United Nations World Tourism Organization engaged diverse stakeholders from around the world to establish 12 sustainability principles that are fully listed below. When summarized, those principles identify goals essential for achieving sustainable tourism. Again, those goals are:

* Conserving environmental quality
* Preserving cultural and social values by means of participatory decision-making
* Creating sustainable economies
* Ensuring positive visitor behaviour, safety, and enjoyment

Though relatively new, polar tourism is old enough to have established recognizable patterns of procedure, and mature enough-even in its newest venue Antarctica-to have accumulated extensive management experiences. Well documented knowledge of tourism management techniques, resource conservation programmes, industry practices, jurisdictional responses, economic strategies, and community opinions and expectations currently exist to provide the basis for sustainable polar tourism policies and practices. Simultaneously, while tourism's presence is growing numerically and spatially, the polar environment itself is experiencing significant change. This section describes tourism management conditions, issues and techniques that are relevant to sustaining the environmental and cultural integrity of the Polar Regions. This information is further reinforced by examples of good polar management practices presented in the final section of this publication.

Management Conditions: Wilderness

Polar tourism most frequently occurs in immense wilderness regions, either de-facto or officially designated, and these vast areas are exceedingly difficult to manage. The Polar Regions contain the world's largest expanses of wilderness-places where human presence and development are virtually absent or not readily apparent. The continent of Antarctica is entirely a wilderness land mass. North America's and Eurasia's largest wilderness regions are located in the Arctic. Fully reliable sets of marine charts and hydrographic information for the Southern and Arctic oceans are not yet available.

These enormous wilderness areas and relatively unknown marine regions provide permanent habitat for highly adapted indigenous wildlife and seasonal habitat for immense populations of migratory wildlife. Arctic wilderness is the homeland of diverse Native Peoples who have practiced cultural traditions for millennia. The Antarctic contains important artifacts of the history of exploration and scientific discovery. Wilderness regions also possess highly esteemed scientific, inspirational and conservation values. For most of their existence these polar resources and values were protected by their remoteness and climatic conditions.

Again, wilderness regions present unique management challenges. Comprehensive inventories of their natural and cultural resources are time-consuming and expensive to obtain. A competent knowledge of their dynamic ecological systems requires long-term investigations that are equally complicated and costly to accomplish. Establishing mutually acceptable methods to facilitate stakeholder participation in wilderness planning and management are difficult to implement, and frequently contentious.

Management Issues

Scarce Management Resources

The absence of development may be essential for sustaining the integrity of wilderness values, but it is also a huge obstacle in the performance of environmental and tourism management. The Arctic's scarce infrastructure in terms of transportation systems, number of trained personnel, and service facilities are severe constraints on managing the impacts of tourism. Operational functions essential for meeting the demands of large numbers of tourists, such as resource conservation, resource monitoring, scientific research, security patrolling, visitor safety, waste collection and disposal, and emergency response capabilities are all affected by the scarcity of infrastructure.

In the Antarctic the situation is even worse. Unlike the Arctic, there are no resources located on the continent specifically dedicated to supporting tourism's expanding presence and growing access. International policy strongly advocates environmental conservation of the entire continent, but the fact remains that because the Antarctic Treaty System cannot tax, there is no money to support on site management. Consequently, there are neither land nor marine Antarctic-based resources dedicated to the management of tourism activities. The Protocol on Environmental Protection to the Antarctic Treaty requires environmental impact assessments of tour operations. Although the inspection regime established under article 14 of the Madrid Protocol could also apply to tourism activities, there are no adequate international monitors to ensure compliance with assessment requirements or that proposed mitigation measures are implemented.

Both Arctic resource managers and Antarctic tour operators are keenly aware of these constraints and have adapted to them. Specialized wilderness management techniques affecting the number and distribution of tourists; educational programmes to promote appropriate behaviour; and self-reliant practices extending from waste collection to the provision of emergency services have been implemented. Valuable information regarding their effectiveness may be found in the wilderness recreation management studies published during the past 40 years.

Environmental Management Issues – Who did what?

Polar tourism must be conducted in a responsible manner and tourism management techniques are often suggested for conserving the polar environment. One of the supreme difficulties for accomplishing this objective is to accurately determine the environmental cause and effect and then manage tourism accordingly. In other words, when an environmental condition changes, the question becomes whether it was caused by a natural event, by tourism activity, or by some combination of both? The capacity to accurately monitor tourism, revise tourism management plans, alter visitor activities and behaviour, and implement appropriate environmental conservation measures depends on the answers to those questions. Realistically, the ability to assess and manage tourism impacts in the Polar Regions is vitally dependent on a competent understanding of those relationships.

Environmental cause and effect relationships affecting the Polar Regions also result from events occurring well beyond the high latitudes. Wildlife populations that seasonally migrate to the Polar Regions from other regions of the world are impacted by changing oceanographic conditions, environmental pollution, hunting and fishing pressures, and habitat transformations that are well beyond the jurisdictional boundaries of polar resource agencies. The cumulative impacts of these complex environmental changes are a colossal challenge to comprehend, much less competently manage. When polar tourism is mixed with this collection of dynamic, naturally occurring events, reliable understanding of those interdependencies is further complicated.

Cultural Management Issues

Numerous cultural traditions pervade the Arctic, many of them derived from centuries of habitation by indigenous people. Others are the culmination of settlement patterns, resource uses, economic systems, and social customs evolved from empire building and the desires of sovereign nations. These very complex heritage and cultural traditions of Arctic societies are simultaneously tourist attractions and sensitive management issues. In Antarctica defining the 'allowable and acceptable' visitor uses of heritage sites and resources is a particularly difficult task.

Internationally significant heritage resources associated with polar discovery, scientific inquiry, historical economic development, and human settlement are located throughout the southern polar region. The abandonment of those sites, the absence of a permanent population to perform conservation, and severe weather has resulted in deterioration. Resource management issues at these sites include environmental remediation, heritage conservation, visitor safety, and the creation of interpretive services that simultaneously preserve the story of these places and enlist the respect of their visitors. These are daunting tasks given the absence of resources dedicated to these purposes.

The sub-polar islands in the southern hemisphere possess sovereignty status and the authority to implement heritage conservation programmes. Many resource conservation activities have taken place, but the scarcity of financial resources and the remoteness of the sites are ever-present impediments to this effort (UNEP-WCMC, 2006,a,b,c).

Managing Tourist Behaviour and Numbers

The history of tourism proves that increased access inevitably leads to increased numbers. This is a serious management concern. In fact, improved access causes various numbers to increase, e.g., number of sites visited, extended use of seasons, greater duration of stay, types of recreational activities pursued, additional support staff required, and more services needed. The results are an increased exposure of environmental resources to additional risks, the economic dependencies of local communities on tourism, threats to privacy, more cultural contacts, and growing demands on infrastructure.

An enduring criticism of tourism is tourist behaviour. Since its inception, tourists have been universally criticized for "inappropriate" behaviour and cultural insensitivities. When tourist behaviour results in resource damage, then condemnations and tough responses are well deserved. On other occasions, criticisms of visitor behaviour more accurately reflect opinion rather than proof of harm. In all instances, efforts are required to hold both the tourist and the tourism industry accountable.

From the tourist's viewpoint, the issue of numbers equates to perceptions of congestion, and this directly affects the quality of their tourism experience. The tourist's perception of congestion in the Polar Regions is an especially critical issue because these locations are strongly promoted as wilderness.

International policy issues

Polar climate and associated ecological changes are fueling international discussions concerning foreign policy. For tourism management, the resolution of those issues will be critical. Decisions regarding sovereign powers and jurisdictional boundaries determine the terms and conditions for allowable uses of Arctic resources. Alteration of wildlife, fishery and marine mammal treaty obligations, management practices and jurisdictional boundaries will directly impact tourism activities such as wildlife viewing, nature tours, angling, and hunting.

Arctic Governance Issues

The wilderness management dilemma faced by Arctic governments is to determine when, where, and how people should be allowed to use areas without destroying the natural character. In other words, what human activity should be permitted in an area universally defined as having no human presence? Governments throughout the world have responded to this challenge in a variety of ways. Management techniques range from strict restrictions of public access to participatory approaches that combine resource inventories, environmental assessments, and public involvement to define allowable uses. The most severe restrictions seek to achieve preservation by preventing human entry. The goal of the more collaborative approaches is to identify allowable uses based on science and citizen input and then test the effectiveness of those decisions by means of careful resource monitoring.

Enormous expanses of the Arctic are governed by the customs and traditional laws established and enforced by Native Communities. The Inuit in Canada, Greenland, and Eastern Russia, the Saami in Scandinavia, and diverse Native Peoples in both Russia and Alaska exercise combinations of traditions and sovereignty to determine the allowable recreational use of their land and water. These customs and the terms and conditions expressed in their management approaches offer valuable experiences that can be replicated in other parts of the Polar Regions.

Finally, it is acknowledged that politics and the competition for budgets are perpetual management issues affecting the governance of Arctic tourism. Officials responsible for wilderness recreation management realize that success in the political and budget arenas depends on providing quality tourism experiences to the public and economic benefits to local communities. They must demonstrate that the fees they collect from recreation activities and associated economic benefits to local communities justify their budgetary requests. Recreation managers have navigated this difficult course for a long time, and make considerable efforts to demonstrate that recreation participation is strong and growing.

Human activities in Antarctica are primarily regulated by the complex of multilateral agreements of the Antarctic Treaty System, in particular the Antarctic Treaty itself and its Madrid Protocol on Environmental Protection. The Antarctic Treaty was adopted on 1 December 1959. Its primary purpose is to ensure, in the interest of all mankind, that Antarctica shall continue forever to be used exclusively for peaceful purposes and shall not become the scene or object of international discord. The Treaty provides for freedom of scientific investigation and promotes international cooperation in scientific research. It also prohibits any nuclear explosions and the disposal of radioactive waste material in Antarctica. In order to further the protection of the Antarctic environment, a Protocol to the Antarctic Treaty on Environmental Protection was adopted in 1991. The main purpose of the Protocol is to provide for the comprehensive protection of the Antarctic environment and dependent and associated ecosystems. The Protocol designates Antarctica as a natural reserve, devoted to peace and science; prohibits mineral resource activities other than scientific research; and sets principles and measures for the planning and conduct of all activities in the Antarctic Treaty area. Guidelines have been developed under this protocol to provide a framework for regulation of the potential negative impacts of tourism in the Antarctic. As tourist activities on the continent continue to grow the ATS is intensifying its focus on these issues.

Management Techniques

The UNEP and UNWTO have established 12 principles essential for accomplishing sustainable tourism. These principles represent guidelines for establishing and evaluating effective tourism management techniques. "The twelve aims for an agenda for sustainable tourism" are presented below and comprehensively discussed in the UNEP/UNWTO publication entitled Making Tourism More Sustainable A Guide for Policy Makers.

1. Economic Viability: To ensure the viability and competitiveness of tourism destinations and enterprises, so that they are able to continue to prosper and deliver benefits in the long term.
2. Local Prosperity: To maximize the contribution of tourism to the economic prosperity of the host destination, including the proportion of visitor spending that is retained locally.
3. Employment Quality: To strengthen the number and quality of local jobs created and supported by tourism, including the level of pay, conditions of service and availability to all without discrimination by gender, race, disability or in other ways.
4. Social Equity: To seek a widespread and fair distribution of economic and social benefits from tourism throughout the recipient community, including improving opportunities, income and services available to the poor.
5. Visitor Fulfillment: To provide a safe, satisfying and fulfilling experience for visitors, available to all without discrimination by gender, race, disability or in other ways.
6. Local Control: To engage and empower local communities in planning and decision making about the management and future development of tourism in their area, in consultation with other stakeholders.
7. Community Wellbeing: To maintain and strengthen the quality of life in local communities, including social structures and access to resources, amenities and life support systems, avoiding any form of social degradation or exploitation.

8. Cultural Richness: To respect and enhance the historic heritage, authentic culture, traditions and distinctiveness of host communities.
9. Physical Integrity: To maintain and enhance the quality of landscapes, both urban and rural, and avoid the physical and visual degradation of the environment.
10. Biological Diversity: To support the conservation of natural areas, habitats and wildlife, and minimize damage to them.
11. Resource Efficiency: To minimize the use of scarce and non-renewable resources in the development and operation of tourism facilities and services.
12. Environmental Purity: To minimize the pollution of air, water and land and the generation of waste by tourism enterprises and visitors.

As stated in the UNEP/UNWTO publication: "The order in which these twelve aims are listed does not imply any order of priority. Each one is equally important."

While all of these principles cannot be applied in the Antarctic and some Arctic regions (because of the absence of indigenous population and the non existence of local economies), they provide a solid basis of management objectives and evaluative criteria for creating, implementing and evaluating sustainable polar tourism. Each principle also contains key words and phrases that identify factors that can be monitored to evaluate the effectiveness, equity and efficiency of those plans, strategies and techniques. Notably, the principles include factors that address both the quantity and quality aspects of the host region and the tourism experience. Given the diverse conditions found throughout the Polar Regions, the principles must be adapted to fit special circumstances.

The remainder of this section outlines tourism management techniques that have been effectively used in the Polar Regions. They are relevant to polar conditions and to the several distinct tourism markets operating in those regions.

Recreation Management in the Arctic Wilderness

As outlined in Section 3, the polar tourism market is now a highly diversified industry that attracts people to many wilderness recreation activities. Nature tourism, wildlife viewing, sport fishing, hunting, and wilderness adventures of all types are actively pursued throughout all regions of the Arctic. In response to these recreation demands, Arctic resource managers have established numerous, specialized techniques to safeguard both the environment and the tourist. These techniques have an extensive history of addressing the Arctic's environmental conservation issues and the opportunity exists to expand their use in the Arctic.

Wilderness recreation approaches used in the Arctic are normally an integral part of comprehensive wilderness resource plans. Responsible stewardship, defined as the conservation of its natural and cultural resources, requires the selection of objectives that define the appropriate and allowable uses of those resources and the establishment of management techniques that protect those resources from loss or damage. In the Arctic, as elsewhere, the primary wilderness management objective associated with tourism is to protect both polar resources and tourists from harm. This approach to wilderness management is employed by all Arctic nations.

Wilderness management plans and the recreation management techniques they endorse are the result of substantial stakeholder involvement. Government agencies responsible for resource management of protected areas seek advice from a variety of stakeholders. Participatory processes and competing interests vary among jurisdictions, but the issue of allowable tourism is always part of these lively discussions. Significantly, polar tourism is only one of many competing resource uses confronting Arctic wilderness managers as they attempt to reconcile economic development interests with the protection of wilderness values. A wealth of tourism management experience can be obtained from the public records that document those decision making processes.

The techniques described below are utilized by wilderness agencies to manage both the independent back country traveller and small groups pursuing recreation activities. The techniques are designed to optimize scarce management resources and, to a considerable extent, hold tourists personally responsible for their own safety. They also respond to the need to manage both general, short term use of wilderness resources and recreation activities requiring special expertise and the use of specific locations. They are especially applicable to three distinct polar tourism market groups: (1) the nature and Eco-tourism market; (2) the sport fishing and hunting market; and (3) the adventure market.

Controlling and Monitoring Back country Use

Arctic wilderness managers implement land and water resource management plans that designate specific recreation entry points. These gateways to diverse wilderness experiences may be trail heads, information kiosks, interpretive centres, ranger stations, boat ramps, hunting zones, fishing sites, or kayak put-in sites. The primary purpose of these widely publicized locations is to intercept the tourist before they venture into the wilderness. When this "capture technique" is successful, managers can dispense vital information while simultaneously learning when, where, and how people are travelling through wilderness lands and waters. This technique requires agencies to designate allowable recreation uses in specific locations and relies on tourists to let them know exactly how and when those resources are being used. Managers then monitor recreation activity locations to determine if current recreational use should be continued, modified or prohibited. Elements of this approach include:

* Before departure the tourists are advised to read all pertinent regulations, obtain maps, essential supplies and equipment, and relevant guide books.
* Given a scarcity of agency personnel or lack of funds for visitor centres, wilderness recreation information is often provided at entry kiosks, or by means of signage. Obviously, selecting the foreign languages to be used will directly impact the effectiveness of this information.
* Back country travellers are requested to identify their route and mode of travel. This is generally done by means of registrations at trailheads and boat launch sites. Identification of their intermediate camp sites and destinations is accomplished by back country permit registrations. Known hazards are identified and they are advised that their personal safety, including clothing and equipment, is their personal responsibility.

* In locations where search and rescue services are available, emergency instructions, such as communication frequencies and weather radio broadcasts, are provided with the assumption that the tourist has compatible communication equipment. Persons travelling by boat or kayak are required to possess proper vessel licenses and to have marine charts, tide tables, and adequate safety and navigational equipment on board. But there are rarely coast guard vessels to conduct inspections.
* Management objectives are enforced by periodic patrolling by authorized resource agency personnel. Patrolling is accomplished from strategically located fixed or seasonal bases. Patrols may be conducted by boat, aircraft and various modes of land travel. The availability and frequency of these enforcement resources is affected by financial and personnel resources, the ruggedness of the terrain, and weather conditions.
* Search and rescue and emergency response capabilities vary widely in the Arctic's wilderness areas. Their availability is generally dependent on agency resources, proximity to communities, terrain conditions, and the severity of the weather. For all remote Arctic settlements, the commitment by volunteers to perform these functions is vital.
* Resource monitoring is conducted by resource agency personnel or designated persons with special skills. The frequency and rigor of these monitoring and evaluation endeavors are dependent on the budgetary and personnel resources of the lead agency and support received from NGO's dedicated to support the agency's resource conservation mission. Arctic NGO's play a vital role in this regard. Their commitment of volunteer personnel, fund raising, public awareness, and political advocacy provide invaluable contributions to the conservation of Arctic resources. Therefore, it is well justified to ask polar tourists to become active supporters of such organizations.

These management techniques have been used by Arctic resource agencies in national parks for more than a century.

National governance of Arctic wildlife refuges, forest reserves, and UNESCO World Heritage and Biosphere sites rounds out a list of prominent environmental settings offering important sustainability experiences. Site management practices, participatory decision making processes, partnerships with stakeholders, and commitment to international resource conservation agreements are all embodied in the roles and responsibilities of these resource agencies.

Licensed Guides and Special use Permits

One of the most successful management techniques for conserving Arctic resources and directly influencing lawful visitor behaviour is guide licensing. Wildlife managers realized long ago that an effective way to insure regulatory compliance was to require anglers and hunters to employ licensed guides. Guide licensing programmes have been established by wildlife management agencies in all Arctic nations. The programmes instruct specialized knowledge of environmental conditions, resource laws and regulations, survival skills, and emergency response skills. Guide licenses are issued based on demonstrated competency of that knowledge and skills. In most jurisdictions refresher courses are required to sustain both educational knowledge and practical skills.

Guide licensing in the Arctic has expanded well beyond angling and hunting. The pursuit of Arctic recreation activities such as mountaineering, rafting, kayaking, and wildlife photography frequently require licensed guides with the special skills required to safely conduct those activities. Licensing requirements vary considerably among Arctic jurisdictions and responsible resource agencies, but fundamental requirements required by all include: proven knowledge of specific locations, technical skills, safe and efficient recreation delivery systems, waste removal, emergency response systems, and detailed reporting of activities and observations. This skill and knowledge takes time to acquire, thus Arctic jurisdictions established a process that evolves from apprenticeship to master status.

States exercising jurisdiction in the Arctic hold guides directly responsible for both resource protection and visitor safety. Critical management issues concerning liability for resource damage and human harm are explicitly addressed by a combination of license requirements that include adequate insurance coverage, bonding, and indemnification. Based on the huge risks they are legally required to accept, guides very diligently monitor the behaviour of their clients. Guides accept the professional and financial risks of their profession for the privilege of pursuing a unique way of life. They generally spend a considerable amount of time teaching their clients appropriate behaviour, and respond quickly to instances when clients willfully disregard this information. Guide licensing regulations not only have beneficial affects on tourist behaviour, but on tourist numbers also. Legal prescriptions effectively limit tourist access by requiring they be accompanied by a licensed guide. Numbers are controlled by means of guide to visitor ratios, length of season, and sometimes duration of stay at a particular location. All of these methods strictly control the maximum number of people that may be on site. These requirements may be further specified in special use permits used to govern recreation activities. By example, the terms and conditions of river rafting, mountaineering, and wildlife viewing expeditions can be defined by special use permits.

Arctic guide licensing and the issuance of special use permits have proven to be effective polar tourism management techniques. They are an integral part of resource conservation programmes, such as wildlife management; they directly affect appropriate visitor behaviour and numbers; and the reports filed by guides provide vital resource monitoring information that would otherwise be unavailable. This approach to sustainable tourism has also established mutually beneficial partnerships between local communities and resource agencies. Native People and local residents who depend on polar resources for their cultural and economic wellbeing often serve as guides or possess special use permits to conduct recreation activities. They are the strongest advocates of sustainable management of polar resources, and as guides, they provide a direct method for accomplishing wise stewardship. The application of a guide licensing programme to Antarctica deserves serious consideration. To date, Antarctic tourism has been conducted by knowledgeable persons who often have distinguished records of scientific service in Antarctica, but no formal training in the skills and techniques of guiding. As the number of Antarctic tourists increase there will be a corresponding need to supply more qualified guides. Proficiency in variety of skills including subject expertise, knowledge of the landing sites, emergency response and communication skills, and tourist management should constitute the basic requirements of the Antarctic guide. These skills would help protect Antarctic resources; enhance the safety of the tourism experience; and advance the development of universal operational and communication protocols needed to respond to emergencies. For ship-based tourism, in particular, an education programme in polar tourism for guides should be considered. Cruise companies interested in high quality educational skills of their guides may support such an initiative and could request a certificate for their guides. Cooperation with environmental organizations in this field could lead to increasing benefits for conservation through advanced education.

The Special Case of Adventure Tourism The Arctic

Significant management challenges confront those responsible for accommodating the adventure tourism market. Principally, it is nearly impossible for Arctic recreation resource managers and licensed guides to competently know if the skill levels, health and psychological preparation of the participant are sufficient to meet the rigors of their sports. Inspection of equipment should be conducted, but managers, guides and operators rarely have that opportunity, and usually do not have spare parts and repair facilities to correct deficiencies. Maps, marine charts, tide tables can be supplied and it is hoped that adventurers will responsibly seek these essential aids to navigation. Emergency communication instructions in the form of emergency radio frequencies, protocols, directional beacons, and Standard Operating Procedures for search and rescue (if available) can also be provided. Again, it is essential for the adventurer to avail themselves of these in order to safely pursue their activities.

The Antarctic

For several decades Antarctica has attracted increasing numbers of adventure tourists. These activities range from relatively traditional outdoor sports to extreme events. More traditional pursuits have included mountaineering expeditions and numerous cross country skiing challenges. The more extreme sports include sky diving at the South Pole and scuba diving. A comprehensive discussion of this market and its management implications are found in Lamers, Stel, Amelung 2007.

Cultural Resource Management

The Arctic

A fundamental Arctic tourism management goal is to achieve balance between the public, commercial display of cultural features and the preservation of cultural integrity. Each culture has its own tolerance level for visitation and sharing its resources. Individual Arctic societies define acceptable visitor behaviour in terms of the types, magnitude, geographic location, and seasons of resource use. Consequently, cultural tourism management in the Arctic is subject to a set of 'host conditions' in which cultural preservation, economic necessity, and scarce natural resources are continuously debated. The conservation of ancestral homelands, scarce resources, and vulnerability to irreversible change are all significant tourism management issues facing Arctic indigenous societies.

From approximately the mid-1970s to the present, Native People have implemented a variety of policies, programmes, and techniques designed to uniquely reflect their approach to cultural tourism. In many instances these approaches are an affirmation of self-rule. When Alaskan Native Corporations and Villages were established they were empowered and capitalized to create economic development programmes. Several organizations pursued very conventional tourism development, such as hotels and similar commercial attractions, others instituted heritage tour programmes that represented their cultures. In the Canadian Arctic, the Inuit attained governance of Nunavut, a territory spanning one fifth of Canada's entire land mass. Nunavut has pursued various forms of tourism development during the past 25 years in response to this opportunity. Attainment of Homeland Rule by the Inuit of Greenland in 1979 resulted in the initiation of a very aggressive tourism development programme that includes ambitious commercial activity in Nuuk and diverse venues in rural areas. The Saami throughout Norway, Sweden and Finland are especially active in designing, funding, and operating numerous types of tourism venues that reflect the diversity of their cultures. And the most recent entrant to the Arctic cultural tourism market is Russia's Association of Indigenous People of the North (RAIPON), established in 1990 to accomplish many goals, one of which is tourism development.

As with other forms of tourism management, there is a substantial history of cultural tourism experience in the Arctic. The lessons learned, both good and bad, provide valuable guidance for those seeking to either establish or modify cultural tourism programmes. But the foremost lesson is that Native People and their governments must be vitally involved in decisions regarding how their culture and resources are shared with others.

The Antarctic

Antarctic heritage sites are popular attractions because of their historical significance and because of family and cultural ties to the pioneering settlers who once worked there. Management responses to these demands for visitation have ranged from prohibited entry to cordial invitations. For example, despite the popularity of Sir Ernest Shackleton's exploits, tourist access is denied to Stromness, South Georgia because of environmental protection concerns, while visitor access to Grytviken, where 'the Boss' is traditionally toasted at his graveside, is encouraged. Antarctic heritage sites in the Ross Sea are permitted with strict, but hospitable controls, and the refurbished 1940s research station at Port Lockroy, in the Antarctic Peninsula Region, actively promotes tourism to share its colorful heritage and to commercially support its postal concession.

Managing the Mass Market

The Arctic

The Arctic's tourism management opportunities and constraints are obviously well known to its people, governments, conservation organizations, and the tour companies that operate there. In response to a strong desire to influence the growth and development of polar tourism, a meeting of affected stakeholders was facilitated in 1995 by the World Wildlife Fund Arctic International Programme (WWF Arctic, 1996). The result of that collaborative effort was the publication in 1996 of Linking Tourism and Conservation in the Arctic which contains ten principles for Arctic tourism and associated codes of conduct for both tour operators and tourists. The participatory process and its product, as described by WWF Arctic, involved:

"Representatives from local communities, governments, different sectors of the tourism industry, conservation organizations and scientific institutions used their experience to create these guidelines for arctic tourism. The principles were also adopted into Codes of Conduct for tourism business and tourists which contain more specific information on what to consider when doing business or travelling in the Arctic."

The Arctic's consensus-based Principles and Codes of Conduct offer a responsible approach to polar tourism management. The ten principles contain an appropriate collection of resource conservation goals, the essential starting point for resource management. Environmental conservation, cultural integrity, economic benefits, visitor safety, and respect for polar resources are comprehensively included in the Principles for Arctic Tourism. The principles are to be realized by two ten point Codes of Conduct for Tour Operators and Tourists in the Arctic, respectively. The direct relationships between the conservation goals and tourism practices by both operators and tourists are clearly described and represent the strength of this approach.

The Principles and Codes are implemented by means of a comprehensive advocacy programme. Stakeholders collectively promote the Principles and Codes through information dissemination, consumer education, and personnel training. To date, they have been diligent in their efforts. The Principles and Codes are described in further detail in the Good Practices section of this publication.

The Antarctic

The first tourism-specific regulations were adopted by the Antarctic Treaty as early as 1966 with the emergence of commercial tourism activities. These regulations were setting rules for visits by tourist groups to Antarctic stations maintained by the Parties. In 1975 a Statement of Accepted Practices was adopted. This was modified and expanded several times and resulted in the Tourism Guidelines adopted in 1994 by the Parties to the Antarctic Treaty. Aside from establishing guidelines for tourist expeditions, the Parties to the Antarctic Treaty also require tourist expeditions to submit reports on their visits.

On August 2005 the UN Secretary General reported on the UN General Assembly on the "question of the Antarctica". The report recognizes that "Antarctic tourism activities are increasing, as is their diversity (camping, climbing, kayaking and scuba-diving), presenting new management challenges". As a first step towards a more rigorous control of tourism activities, the Antarctic Treaty Consultative Meetings (ATCMs) adopted two resolutions to enhance information exchange and consultation and to further the development and implementation of site-specific guidelines. However, according to the Secretary General report, "no consensus has yet been reached on critical issues, such as land-based and high-risk (adventure) tourism, leaving tourism to be regulated to a large extent by the industry itself". The annual Antarctic Treaty Consultative Meetings (ATCMs) have been discussing tourism and tourism regulation in details since 2001. The Antarctic Treaty parties have adopted guidelines for visitors to the Antarctic. These guidelines are intended to ensure that wildlife and vegetation are not disturbed, protected areas and research programmes are respected, and activities are conducted with a high regard for safety. Guidelines for operators request that they provide advance notification of their activities, confirm visits to scientific stations, ensure that their passengers are properly supervised and report on their expeditions.

The requirements of the Madrid Protocol and other components of the Antarctic Treaty System are implemented by each Treaty party in its own laws, according to its legal system. Visitors to the Antarctic should ensure that they are familiar with the legal requirements that apply to them-for example, the applicable laws may be those of the country where the expedition is being planned, or the country from which the expedition departs. The most important legal requirements relate to prior environmental assessment of the proposed activities, prohibition on taking or harming flora and fauna, waste disposal, contingency planning and the need for permits if visits to protected areas are contemplated.

Complimentary to the regulatory framework created by the Antarctic Treaty System, one on-site management technique currently available for conserving the resources of the entire continent is self regulation of tourist operations and behaviour. The International Association of Antarctic Tour Operators was founded by seven private tour operators in 1991 and, as of 2007, had grown to include 80 members from 14 countries. The majority of tourist ships to Antarctica are members of the Association and some yacht operators are joining them. The members of IAATO endeavored to comply with Recommendation XVIII-I: Guidance for Visitors to the Antarctic by creating visitor guidelines that addressed the environmental protection of landing sites, the safety of the guests, and the establishment of operational protocols to provide emergency assistance. Both guests and all tour operator personnel receive these instructions.

As the UN Secretary-General's Report to the GA in 2005 on the Question of Antarctica states, "since the Twenty-fifth Antarctic Treaty Consultative Meeting, the IAATO has continued to focus its activities on increasing cooperation and field coordination among its members; promoting effective environmental impact assessments; preventing the introduction of alien organisms; promoting self-sufficiency and proper conduct among visitors; developing emergency response and contingency plans; and promoting specific guidelines for sites where the growing bulk of tourism occurs".

The self-regulated approach to tourism management in Antarctica, developed in accordance with the existing regulatory framework, currently depends on the following premises: (1) the tourist industry instructs their clients about appropriate behaviour and does not alienate them; (2) voluntary coordination among cruise and tour directors is the only means of managing site visits; and (3) responses to emergency situations are completely dependent on voluntary efforts and the skills of those who, fortuitously, are willing to respond. To date this approach has been effective, but the inherent environmental conditions of Antarctica, its remoteness, and, most importantly, the growing number of tourists will test the sustainability of this approach. As passenger numbers increase, there is a need for increased vigilance at some of the sites. Towards this end, the indicators proposed by UNWTO for the assessment of the sustainability of tourism in Antarctica provide a good base for a monitoring programme.

Conclusion

Key elements of an agenda for sustainable tourism development in Polar Regions have been developed through the efforts of a combination of governments, inter-governmental bodies, NGOs, business initiatives. They are:

* The 12 principles for sustainable tourism development that have been endorsed by UNEP/UNWTO. While all of these principles cannot be applied in the Antarctic and some Arctic regions (because of the absence of indigenous population and the non existence of local economies), they provide a solid basis of management objectives and evaluative criteria for creating, implementing and evaluating sustainable polar tourism.
* In response to unique circumstances, Arctic governments, Arctic natural resource agencies, NGOs, the tour industry operating in both hemispheres, and Native People have created innovative management techniques that are now applied in both Polar Regions. Some of the most important of these techniques include the Antarctic Treaty tourism Guidelines, and the WWF 10 Arctic Principles.
* Recognizing the need to simultaneously protect many resources from adverse impacts, existing tourism management techniques employ a comprehensive approach to influence appropriate tourist behaviour and resource conservation practices.
* An immense amount of information pertaining to the laws, participatory decision-making process, native customs, and numerous techniques employed to manage polar tourism and polar resources has been produced.

* A multitude of good tourism management practices exist throughout both the Arctic and Antarctic that should be evaluated for either expansion to new regions or modified for current tourist activity zones.
* Improved knowledge of the many natural events affecting the environmental conditions of the Polar Regions is growing rapidly. This knowledge is an essential ingredient in the design of tourism management policies and programmes, which must also be adjusted and as necessary reinforced in the face of growing tourist numbers.

What is now needed to advance sustainable polar tourism policies and programmes is the assembly of existing information and open access to that information. Since virtually all polar tourism management documents are in the public record and the Arctic is supremely well connected in this digital age, this is a very feasible agenda that can produce immediate positive results. Remote Arctic communities seeking to manage tourism in a timely manner need immediate access to this type of information. Stakeholders concerned about Antarctic tourism should have access to the full spectrum of available resource conservation and tourism management techniques.

The collection and dissemination of appropriate tourism management and resource conservation laws, customs, treaties, codes of conduct, techniques, and customs will provide significant benefits to both Polar Regions.

This free flow of information will allow the benefits derived from tourism in Antarctica by a limited number of persons or commercial entities to be weighed against the global values at risk. Antarctica offers unique opportunities for scientific monitoring of, and research on processes of global and regional importance and was declared a natural reserve devoted to science and peace. A regime for its protection was also developed in the interest of mankind as a whole. As stated in the SG report, "the tourism industry has increased tremendously over the last decade. [...] Efforts should be continued to ensure that commercial activities will not impact on the successes of the Antarctic Treaty system, in particular in securing Antarctica as a natural reserve, devoted to peace and science".

Defining 'Nature Tourism'

Nature in Tourism

In its broadest sense, nature in tourism involves experiencing natural places, typically through outdoor activities that are sustainable in terms of their impact on the environment. These can range from active to passive and include everything from bush walking and adventure tourism experiences to sightseeing, scenic driving, beach experiences and wildlife viewing. In many instances a visitor may combine several of these in the one trip. For keen outdoor enthusiasts, and there are many, the great majority of adventure activities directly depend on nature and natural environments for their successful conduct. Fundamentally, the role of nature can vary from 'crucial to the visitor experience' to 'enhances the visitor experience'-particularly in relation to such variables as active or passive measures of the activity involved.

For passive and active visitors alike, nature is also playing an increasingly important role in giving something back to people (relaxing, enriching the spirit, getting back to basics). By doing so, it is able to enhance their broader experience of a destination. And for mainstream domestic visitors, these benefits tap more accurately into nature's deeper meaning-see resource paper No 3, The deeper significance and role of 'nature' in tourism. Nature-based experiences are intimately linked to all other aspects of the visitor's total experience of a destination, such as food, culture, relaxation, health, escape, family needs, accommodation, transport, etc. All serve to complement each other and together form the basis of a visitor's overall satisfaction with their holiday.

Eco-tourism

Eco tourists, with their strong focus on learning about the natural environment, minimising negative impacts and contributing to its care, lie at one specialist end of the nature in tourism spectrum, albeit an important one. They are in effect ambassadors (or early adopters) for a set of personal values towards which it now appears many other market segments, potentially comprising much larger visitor numbers, are moving. Conserved and protected areas (including Marine and National Parks), the Earth's biodiversity, and respect for local culture and those who have been traditional guardians of our natural environments, can be central to their interests. Eco tourists are also characterised by knowing what they want and being strongly self-active in accessing it. They will often plan and book their experiences and travel needs themselves, leaving tourism operators with more time and the broader opportunity to pursue tourists with more mainstream nature-based interests, and those seeking adventure activity.

Soft and Hard Adventure Tourism

Soft and hard adventure tourism activities also comprise a subset of activities strongly associated with the natural environment and nature-based tourism. Related market segments include 'adventure sports' such as mountain biking. Anecdotal evidence from Australian tourism operators suggests that demand for both soft and hard adventure tourism is growing. Research suggests that spending by nature-based tourists (particularly those with an interest in adventure activities and visiting significant nature destinations including national parks) is often substantially above average, per visitor and per night (Tourism Tasmania: Nature-based Tourism Report: 1998-99 Update).

It is important to recognise that international source markets can culturally differ over which activities they will describe as 'soft' and which as 'hard' (e.g. snorkelling, surfing, ballooning and orienteering may be viewed as soft by one market and hard by another). Similarly, differences in outlook can arise between younger and older visitors from the same source market. For many major international markets (e.g. Asian and American), soft activities rather than hard are more frequently preferred by those interested in adventure-based experiences in natural areas. Soft adventure activities commonly require a moderate level of physical involvement by participants and are less physically challenging than hard activities.

They can include– hiking/bush walking, mountain biking/ bicycling, camping, horseback riding, orienteering, walking tours, wildlife spotting, whale watching, river and lake canoeing and fishing. The numbers undertaking such activities can be substantial – e.g. the NSW Fisheries estimates that recreational fishing is enjoyed by over 1 million New South Wales residents each year, as well as around 300,000 visiting anglers. There is evidence from leading natural destinations that bush walking activity rates are also significantly increasing, particularly when support facilities are good, with highest participation rates in the 'under 2 hours' and '2 hours to a full day' categories. Wildlife viewing also achieves high levels of participation. Hard adventure activities commonly involve a higher level of physical or rugged involvement or a potentially greater personal challenge for participants. The risk factor can also increase. Hard adventure activities with a nature basis or need include – caving, scuba diving, trekking, white water rafting, kayaking, rock and mountain climbing, cross-country skiing, safaris, surfing, windsurfing, ballooning and ocean sailing. By contrast, bungy jumping does not depend on a nature setting. At the more challenging end of the hard adventure scale, support equipment can be involved or be absolutely necessary-e.g. climbing gear, oxygen tanks, ocean-going kayaks.

Special interest tourism

Nature-based tourism and its various subsets can also encompass some particularly challenging, but potentially high spending, special interest market segments. These often comprise socially and environmentally aware, highly educated and potentially demanding visitors who travel both to learn and to achieve personal and social goals. Most of these visitors are serviced and targeted by specialist tourism operators and suppliers who often provide highly expert guides as part of the service. Examples include the 'not for profit' travel sector in the United States whose interests can range widely, encompassing anything from wildlife expeditions to scientific and cultural tours.

The major non-profit institutions of North America, such as natural history museums, zoos, universities and botanical societies, commonly promote their own worldwide travel programs to membership, alumni and donor bases that can run into the millions. Accessing and converting their small groups travel market can be difficult. It takes time, effort and a great commitment to high quality standards and delivery. An equally dedicated nature-based special interest visitor segment exists with bird-watching. Enthusiasts will travel long distances (and often at short notice) to sometimes remote and hard-to- access destinations, in order to sight new and rare species. In addition, readily identifiable communication channels (such as the ornithologists' special interest newsletters) can exist for accessing such market segments.

Wildlife Tourism

Wildlife tourism involves travel to observe wildlife in natural environments and preferably their native habitat. It is a further subset of nature tourism and one in which significantly high levels of domestic and international interest exist. Wildlife tourism involves wild and non domesticated animals and can encompass free-ranging and captive circumstances. Given the unique character and special appeal of most of Australia's wildlife, this suggests it may represent a tourism opportunity area for some destinations. The Blue Mountains, Barrington Tops, North and South Coast areas and Outback New South Wales possess great potential in this regard given their species diversity and relative convenience as destinations from major source markets and ports of entry.

Wildlife tourism encompasses the chance to encounter fauna (and flora) in terrestrial, aquatic/marine and aerial settings and to gain some further understanding of a wide variety of species (including viewing kangaroos, koalas, whales, dolphins, seals, fish and birds). Undertaking this activity in a manner that is environmentally responsible is important to ensure less disturbance to wildlife and habitats. In terms of major visitor trends, 'appreciative tourism' involving observation, photography and interaction with wild animals is large scale, prominent and growing. Consumptive tourism involving such activities as hunting and (non-catch and release) fishing is also large scale, but declining. Ideally, wildlife tourism should include some element of education and an increased appreciation of nature and conservation issues. Potential new models for wildlife tourism in Australia are being developed. These involve wildlife sanctuaries with feral free habitats attempting to use tourism and other enterprise based revenue sources as a means to help protect endangered native species and develop recovery plans for the species. Activities directly related to wildlife viewing, such as scuba diving and whale watching, are experiencing rapid worldwide growth in popularity and it is clear that the concept of wildlife viewing itself is gaining global currency with visitors. It has been estimated to generate $30 billion worldwide in revenues each year. Alaska has experienced strong tourism growth in recent years, particularly in wildlife tourism, with more than 46% of its visitors engaging in this activity.

Nationally in the USA, wildlife viewing is the third highest purpose for trips each year (671 million) after sightseeing (1037 million) and family gatherings (778 million). It is expected that wildlife activities will increase 61% nationally over the next 52 years to Year 2050 (Outdoor Recreation in American Life: A National Assessment of Demand and Supply Trends, 1999 – quoted in Nature: The leading edge for regional Australia). 43% of Canadians are involved in outdoor recreation each year and 18.6% have a wildlife component to their trip. 74.5% watch wildlife on the media and this is a major influence on driving wildlife tourism.

The worldwide value of whale watching is estimated at over $2 billion. In Australia it has been estimated to generate $100 million with almost one million people watching each year. In New South Wales alone, more than 200,000 people annually pay for whale watching tours – double the number of 10 years ago. Wildlife tourism should also seek to maximise the benefits to local communities, while avoiding problems such as disturbance to wildlife and pollution. Types and magnitudes of environmental impacts associated with wildlife tourism vary with the type of tourist activity pursued – some impacts are obvious and easily identifiable while others are indirect and difficult to quantify. The impacts on particular animals should not be considered in isolation from the broader environmental settings and wider animal population. The conservation benefits of wildlife tourism can include – its financial contribution; practical (in kind) contribution; socio-economic incentive for conservation; and education.

Sustainable Tourism

Sustainable tourism is envisaged by the World Tourism Organisation (WTO) as "leading to management of all resources in such a way that economic, social and aesthetic needs can be fulfilled while maintaining cultural integrity, essential ecological processes, biological diversity and life support systems". Sustainable tourism might also be defined as "tourism which is economically viable but does not destroy the resources on which the future of tourism will depend, notably the physical environment and the social fabric of the host community".

Furthermore, "A clear distinction should be made between the concepts of Eco-tourism and sustainable tourism: the term Eco-tourism itself refers to a segment within the tourism sector, while the sustainability principles should apply to all types of tourism activities, operations, establishments and projects, including conventional and alternative forms".

The goal of 'ecologically sustainable development' is to improve the total quality of life, both now and in the future, in a way that maintains the ecological processes on which life depends. Supplementary definitions with significant relevance to nature in tourism.

Geotourism

Geotourism is concerned with sustaining or enhancing a destination's geographic character – the entire combination of natural and human attributes that make one place distinct from another. Geotourism encompasses both cultural and environmental concerns regarding travel, as well as the local impact tourism has upon communities and their individual economies and lifestyles. Aesthetics, heritage and the wellbeing of residents are included as some of its concerns. Geotourism has also been summarised as restorative and reconstructive forms of tourism that enhance a destination's natural and cultural distinctiveness, as well as provide a high- quality visitor experience. Geotourism is obviously closely related to sustainable tourism, even though it has its own refined concerns and focus.

Ecologically Sustainable Development

"Using, conserving and enhancing the community's resources so that ecological processes, on which life depends, are maintained and the total quality of life, now and in the future, can be increased."

Conservation

"The management of human use of the biosphere so that it may yield the greatest sustainable benefit to present generations while maintaining its potential to meet the needs and aspirations of future generations." (National Conservation Strategy for Australia.) "The protection, presentation, maintenance, management, sustainable use and restoration of the natural environment (and its ecosystems)." The issue of management is vital in reltion to tourism.

The environmental impacts of tourism as a service industry must be recognised and never dismissed, but they also need to be placed in perspective. Ecological sustainability will never be achieved through a focus on environment and biodiversity alone. Social and economic values and needs must become integral concerns of nature conservation management. Likewise the tourism industry must address the concerns of natural area managers and recognise them as important partners in delivering sustainable experiences to visitors. Managed protected areas and other conservation sites now provide accessible means by which all visitors can experience at first hand nature in its wider diversity (and come to appreciate its values). Effectively planned and managed, this can foster conservation benefits – the basic challenge is to deliver good management, planning, education and resourcing. Interpretation (directed at visitors)

1. "A special process of stimulating and encouraging an appreciation of the natural and cultural heritage of a region, as well as a means of communicating nature conservation ideals and practices."
2. "A means of communicating ideas and feelings which helps people enrich their understanding and appreciation of their world, and their role within it." The first definition sees interpretation from a visitor's perspective as a means of value-adding to their experience because of the added interest it creates when more is known about an attraction or experience. The second definition places the responsibility back with the visitor to arrive at their own understanding based on their collective experiences.
3. "An educational activity which aims to reveal meanings and relationships through the use of original objects, first hand experience and illustrative media, rather than simply by communicating factual information."

Principles for Successful Interpretation

Successful interpretation typically reflects a number of key principles: People learn better when they are actively involved in the learning process. People learn better when they are using as many senses as appropriate. It is generally recognised that people retain approximately 10% of what they hear, 30% of what they read, 50% of what they see and 90% of what they do. Insights that people discover for themselves are the most memorable as they stimulate a sense of excitement and growth.

Learning requires activity on the part of the learner. Being aware of the usefulness of the knowledge being acquired makes the learning process more effective. Enhancing the quality of interpretation at visitor centres, attractions, on tours, along trails/ drives and 'in the field' or on site, is a major opportunity area for 'nature in tourism' in New South Wales.

As far as possible, interpretation needs to capture a visitor's imagination, intellect or emotions (even momentarily) and in so doing grab their interest. Differences such as age, and cultural background are also obvious considerations. When pursuing excellence in interpretation, there are as many paths of possibility open to visitor managers as there are creative ideas in the world. To fail to explore these is to risk having an audience label the interpretive approach adopted as too dull, tired, serious, patronising, over- complicated, overwhelming, superficial, cautious, etc.

Great creative ideas resulting in exciting interpretation outcomes are often achieved more successfully if more innovative creative development processes (e.g. those developed by Edward De Bono) are applied, and the creative net cast more widely. Building wider creative alliances by involving other people with different 'skill sets' (e.g. who are known for their innovative & 'wildcard' thinking capacities as well as essential sense of humour & fun) can often prove of value-particularly if they are properly rewarded for the business significance of their personal contribution to the results.

A capacity for simple but effective delivery coupled with good commonsense and empathy also helps.

Summarising its benefits, interpretation is an effective way of adding value to the experience, employing more locals, creating a cultural connection for visitors, building understanding and differentiating an operator's product in the market.

Tourism Feels the Heat of Global Warming

The promoters of 'adventure-' or 'Eco-tourism' have popularized slogans such as: "Go visit the last paradises... before they'll be destroyed by tourist hordes." In a similar fashion, the British daily The Observer recently suggested that world travellers need to hurry up if they want to see the '10 wonders of a vanishing world'. According to the related article, the most wondrous natural tourist attractions we can no longer take for granted due to global warming include:

Africa's highest mountain-the spectacular Kilimanjaro in Tanzania will never look the same as snows are disappearing at an alarming rate.

The Caribbean coral reefs – particularly the Meso-American reef, the world's second biggest, stretching from the coast of southern Mexico down past Belize and into Honduras, is threatened by a three-fold environmental disaster: Warmer water disrupts coral growth; acidic water affects coral's abilities to secrete new skeletons; and increasingly intense hurricanes break it up. As a result thousands of marine species are on the brink of extinction.

The Maldives in the Indian Ocean-many tropical islands forming the Indian Ocean archipelago are likely to become submerged in the next two decades as a result of rising sea levels and increasing numbers of heavy storms.

Traditional ski resorts in the Alps such as Kitzbuhel in Austria for example will disappear from the tourist map within 20 years because of the lack of snow.

Furthermore, the future of many unique animal species that have attracted wildlife tourism is in jeopardy as habitats, breeding grounds and migration routes are changing. If global warming gets worse, entire populations of polar bears in the Arctic region, Wildebeests in East Africa, Mountain Gorillas in Uganda and Rwanda or Monarch Butterflies in Mexico may be destroyed.

Tourism World Wakes up to the Climate Crisis

Climate is an essential resource for tourism, and especially for beach, nature and winter sport tourism, and the phenomenon of global warming already gravely affects the industry and an increasing number of destinations. In 2003, the Madrid-based UN World Tourism Organization (UNWTO) convened the 1st International Conference on Climate Change and Tourism in Djerba, Tunisia, to help the travel and tourism industry to respond to these issues. The UNWTO, that only a few years ago became a special UN agency, is traditionally driven by a strong Business Council that aggressively advances the interests of the world's most powerful tourism-related corporations.

That the UNWTO declared climate change a priority issue shows the growing awareness among industry leaders and policy-makers that the impacts of global warming pose a serious threat to tourism-one of the world's largest and fastest growing industries, generating over 10.4 per cent of world GDP, according to the World Travel and Tourism Council (WTTC).

Notably, the Djerba conference recognized that the relationship between climate change and tourism is two-fold: Not only is tourism affected by a changing climate, at the same time it contributes to climate change by the consumption of fossil fuels and resulting greenhouse gas emissions. It was concluded that there was an "urgent need for the tourism industry, national governments and international organizations to develop and implement strategies to face the changing climate conditions and to take preventive actions for future effects, as well as to mitigate tourism's environmental impacts contributing to climate change.". Also the burgeoning international Eco-tourism industry feels challenged. At the recent Global Eco-tourism Conference 2007 (GEC07) that was jointly organized by The Eco-tourism Society (TIES), Eco-tourism Norway and the UNEP in Oslo, Norway, it was agreed that "Climate change has increasingly become a major threat affecting the very resources on which Eco-tourism depends – natural areas and local and Indigenous communities around the world....Stronger leadership and strategies are needed in order to substantially decrease Eco-tourism's carbon footprint generated from multiple sources including facility operations and transport-related greenhouse gas emissions."

This article will offer some explanations as to why travel and tourism leaders are now feverishly working at the climate change front. Firstly, the economic costs of climate change for the industry will rise inexorably if it takes a business-as-usual attitude. Secondly, tourism relies more than other industries on a good image, but its reputation as a beneficial and environmentally acceptable activity has rapidly faded during recent debates on the causes of global warming.

Economic Factors

Critics have always pointed out the fickle nature of tourism, and indeed the industry's special vulnerability to bad news and events has been proven many times in recent years; just consider the slumps following terrorist attacks such as 9/11 and the Bali bombings, the threat of diseases such as SARS and avian flu or environmental crises. The Indian Ocean tsunami in 2004 and Hurricane Katrina that hit New Orleans in 2005, caused immeasurable costs for the travel and tourism industry. What needs to be calculated here are not only the costs of lost property and for the reconstruction of tourist infrastructure in case of disasters, but also the costs of tourists staying away from crisis-hit destinations for a long time as well as the high expenditures for promotional campaigns to get tourists visiting again.

To enable the tourism sector to respond promptly and effectively in cases of emergency, the UNWTO and international business associations such as the Pacific Asia Travel Association (PATA) have already made major investments to establish crisis centres and risk management task forces. Further efforts are underway to develop climate change policies for the tourism sector that offer adaptation and mitigation measures aimed to prevent or reduce high expenditures in tourist areas affected by climate-change-related problems.

How urgent it is to take action is shown by the case of Fiji. Like uncountable other small islands around the world, Fiji's islands are highly vulnerable to climate change, and the tourism industry is already suffering from the impacts in the form of cyclones, storm surge and flooding, sea level rise, erosion, transport and communication interruption, and reduced water availability. These are the findings of a research by Susanne Becken, published by the University of the South Pacific in August 2004. The "climate-change-related hazards have the potential to destroy existing tourism capital and severely undermine efforts to attract new investment from within Fiji and overseas. Increasing insurance premiums aggravate the risk.".

Aviation, Cruise Ship Industry Major Climate Change Culprits

The aviation industry in particular is now facing enormous pressure since the Intergovernmental Panel on Climate Change (IPCC) and environmental campaign groups have singled out the responsibility of air travel in accounting for a considerable portion of global greenhouse gas emissions. Globally, the world's 16,000 commercial jet planes generate more than 600 million tones of CO2 per year, almost as much as from all human activities in Africa each year, according to Friends of the Earth.

The huge increase in aircraft pollution is largely due to the rapid growth of tourism and related air traffic. A WWF briefing paper on 'Tourism & Climate Change' (2001) states that the actual tonnage of CO2 emitted will increase by over 75 per cent by 2015; concomitantly, from almost 700 million international travellers in 2000, numbers are expected to jump over one billion by 2010 and 1.6 billion by 2020. "As a consequence, the role of air travel within the tourism industry is likely to expand, cause considerable environmental damage, and to have knock-on effects on the tourism industry itself," concludes WWF.

Given the recent negative publicity, tourists in Western countries are changing their behaviour and tend to fly less. There are now even voices in Europe that go so far to suggest that flying away on holiday is immoral and should be stopped altogether.

"Warming stops global roaming", wrote the Australian newspaper Daily Telegraph recently. A survey in Australia done by a holiday website found nearly 20 per cent of respondents considered giving up air travel as it causes irreparable harm to the environment, while only 16 per cent said they do not care about climate change and it would not affect their travel choices at all. Similarly, a study prepared for Greenpeace in the UK showed a clear shift in consumers' perception: 61 per cent of the respondents were of the opinion that "We should limit our air travel voluntarily", 33 per cent agreed that "Air travel is now too cheap", 52 per cent agreed that "There should be a tax on fuel for air travel", and 61 per cent of the respondents supported the idea that "There should be a pollution warning on air tickets".

Apart from aviation, the worldwide booming cruise ship industry has also come under fire. Cruise ships that can carry up to 5,000 tourists are not only notorious for creating tremendous amounts of waste and sewage but also belong to the biggest contributors to greenhouse gas emissions within the travel and tourism industry. The US-Bluewater Network that campaigns against the pollution of the world's oceans by ships has found that in one port visit, a single cruise ship can generate the emissions of more than 12,400 cars. The ship smokestacks release toxic emissions that lead to acid rain, global climate change, and damaging health effects to communities situated near ports. Despite the fact that ocean cruise liners are more energy efficient than other forms of commercial transportation, marine engines operate on extremely dirty fuels, known as 'bunker oil'. To compound the problem, engines on these ocean-going ships are currently not required to meet the same strict air pollution controls as cars and trucks are required to do.

Global travel and tourism could only grow by leaps and bounds because the transport networks that enable the movement of people and goods around the world are heavily subsidized. Tourists can enjoy to travel the world at incredibly low prices. As the New Economic Foundation study 'Up in Smoke?' explains "...much international trade lives in a bubble. International aviation and marine fuels are immune from any kind of taxation that would indicate and internalize the real environmental cost of freight and shipping. Greenhouse gas emissions from international freight are also exempt from the emissions targets set for rich countries to meet under the Kyoto Protocol of the UN Climate Change Convention." Growing consumer awareness on these issues and a burgeoning citizens movement calling for fuel taxes and stricter regulation of the transport industry can severely curb future tourism growth targets and, thus, cut deep into the profits of plane-makers, airlines, travel agencies, cruise ship-operators and other tourism-related businesses. No wonder then that companies are now scrambling to talk about hard-earned environmental advances and new initiatives to protect the environment.

At the Paris Air Show in June, for example, Airbus' top salesman John Leah, told a press conference that Airbus is "saving the planet, one A380 at a time". The company's promotional brochures featured a silhouette of the new two-deck super-jumbo-dubbed the "gentle green giant"-set against images of dolphins, rain forests and fishing boats on a misty pond. Boeing representatives were also keen to display ecological bona fides and claimed the industry has reduced fuel consumption by 70 per cent since the jet age began, reported Dow Jones Newswires.

While the global travel and tourism lobby has adopted the rhetoric of corporate social and environmental responsibility, reality checks on the ground show that tourism's environmental performance has remained very poor. Neither the UN-initiated International Year of Eco-tourism 2002 or multilateral environment agreements such as the Tourism Guidelines under the Convention of Biological Diversity (CBD), have achieved anything to stop tourism from pervading pristine coastal areas, islands, forests and mountainous areas.

On the contrary, more fragile ecosystems and biodiversity are destroyed, local communities displaced and traditional livelihoods destroyed-all for the establishment of huge exclusive resorts, golf courses and marinas. These massive tourism complexes are also notorious for high per capita consumption of energy and water. But however damaging and wasteful these projects may be, with the right PR efforts, they can still pass as 'Eco-tourism' developments and even raise their profile thanks to eco-accreditation schemes, or environmental Best Practices awards.

As long as no proper legally binding frameworks are in place to check and redress excessive and damaging tourism activities, 'green-washing' continues and climate change culprits are likely to get away scot-free. Eco-tourism promoters' intention to help minimize tourism's carbon footprint is laudable. The GEC07 Oslo

Statement, for example, outlines an action plan that aims at "encouraging adapted travel patterns (e.g. increase length of stay per trip); promoting more energy-efficient, alternative or non-motorized transport options; utilizing reduced and zero-emission operation technologies; and increasing participation in reliable high-quality carbon offsetting schemes."

But many of the new initiatives that promote 'zero-carbon' or 'carbon-neutral' tourism businesses need critical examination because they may just be marketing gimmicks. For instance, The Guardian (UK) announced in January that Per Aquum, the brand behind some of the world's most luxurious resorts, was the owner of the first 'zero-carbon' five-star beach resort designed by architects in London. The developers of the resort, due to open in 2008, claim the project will have no negative environmental impact and will be totally self-sufficient, using only energy from the sun and wind and producing little waste or carbon emissions. "The only drawback, environmentally speaking, is its location-thousands of fuel-guzzling miles away in Nungwi, Zanzibar," cautioned The Guardian.

Six Senses Resorts and Spas, a Bangkok-based luxury hotel chain with properties in Thailand, Vietnam and the Maldives is now specialized in 'carbon-cutting getaways' for millionaires who do not want their "vacation dampened by global warming guilt". Apart from introducing energy-saving innovations at the luxurious island resorts, all visitors are required to pay a tax for their flight, which goes into a carbon offset fund. The project owners say the fund will be spent on renewable energy projects for villages in Sri Lanka and India, thus, offsetting among the poor the carbon emissions caused by jets transporting the rich to their holiday destination. Yet, can Six Senses really be called an environmentally friendly company considering that it consumes exorbitant amounts of water to run their spa facilities, for example?

Controversial Carbon Offsetting and Trading Schemes

A growing number of airlines have included carbon offsetting into the price of tickets. However, there are increasing reports about shady 'think green – see cash' carbon trading businesses that are trying to take advantage of well-intentioned air travellers.

When Lufthansa earlier this year was looking for a partner to offer a carbon offsetting scheme to customers, half of the 13 studied companies were considered unreliable.

Last year, the activists Timothy Byakola and Chris Lang exposed a Dutch company called GreenSeat which promised to invest airline passengers' carbon offset contributions in climate friendly projects in poor countries. For the paltry sum of US$28, one would be able to cover the costs of planting 66 trees to 'compensate' for the CO2 emissions of a return flight from Frankfurt to Kampala. But looking closer at one of these projects, in Mount Elgon National Park in Uganda, the activists found that local people were harassed and even driven from their land to pave the way for the tree plantations. GreenSeat has since stopped selling carbon credits from Mount Elgon – because of the problems there. Earlier this year, farmers cut down half-a-million of the project's trees and planted crops and fruit trees on the land.

Carbon trading that enables companies and consumers to buy themselves out of responsibility are highly controversial. It "dispossesses ordinary people in the South of their lands and futures without resulting in appreciable progress toward alternative energy systems," argues Larry Lohmann of the UK-based The Corner House, who has co-edited the book 'Carbon Trading: A Critical Conversation on Climate Change, Privatization and Power'. "Tradable rights to pollute are handed out to Northern industry, allowing them to continue to profit from business as usual. At the same time, Northern polluters are encouraged to invest in supposedly carbon-saving projects in the South, very few of which are actually helping to halt dependence on fossil fuels."

4

Tourism as a Development Strategy

Introduction

Since the Revelstoke Tourism Strategy was developed in 1997, the community has made extensive progress in promoting and marketing tourism opportunities in Revelstoke. The identification of the Chamber of Commerce as the lead tourism marketing and coordinating 'agency', the formation of the Revelstoke Tourism Advisory Committee, the hiring of a full-time Tourism Development Coordinator, and the commitment of the City of Revelstoke and the CSRD to provide long-term funding for tourism marketing activities have all been positive developments. The community has won awards for the quality of the electronic marketing initiatives which have been undertaken, and the quality, variety and distribution of the print-based promotional materials has also improved dramatically over the course of the past six years. The intent of the Revised Tourism Strategy is to identify the opportunities which will further enhance the tourism sector over the next 5 year period.

While the initial Tourism Strategy was prepared several years ago, many of the observations regarding the potential of Revelstoke to capitalize on its tourism assets are still valid today. The 1997 Strategy stated:

Revelstoke is very well positioned to take more effective advantage of the community and economic benefits associated with tourism. In addition to a very scenic location on a well travelled highway corridor,

Revelstoke is unique among B.C. communities in terms of the range and quality of activity options, the uniqueness and visual appeal of the town itself, and the availability of related support services and infrastructure.

Since that time, the infrastructure to support tourism has expanded and the quality has improved, increasing the potential for further tourism related development.

Revised Strategy Format

The revised strategy identifies eleven (11) objectives that will set the framework for tourism development over the next five years. These objectives build on the work that has been done since 1997, and have been endorsed by the Tourism Advisory Committee and the tourism industry and wider community through their participation in the Tourism Forum held in October, 2003.

Tourism Strategy Objectives

This has been partially achieved. Following the 1997 strategy, the Chamber of Commerce was identified as the lead agency for tourism development. It is important that the Chamber of Commerce continues to inform the funding agencies and the wider community of the work that it does in coordinating and promoting tourism. The Tourism Advisory Committee and the Chamber of Commerce will work to secure consistent and stable long-term funding for the position. In addition, to raise the profile of the tourism promotional activities that are underway, the Chamber of Commerce will establish an identity exclusively for tourism promotion.

The Tourism Advisory Committee functions as a communications body between the Chamber of Commerce, the Tourism Development Coordinator, and the community. The committee meets on a monthly basis. The Committee will organize an annual Tourism Forum to facilitate communication with, and to solicit input from, the wider tourism industry and the community. Articles by the Tourism Development Coordinator will also be included in the quarterly publication, Development News.

While several tourism businesses have participated in professional development activities such as the Superhost program since 1997, there is still room for improvement in the level of service offered to visitors. The Chamber of Commerce will initiate a Tourism Service Awards program. In addition, the Tourism Development Coordinator will work on a one-to-one basis to encourage tourism businesses to maintain or develop high levels of customer service.

Many of the recommendations and strategies identified in the 1997 study are still valid, and not all marketing and promotional activities have been undertaken. The role of the Tourism Development Coordinator will be to assist local operators and tourism companies to package and promote winter activities e.g. a weekend visit including cross-country skiing and snowshoeing; a 4-day package including downhill skiing and snowmobiling.

These packages (i.e., getaway and destination) can be marketed via:

- *Canadian, American and European tour wholesalers;*
- *Tour wholesaler fam tours;*
- *Direct advertising to Canadian, American and European winter sport clubs;*
- *Ongoing publication of travel articles; and*
- *The Internet.*

Revelstoke needs to do a better job of positioning and marketing itself as a summer destination.

The role of the Tourism Development Coordinator will be to assist local operators and tourism companies to package and promote summer activities e.g. hiking and kayaking; canoeing and bird-watching; trail-riding and visits to local museums; or a combination of any of the above.

Marketing activities will be the same as Objective #4.

Despite improvements to the appearance of the entrances to the community from the TCH, this remains a critical activity for the community to pursue. Further improvements to signage and to areas adjacent to the highway west of town are required to help entice more travellers to visit Revelstoke. In addition, new signs need to be developed to attract more visitors who stop at Woodenhead Park and the fast-food outlets into the community.

The Tourism Advisory Committee will continue to provide support to the Enhancement Committee and the City in the highway revitalization efforts. The areas west of town (before the bridge, on either side of the highway) need to be developed and made more attractive.

A specific long-term strategy will be developed by the Tourism Development Coordinator with input from the Tourism Advisory Committee, the City of Revelstoke, and the community. This objective was identified in the 1997 Tourism Strategy, and very little progress has been made over the past six years. The objective and rationale described in 1997 are still relevant today. An Events Committee was formed in 2003, and includes the Tourism Development Coordinator. The Events Committee will ensure that this important objective is pursued during the life of the strategy. There are excellent opportunities to attract small and medium-sized conferences and conventions to Revelstoke. There are a number of high quality accommodation properties, and the community offers a wide range of recreational and cultural activities which can be packaged to enhance a conference program. The community needs to promote Revelstoke as a Conference Centre and aggressively pursue opportunities that arise.

According to the Tourism Activities and Motivations Study, the Visual Arts, Performing Arts and Heritage Tourism sectors are projected to be the fastest and greatest growth activities in tourism over the next 25 years. Revelstoke has a wealth of cultural and heritage tourism attractions which can be marketed further. A strategy will be developed to increase the promotion of this sector to the appropriate markets.

More initiatives should be undertaken to jointly market with regional and neighbouring communities. For example, preliminary discussions have begun with Nakusp to organize a Kayak the Columbia event, a recreational kayak/canoe race between Revelstoke and Nakusp. Similarly, and the idea of a Peddle the Pass bicycle race between Revelstoke and Golden is being considered. The Revelstoke Golf Club is examining the potential of a TCH golf tour, in partnership with other neighbouring communities on the TCH, Golden, Sicamous and Salmon Arm. These type of events increase the number of visitors to each community and help raise the profile of all communities involved. The Tourism Development Coordinator will also work with the Tourism Action Society of the Kootenays to seek opportunities for partnering with the Product Club initiative.

It is critical that some objective measures be developed and implemented to try and measure the success of the activities described above. Obviously, the primary measure of success will be increased tourism visitation, resulting in increased expenditures in the community and increased employment in the tourism sector. The Tourism Development Coordinator, with input from the Tourism Advisory Committee, will work to develop some indicators which can be used to measure success.

Tourism Development Strategy: 2001-2010

The Tourism Development Strategy for the Borough of Coleraine can be downloaded from the link below:

Tourism Development Strategy: The background and objectives of the report can be read here:

Background/ Objectives

The Coleraine Borough Council commissioned TTC/ Tourism & Leisure Partners to assist it in developing a strategy to develop the area's tourism into the 21st century.

The key aims of Coleraine Borough Council in commissioning this study were:

- to review tourism's role as a vehicle for economic growth;
- to develop a strategy for the future, particularly identifying the constraints which need to be addressed; to set the priorities for the sector, including targets, product development and marketing strategies;
- to identify factors which would improve profitability of the sector and attract investment; and,
- to review the role of government and the commercial sector; to quantify the resources necessary, and support the case for public sector funding where appropriate.

The Terms of Reference for the Tourism Development Strategy clearly defines the key aim of the study as follows:

"To produce a Tourism Development Strategy for the Borough which is soundly market-based-identifies the opportunities and the needs of the Borough-attracts support from the private, public and community sectors; and,-provides a dynamic framework for action over the next ten years". In meeting the key aim of the study the Council also specified the importance of:

- maximising sustainable economic benefits from tourism; and
- a clear and definite action plan to deliver the economic and social benefits.

The strategic framework is intended to assist a number of different stakeholders involved with tourism. These include policy makers, businesses engaged in tourism, financial institutions and professional advisors to the sector.

This report aims to provide information, guidance and direction to all involved in the future development of the industry within the area.

East London Tourism Development Strategy and Action Plan 2004-2006

The completed strategy and action plan for East London aims to support the growth of the east London tourism industry and ensure that the area is firmly on the visitor map. The strategy was launched on 28th September 2004. The plan will make the most of east London's diverse attractions and communities, its rich culture and history and its vibrant new businesses.

The plan is an innovative joint venture between the LDA, Tour East London and Visit London and has been completed with input from all key stakeholders. The plan covers the London Boroughs of Barking and Dagenham, Bexley, Greenwich, Hackney, Havering, Lewisham, Newham, Redbridge and Tower Hamlets, plus the Corporation of the City of London.

The plan has a number of priority actions including research to quantify the benefits of tourism to each borough, specific research into the views of visitors to the area, target markets and product clusters in order that the area can be marketed more effectively in the future

Dcms Sustainable Development Strategy: Sectors Tourism

Tourism is the Fastest Growing Sector in the World Economy

Tourism has a significant input to the economic strand of sustainable development; tourism in rural England alone supports 380,000 jobs and underpins 25,000 small and micro businesses.

Sustainable tourism is about adopting a long-term perspective on quality, competitiveness, impacts on the environment and local distinctiveness.

Tourism's Potential as a Sustainable Development Strategy

This publication contains the proceedings of the 2004 WTO Tourism Policy Forum, organized by the WTO Education Council and held at the George Washington University in Washington, D.C. It includes over thirty speeches and academic papers from Tourism Ministers, development agency representatives, WTO officials, academics, and other tourism experts who presented at the main session of the conference. Also included are summaries of the parallel sessions in which case studies were presented. The Forum was organized with the aim of exchanging views with bilateral and multilateral donor organizations, as well as representative recipients; discussing sustainable tourism development policies in relation to the MDGs; reporting on WTO general initiatives in relation to sustainable tourism and development and particularly the WTO ST-EP program to bring sustainable tourism development into the service of poverty elimination; sharing promising practices for sustainable development and considering lessons learned from exemplary tourism projects supported by donors; and formulating recommendations for utilizing tourism as a sustainable development tool for achieving MDG outcomes.

Fifteen years ago, a group of university professors, professionals and public tourism officials gathered together at The George Washington University to attend the first Tourism Policy Forum (TFP), which was held at the initiative of Professor Donald Hawkins. Some of us in attendance were seriously concerned about the exhaustion of the tourism paradigm of the 1970s and 1980s, the so-called mass tourism model, which we later re-named Fordian tourism. The externalities of this tourism business paradigm were already threatening the very sustainability of tourism activity, and called into question tourism's capacity to contribute to development.

The 1990 TPF made it possible—I believe for the first time ever—to carry out a deep, collective reflection at the global level regarding (i) tourism scenarios in the 1990s (taking into account economic, technological, socio-cultural and environmental aspects), (ii) Tourism Policy objectives going beyond simply maximizing the number of tourists and/or tourism revenues, and (iii) the instruments of this sectoral policy. Using today's terminology, it could be said that 1990 TPF was an international exercise in knowledge management in tourism, which had a considerable influence on the development of tourism policy in the 1990s.

Indeed, some of the key tourism policy documents of the 1990s (e.g.: Australia's Passport to Growth: A National Tourism Strategy, 1992; Futures: Plan Marco de Competitividad del Turismo Espanol, 1992; or White Paper: Development and Promotion of Tourism in South Africa, 1996), it seems to me, show the impact of many of the concepts discussed at 1990 TPF, whether due to the direct participation of their authors in the TPF, or thanks to the dissemination of such concepts through the academic and governmental publications and forums of the time (e.g.: meetings of the International Academy for the Study of Tourism, academic activities and research work supported by the European Union's DGXXIII, General Assemblies and knowledge management activities of the WTO, etc).

In September 2003, on the occasion of the awarding of the WTO's Ulysses Prize to Professor Hawkins, and the tribute event held in his honour in Andorra by the WTO·Themis Foundation, the idea arose to revive the TPF, this time as a permanent programme of the WTO under its Department of Education and Knowledge Management (WTO.EKM) and in close collaboration with the WTO Education Council (WTO.EdC). As everybody knows, the WTO.EdC is composed of some fifty educational and research institutions from around the world, which have received the WTO's TedQual Certification through a quality audit. The WTO.EKM, for its part, carries out the Programme of Work of the WTO in the areas of research, education and training, and the application of knowledge to tourism policy and governance in tourism.

For one thing, it was decided to make it a biannual event, thus allowing constant interaction with the WTO's deliberative bodies and decision-making organs (the Executive Council and the General Assembly). For another, the new WTO TPF was to place greater emphasis on practical results and encourage the active participation of public bodies, both national and international, as well as of civil society entities with the capacity to support and implement the conclusions reached by the forum.

It remained only to decide the subject areas to be tackled by this new WTO TPF, and this task was made relatively easy in view of the full integration of the WTO in the UN system in December 2003, and its consequent dedication to the Millennium Development Goals, and especially to the issue of development and poverty reduction (e.g., ST-EP Foundation, WTO. Scholars programmes in collaboration with the cooperation agencies of Italy and Mexico, etc.). Thus, the 2004 TPF took shape with a focus on the issue of tourism as an instrument of development.

This issue is both old and new at the same time. Tourism's capacity to generate income and wealth, to consolidate cultural and environmental assets and to transmit knowledge and information has been discussed and analysed from very diverse perspectives-academic, professional, and governmental-over the past several decades. And yet, actual tourism policies have paid much more attention to the purely promotional and microeconomic/entrepreneurial aspects of tourism.

For this reason, the WTO, in organizing the 2004 TPF, had two great hopes from the outset: (i) that it would contribute to clarify the methods and instruments of tourism as a motor of development, and (ii) that it would lead to broad consensus among governments, institutions of the United Nations, development agencies, educational and knowledge management institutions, NGOs, and the private sector regarding best practices, initiatives and recommendations. We believe that the results have lived up to expectations, although it is clear that we have a huge task ahead of us. The 2004 TPF, which was held at The George Washington University (Washington D.C.) in October 2004, drew some 200 participants representing the upper echelons of decision-making in tourism, plus another 200 highly qualified observers. In my view, the event constituted a milestone in the WTO's Programme of Work, and a high point in the effort to tackle the issue of tourism as an instrument of development. Someone once said that humanity's development has been a race between knowledge and chaos. I believe that the 2004 TPF has given a substantial lead to knowledge-and I trust in its concrete application as well.

Tourism Development Strategies

Recognising its importance, the Lao government has declared tourism to be one of the top three priority areas for socio-economic development, with a target of 1.2 million tourist arrivals by 2010. Significant investment has already been committed to the upgrading of the tourism infrastructure and plans are currently being prepared for the establishment of a tourism marketing and promotion board and the adoption of a master plan for tourism development.

At the present time by far the greatest proportion of foreign tourists visiting Laos are those from neighbouring countries of the Asia Pacific region. In 2004 this group made up 81.59 per cent of the total number, incorporating the two largest visitor groups from Thailand (489,677, 54.72 per cent of the total) and ViCt Nam (130,816, 14.62 per cent of the total). Other major national groups visiting the country in 2004 included Americans (37,181, 4.16 per cent of the total), Chinese (33,019, 3.69 per cent of the total), French (27,806, 3.11 per cent of the total), British (27,402, 3.06 per cent of the total), Japanese (20,319, 2.27 per cent of the total), Australians (15,149, 1.69 per cent of the total) and Germans (14,009, 1.57 per cent of the total). At present few figures are available for domestic tourism, but this is also believed to be on the increase.

Market research of recent years has shown consistently that the cultural heritage scores highly amongst the country's visitor attractions – in 2004 56 per cent of the 1,417 international visitors surveyed at Wattay International Airport claimed to have been drawn to Laos mainly by its culture, 39 per cent by its temples and monuments, 54 per cent by its natural beauty and 23 per cent by its ethnic minorities. The consequence for tourism has been that to date around 80-90 per cent of all tourism has focused on relatively short visits to the country's two main cultural centres of Vientiane and Luang Prabang.

In practice, the main focus of cultural tourism to Laos has been the former royal capital of Luang Prabang, which was awarded World Heritage status in 1995 for its 'exceptional example of fusion' between traditional architecture, Lao urban design and the structures built by colonial authorities in the 19th and 20th centuries. In the years which followed that award the town's tourist infrastructure expanded exponentially. Many local people were displaced as hotels, guest houses, restaurants and souvenir shops sprang up everywhere, often in contravention of building regulations, while at the same time numerous historic buildings were renovated with little regard for authenticity.

Realising that urgent action was required to deal with the unplanned and inappropriate development in Luang Prabang, the government established a National Inter Ministerial Co-ordinating Committee for the Protection and Development of Cultural, Historic and Natural Heritage by Prime Ministerial Decree in 1996. This was followed in 1997 by the Presidential Decree on the Preservation of Cultural, Historic and Natural Heritage, which outlined regulations and measures for the management, conservation, preservation and use of the national heritage, including the upgrading of movable and immovable assets with historical or cultural or natural value into national heritage.

In Luang Prabang itself an inter-institutional body known as the Provincial Committee for the Protection and Development of Luang Prabang Heritage was also set up in 1996 with support from UNESCO to bring together the key stakeholders in the Luang Prabang World Heritage site, namely the Luang Prabang Provincial Government, the Luang Prabang Provincial Service of Information and Culture, the Luang Prabang Provincial Tourism Office and the Luang Prabang Service of Construction, Transport, Posts and Communication. Since that time all construction work carried out within the protected area-whether for new structures or for renovation of old buildings-has required its agreement. In the same year the Maison du patrimoine (Heritage House) was established under the auspices of the Luang Prabang-Chinon

(France)-UNESCO World Heritage Centre Cooperation Project as a technical office within the Luang Prabang Provincial Service of Information and Culture; this now acts as the Committee's executive arm and secretariat, offering advice on all building permit requests and developing regulations and plans for safeguarding and developing the Luang Prabang World Heritage protected area and buffer/support zones. A parallel initiative, UNESCO's Cultural Survival and Revival in the Buddhist Sangha Project, is currently training monks in the traditional arts and crafts skills needed to properly care for, preserve and conserve their temples.

Similar measures are currently being implemented for the heritage sites of Wat Phu Champassak and the Plain of Jars, regulating construction and requiring all new buildings in those areas to conform with regulations in respect of size, style and building materials used.

However, with 105,513 foreigners and an unquantified but undoubtedly substantial number of Lao tourists visiting Luang Prabang (a tiny city of 30,000 inhabitants) in 2004 and visitor numbers at Wat Phu Champassak and the Plain of Jars also showing significant increases in recent years, the Lao authorities recognise the urgent need to diversify the tourism sector in order to take spread the load more evenly. As a result, the LNTA is currently placing the development of ecotourist attractions at the core of its official tourism development strategy.

In 1993 the government identified and designated 20 locations as National Biodiversity Conservation Areas (NBCAs). These areas now fall under the jurisdiction of the Division for Resource and Development of the Ministry of Agriculture and Forestry's Department of Forests. Zoning, management and safeguarding guidelines and regulations for both the environment and people living within the protected areas are in the process of being created.

The LNTA's National Ecotourism Strategy and Action plan 2004-2010, produced with advice from the SNV Netherlands Development Organisation, sets out the framework for the development of ecotourism in Laos by: strengthening the institutional arrangements for planning and managing ecotourism growth; supporting training, capacity building and the promotion of good practice; supporting environmental protection and nature conservation; providing socio-economic development and cultural heritage protection for host communities; and developing ecotourism research and information.

One particular Lao ecotourism project has been operating with success for several years. The UNESCO Nam Ha Ecotourism Project in Luang Namtha Province is being implemented by the LNTA in cooperation with the Lao Ministry of Agriculture and Forestry, the Luang Namtha Provincial Service of Forestry Resource Conservation and the Luang Namtha Provincial Service of Information and Culture. The UNESCO Office of the Regional Advisor for Culture in Asia and the Pacific is the project's executing agency and provides technical assistance and monitoring. The project itself is funded by grants from the government of New Zealand and the International Finance Corporation (IFC).

The objectives of the project are: to ensure that tourism contributes to the conservation of Laos' natural and cultural heritage; to involve local communities in the development and management of tourism activities; to use tourism as a tool for integrated rural development; to provide training and human capacity building skills to tourism providers and local communities; to integrate public and private sector investment in culturally and environmentally sustainable tourism; and to assist communities to establish cultural and nature tourism activities in and around the Nam Ha National Biodiversity Conservation Area (NBCA). The UNESCO Nam Ha Ecotourism Project has received the UNDP Award for Poverty Alleviation and the British Airways Tourism for Tomorrow Award.

Promotion of community-based ecotourism is also an important focus of the four-year US$14.2 million Mekong Tourism Development Project, currently the LNTA's flagship programme, which was launched in 2003 in partnership with the Asian Development Bank. This project, which also covers Cambodia and Vietnam, seeks to improve tourism-related infrastructure, support pro-poor, community-based sustainable tourism in rural areas and strengthen sub-regional cooperation with a view to facilitating the flow of tourists in and between the three countries.

An important component of the Mekong Tourism Development Project is the Pro-poor Community-based Tourism Development programme, which is similar in format to the Nam Ha project but covers four provinces-Luang Namtha, Luang Prabang, Khammouane and Champassak.

This programme aims to assist local communities with distinctive rural lifestyles or living in areas with pristine ecosystems to manage and determine their limits to tourism growth, to increase control over the selection of tourist types and modalities, and to equitably distribute tourism benefits. It is envisaged that it will develop pilot ecotourism and village-based tourism projects, foster the conservation and improvement of the cultural and environmental heritage of selected areas, monitor social impacts, promote the role of women, and establish mitigation measures to minimise negative impacts due to increased tourism.

Development Strategy to the Challenge of a "Plan de Excelencia"

History, Context and Background of the Cultural Tourism in Cáceres

The city of Cáceres is located in the mid western part of Spain, about 300 km from Madrid, at an altitude of 459 m. above sea level. It is the capital of its province, and belongs to the *Extremadura* region. According to the population services, the town counts 90.930 inhabitants, of which 60% is comprised between 20 and 60 years old, and 20% under 20. To these figures we have to add an extra population of 15.000 non-residents, most of them students.

The economy of the city has been traditionally based on the primary sector, though in the last half century Cáceres has evolved into a third sector city, with a small presence of textile and food industries. Nowadays it is the main commercial, economic and administrative centre of its province, and the most important tourism destination of the region.

Cáceres was founded as colony by the Romans in 25 B.C., with the name of Norbensis Caesarina (Home-page of the Municipality of Cáceres), close to an important way of communication that will be later known as "The Silver Route". The settlement is destroyed by the Visigoths in the 5th Century, and the city remains abandoned until the arrival of the Muslims from the north of Africa in 8th Century. This population takes advantage of the strategic position and transforms the ruins into a military base to face the Christian kingdoms of the north during the first centuries of the reconquest.

Part of the walls are rebuilt under the rule of Almoarab leader Abu Ya'qub. In 1229 the town is definitively occupied by the troops of Alfonso IX, monarch of the Leon Kingdom. The city is granted a free status, and is ruled by 12 *Regidores* (Rulers) elected by the citizens. This status makes the city prosper, and new churches and palaces rise on the foundations of previous mosques and Muslim palaces. The 15th, 16th and 17th century are the most important centuries from the built heritage point of view, since the fortunes brought back from America by adventurers and emigrants transform the downtown into the monumental city we see nowadays. Palaces and sumptuous residences spread around two focuses:

Santa Maria Square and San Mateo Square. The most impressive palaces are built by the powerful families between the 15th and 16th century. In the following centuries Cáceres evolves into a quiet, forgotten province's capital. The situation essentially remains the same until the 1950's when immigration from the countryside starts to make its economy shift from the first to the third sector. In 1986, following a gradual growth of tourism, Cáceres was included in the list of World Heritage Cities.

Tourism Development Strategy: Plan de Excelencia (Excellence Plan)

The tourism vocation of the city has developed at the end of the 20th century: the number of beds grew of almost 50% in the last decade.

However, it is difficult to calculate the average number of tourists per year, since the indicators we have are partial or can't be compared between them. For example, the "Institute de Estudios Turisticos" of the Ministry of Industry Tourism and Commerce provide figures related to the whole region, and can vary from the first available estimation of 1.562.000 Spanish tourists in year 2001 to the 1.227.000 in year 2002. Other indicators, provided by the Municipality, are the number of visitors of different cultural attractors in Cáceres in the year 2003: 20.791 visitors to the Museo de Historia Cultura "Casa Pedrilla"; 34.677 to the Sala de

Exposiciones permanente municipal "Ciudad de Cáceres"; 28.505 to the Museo Vostell; and 68.813 to the Centre de Interpretacion "Torre de Bujaco".

We will have to wait until the launch of the planned Tourism observatory before we have reliable estimations of the number of tourists that arrive to Cáceres every year. The offer of tourism in Cáceres has traditionally been related to Hunting, and thus concentrated in the autumn season. The progressive increase of city-breaks and of cultural tourism in general opened an interesting perspective of development. This lead the local authorities to try to develop a tourism of quality (in terms of purchasing power of the visitor), and improve the ratio of overnight stays rather than just the number of visitors.

However, in the late 1990's the lack of a defined strategy was evident: the offer was a monothematic, un-structured, and initiatives were taken mostly by private actors. The chance to put some order and to exploit the sector according to sustainable and also rational criteria came with the *Plan de Excelencia* started in 2000. In Spain this kind of plan comes out of a series of national framework plans for tourism competitivity: FUTURES (1992-1995) and PICTE (2000-2006), launched in the early nineties by the Ministry of Industry, Tourism and Commerce.

The first framework plan was created to reduce and correct the negative impacts (mainly ecological and in terms of town planning) of thirty years of wild tourism development, and the second one was created after assessing the success of its predecessor, with the same goals.

The *Planes de Excelencia* are the operative tools developed to accomplish these goals: they are addressed to "mature" destinations: mostly traditional "sun & beach" destinations, but also to cities of great historic value, where the main issue is to rise or control the tourism capacity. The investments, financed equally by a Collective Agreement of local, regional and national administrations, are distributed over three or four years. The objectives of the *Planes de Excelencia* are usually focused on the diversification of the tourism seasons and the development of a care for details in the offer: improvement of marketing strategies to attract tourists in low-season, embellishment of historical centres, renovations and reforms of infrastructures, and adaptation of hotels and restaurants to quality standards.

In the specific case of Cáceres, the *Plan de Excelencia* was launched by a collective agreement between the Ministry of Economy, the Region of Extremadura, the Municipality of Cáceres and the representatives of the private sector of the city. Its planned length was of three years, from 2000 to 2003, and the total budget amounted to 2,7 Millions of Euros. The generic goal of the *Plan* was to transform the city in a tourism benchmark at national and international level, but developing a tourism of quality, different from the mass-tourism models of the sun & beach offer.

Concrete Actions Within the Cultural Tourism Strategy

A series of objectives were defined, in order to achieve the generic goal source: Ministry of Industry, Tourism and Commerce):

- Urbanistic rehabilitation of the downtown.
- Improvement of the management.
- Recovery of the Historical built Heritage.
- Construction and development of infrastructures.
- Promotion.
- Equipment
- Definition and diversification of the tourist offer.

The objectives generated a series of actions, presented in a publication of the Municipality of Cáceres in 2003 and 2004. Regarding the urbanistic rehabilitation, it involved restoration of facades, from specific and isolated cases to whole districts in close cooperation with the urbanism councillor. This objective also lead to the creation of a limited traffic area in the downtown, equipped with sophisticated access monitoring systems. Another action issued from this objective was the creation of a pneumatic system for the automatic collection of the rubbish in the downtown area. Concerning the improvement of management, it meant the provision of the funds needed to have a full-time staff devoted to the accomplishment of the Plan, and development subventions to the tourism-related enterprises of the city.

The Historical built Heritage recovery activities consist in the lighting of historical buildings, as well as the rehabilitation of representative places for its public use (for example, the transformation of Torre de Bujaco into a visitors centre with a viewpoint, and the enhancement, in different phases, of several stretches of the city walls). Regarding the construction and development of infrastructures, the actions undertaken have been the improvement of the streets of the downtown, and the construction of a bus parking area. The promotion actions, varied from the organisation of fairs and seminars, to the advertising of the city in newspapers and specialised magazines, as well as the publication of a *Plan de Excelencia* bulletin.

Concerning the equipment objective, it entailed the installation of street furniture, as well as urban and tourism signpost, and information panels on the facades of representative built heritage elements. Finally, the definition and diversification of the tourist offer entangled the preparation of strategic plans and the development of cultural tourism offer: the most relevant actions in this context were the preparation of tourism routes in cooperation with the Church administration, the inauguration of two visitor centres (in the Parking Galarza and in Torre de Bujaco), and the creation and/or promotion of events in low season, in order to increase the number of visitors (i.e., the medieval market, the "Semana Santa", theatre festival).

The *Plan de Excelencia* expired in 2003 but some actions have been achieved in the following years. In October of 2006 according to a press note released by the Municipality to *El periodico de Extremadura,* the *plan* isn't still fully accomplished (98%).

Beside the concrete actions awaiting to be completed (mainly the enhancement of the Wall and a second tower for visit purposes), the strategic plans and the objectives fixed by the plan are still defining the policies of the municipality. For example, there is the idea, presented in the second issue of the Plan de Excelencia's publication, of launching a "Tourism Observatory", as the one in Avila, a platform devoted to the monitoring of Tourism flows, to visitor studies and to macroeconomic studies that will show the incidence of tourism in other productive sectors of the city. This will also analyse the offer of the sector and the national and foreign demand, in terms both quantitative and qualitative, providing info to establish coherent future strategies. The Tourism Observatory, which hasn't been launched yet, is the result of a mature and professional approach to audiences management issue, and arrives in due time, since one of the gaps in the tourism policy of Cáceres detected by PICTURE surveys was precisely the absence of monitoring tools.

In this sense, the Tourism Observatory, if organised as the one of Avila or the one of Cordoba, will probably be very close to the Cultural Offer Quality Monitoring Tool developed by the UAM team. The techniques and methodologies are different, but both tools are conceived as part of the whole process of management of cultural resources. They do not just complement the management process and strategies, they are integrated into it. The main difference between a Tourism Observatory and our (UAM) tool is that our tool provides more qualitative analysis of the city's cultural offer quality, while other Observatories aim more to statistical results. This is why the testing of our tool offers complementary information suitable to improve the cultural offer of the cities, and Cáceres in this particular case. The detailed survey and conclusions of our tool can be found in the final report.

However we would like to mention here the most remarkable outcomes in relation to the strategies of the *Plan de Excelencia*. Regarding the urbanistic rehabilitation of the downtown, and the recovery of the Historical built Heritage, the results proceed adequately, gathering the visitor's full appreciation of the value of the downtown's built heritage; however, there seems to be a problem with the promotion, because our tool has detected a mismatch in the perception of Cáceres between real and potential visitors. The first group is already aware of the rich tangible and intangible heritage of Cáceres, and comes to the city for that reason, while the secónd group has an idea of the city as a place with little or no cultural offer at all. This means that the efforts in promotion must continue and strengthen the image of Cáceres that the municipality wants to export.

Concluding Comments and Transferable Key Lessons

The experience of Cáceres is for many reasons a reference model in the management of Heritage cities. Here are the main keys that have contributed to its success.

- Holistic approach: understanding that the dynamics of Tourism are not separate from the dynamics of other domains (social, economical, environmental...), they all are interconnected parts of a system where any action may alter the inner balance;
- Existence of a strategic plan where the tourism policies are integrated into the general policies of the administration;
- Tight cooperation and coordination between different departments (Culture, Urbanism, Environment);
- Integration of assessment and evaluation tools in all the stages of the strategic plan;
- Investment of external funds (*Plan de Excelencia*) not only in short-term and isolated actions (i.e., built heritage conservation and embellishment) but also defining and launching development strategies that will survive after the aid is over.

National Sustainable Development Strategies

The United Nations Conference on Environment and Development (UNCED) held in Rio de Janeiro in 1992, recognised the pressing environment and development problems of the world and, through adoption of Agenda 21, produced a global programme of action for sustainable development into the 21st century.

Agenda 21 states that countries should adopt national strategies for sustainable development, which "should build upon and harmonize the various sectoral economic, social and environmental policies and plans that are operating in the country".

The 1997 Special Session of the UN General Assembly set a target date of 2002, for "the formulation and elaboration of national strategies for sustainable development". It confirmed the approach and purpose of national sustainable development strategies as "important mechanisms for enhancing and linking national capacity so as to bring together priorities in social, economic and environmental policies". It also reaffirmed that "all sectors of the society should be involved in their development and implementation".

The Millennium Declaration was signed in September 2000. The associated Millennium Development Goals includes onerelating to environmental sustainability, to "integrate the principles of sustainable development into country policies and programmes and reverse the loss of environmental resources". Activities towards developing and implementing national sustainable development strategies will, thus, contribute to the achievement of this goal.

Finally, the World Summit for Sustainable Development (WSSD), held in August 2002, urged in its Plan of Implementation that "States should take immediate steps to make progress in the formulation and elaboration of national strategies for sustainable development and begin their implementation by 2005".

Since UNCED, governments have made extensive efforts to integrate environmental, economic and social objectives into decision-making by either elaborating new policies and strategies for sustainable development, or by adapting existing policies and plans.

To assist in this process, an International Forum on National Sustainable Development Strategies was held in Ghana in November 2001. The Forum adopted a guidance document containing a number of recommendations on approaches for integrating the principles of sustainable development into policies and programmes of both developed and developing countries. The Forum agreed that a national sustainable development strategy is a tool for informed decision-making that provides a framework for systematic thought across sectors and territory. It also helps to institutionalize processes for consultation, negotiation, mediation and consensus building on priority societal issues where interests differ. Development of a strategy empowers countries to address inter-related social and economic problems by helping them to build capacities, develop procedures and legislative frameworks, allocate limited resources rationally and present timetables for actions.

It was strongly reiterated, that countries would benefit from formulating strategies both directly (as a result of making development more sustainable) and indirectly (from the process itself)

United Nations Department of Economic and Social Affairs Division for Sustainable Development

"The next 50 years could see a fourfold increase in the size of the global economy and significant reductions in poverty but only if governments act now to avert a growing risk of severe damage to the environment and profound social unrest. Without better policies and institutions, social and environmental strains may derail development progress, leading to higher poverty levels and a decline in the quality of life for everybody."

Tourism Development Strategy (2006 – 2010)

Vision

By 2010 Linden has become a tourist destination topping 10,000 visitors per year. More than 300 beds are offered by hotels and bed & breakfast providers. Linden and Region 10 offer attractive events and particularly Linden serves as a hub for tourists to other destinations in the interior. Tourism has developed into the third biggest industry in the Region after mining and forest production. The enterprises working in the tourism sector are well-trained and developed into hospitable entities serving satisfied clients. The Region 10 Tourism Development Association (RTTDA) offers professional services, avails of a well-functioning office and counts more than 100 members. The Region 10 tourism industry is well integrated into national efforts to attract even more tourists to Guyana.

Summary

The Tourism Development Strategy centres around three axes:

1. Development of Region 10 into a genuine tourist destination (identification of destinations, creation of events),
2. Improvement of services through local enterprises (training, information),
3. Institutional strengthening of the Region 10 Tourism Development Association (organisation, coordination).

The three axes are accompanied by an aggressive marketing of Region 10 as a tourist destination (external marketing) and of the RTTDA as the major platform for local enterprises earning their livelihood from tourism (internal marketing of the association). Logic of this strategy: the creation and identification of tourist events and destinations trigger a higher influx of visitors who will be professionally hosted and catered for by the local tourism industry to make them come back again in future. RTTDA is the institutional backbone ensuring organization, coordination, promotion and services to its members.

Target Market

Given the comparatively low attraction of Region 10 destinations and events to foreign tourists at present, focus will be laid on national and Caribbean visitors. Some potential for European and American tourists is identified in bird watching possibilities, Linden as a transition to more attractive destination in Region 9, and in linking Linden to other cities during flight hopper tours (such as Bartica – Linden– Georgetown on a day tour). Greatest market potential lies in the Diaspora Lindeners having keen interest in revisiting their birth town while some are expected to resettle and invest in Linden after retirement. The influence of this target market became clearly visible with the announcement of 300 Diaspora Lindeners visiting the Linden Town Week 2006 celebrations with the dedicated assistance of the Linden Fund/USA.

Tourist attractions (events + nature)

New tourist attractions will be created if the tourism industry is to grow. The starting point is the successful operation of singular events (such as the Kashif & Shanghai Football Tournament and the Linden Town Week). More events preferably stretched over several days will be identified to improve the influx of tourists. The Rockstone Fish Festival planned for August 2006 is the first step into this direction. Other ideas emitted so far are: Jazz Festival, Cycling race Georgetown – Linden with finish in Linden, extended carnival festivities (LICA = Linden Carnival), and regattas. It is evident that developed event ideas need to be marked by a great uniqueness.

Apart from the event attractions, other destinations and related services will be offered. Some have already been identified and will be further explored: bird watching and *Victoria Regia* on Gluck Island *(ecotourism niche for short one-day* visits, and possibilities of setting up larger tourist facilities such as a guest-house *or professional boat services*), museum, fishing and hunting tours around Rockstone, visits to reclamation activities in the mined-out areas with scientific guidance, regular weekend visits of the bauxite mine, etc.

Events and nature will be accompanied by a comprehensive signage system leading tourists to and guiding them in Linden. A huge signboard at the Soesdyke- Linden junction will indicate the way to Linden. Arriving in Linden a tourist signboard with map and important destinations of relevance for tourists in Linden will be established (another one for visitors coming from the South). In collaboration with the Town Council traffic signs will be placed in Linden and on the routes to Kwakwani, Ituni, Rockstone, Lethem and other destinations in Region 10. In Linden itself, buildings of relevance for tourists (such as the waterwheel, museum, etc.) will be indicated by special boards explaining the history in brief. Differently coloured sign posts will guide the tourists to these destinations.

Tourist services

Existing and new tourist attractions and events can only be marketed successfully if the clients' needs are satisfied. Hence, we favour competition and we welcome any investor in the tourism sector from abroad or from other areas in Guyana. Tourist services will be provided through the "Linden Office for Visitors" (LOV) as the most important entry point for client information and through individual service providers being members of the association.

a. The "Linden Office for Visitors" (LOV) is the executive branch of the association where contacts with clients are made. Hard copies of all promotion material are made available to incoming visitors. Email queries are answered and the association's activities are coordinated by an executive secretary. More personnel might be hired if the financial situation allows for that. The office is located in the museum; it is equipped with PC, printer, photocopier, display shelves. LOV serves as a facilitating and mediating agency linking customers to the Region 10 tourism service providers. It will concentrate on association members in the first place, hence creating a need for service providers to join.

b. Individual service providers: existing hotel accommodations in Linden, Ituni and Kwakwani will be inspected and rated according to existing standards. A four-tier categorization will be applied as this is currently done with the B&B providers.

The rating (stars for hotels and restaurants, diamonds for B&B providers) will be officially acknowledged through specifically designed signs (size: 1x1 ft) which can be fixed on the walls of the establishments. These signs carry high promotional value and may also attract other service providers to join the association.

Assessments and inspections will be done on a yearly routine basis providing room for all members to improve their standards and services. Tourists can easily locate recommended establishments. While rating criteria exist for hotels and B&B providers, a similar rating system for restaurants will be elaborated and applied.

Service providers will be trained in areas common for all such as client reception, customer care, monitoring of customer satisfaction, pricing of services, importance of insurance systems, safety regulations and cleanliness issues. These training offers will be binding for the association's members in order to maintain and eventually improve their grades. Furthermore, there will be sector-specific training arrangements on a needs basis such as cooking of speciality dishes, accommodation standards and design, kitchen hygiene, etc. The needs of the different tourism sectors will be analysed during meetings with the committees to be established under the umbrella of the RTTDA.

Institutional Strengthening

RTTDA is a certified and recognized institution under the Friendly Societies Act. However, in the past the internal functioning was based entirely on the voluntary work of dedicated members who were never asked to pay any fees.

The newly developed fees structure distinguishes between a general admission fee of $2,000 for all and sector-specific yearly fees which have been developed in accordance with income prospects. In future, only those individuals and enterprises are considered members who have paid their dues and will be eligible to vote and to decide during the internal meetings.

At the end of each fiscal year, RTTDA will conduct "Certificate Award Functions" during which members who provided excellent services and other personalities and institutions which contributed significantly to the tourism development in Region 10 will be awarded with certificates and plaques. These functions are also meant to enhance visibility of the association and the sector. Increase in (paid) membership will be achieved through the provision of services which consist primarily of marketing, training and lobbying. The services will be organized according to our members' needs and in cooperation with the regional and national bodies in which RTTDA is organized.

Sector-wise committees (for example: B&B providers, restaurant owners, etc.) will be established whenever desired by the members in order to make sure that specific questions can be professionally dealt with by the concerned business people. Chiefs of committees will be elected who report to the RTTDA General Assembly during its official meetings.

RTTDA will become a paying member of the Linden Chamber of Commerce, Industry and Development to ensure the best representation of its interest on the regional level. Interests on the national level will be defended through membership in THAG and close cooperation with the Ministry of Tourism, Industry and Commerce (MINTIC) and particularly the Guyana Tourism Authority (GTA).

We will develop special relationships to identified sponsors and donor agencies because it is acknowledged that the membership fees will hardly suffice to pay for overhead costs and association staff. A particular relationship exists with the Linden Fund representing the largest tourism target group at the time being, GTIS and LEAP which provided valuable assistance in the past. Inputs in institutional strengthening are required in the following areas: preparing requests for external assistance, internal functioning of the association and membership care, linkage to potential visitors overseas, tourist product development, assistance in design of marketing devices.

Marketing

The printing of the "Discover Linden" glossy magazine will serve as a starter in Region 10 tourism marketing efforts. The Linden Town Week is the catalyst to get more diversified marketing efforts on stream.

The RTTDA Web Page is the central long-term marketing tool informing customers about tourist destinations and accommodation facilities. The office in the museum building is centrally located; it will be staffed with at least one competent person who answers questions on the telephone, replies to email inquiries, links visitors to accommodation facilities, distributes tourist brochures and sells tourism articles and literature.

Brochures on the following issues are circulated per hard copy: B&B facilities, hotel accommodation, restaurant and catering services, travel-, boat and fishing tours, Linden tourist map, other tourist services such as bars, taxi and other transport services, offer of handicraft products, and a general flyer summarizing key information of interest to tourists.

To attract visitors from Georgetown, regular ads are published in national newspapers, particularly in conjunction with the different events to be organized. On very special occasions, TV ads will be made on the national TV station. All published information material will also be accessible to interested persons at the "Tourism & Hospitality Association of Guyana" (THAG) of which RTTDA becomes a member. National seminars and workshops on tourism will be used as a platform to attract visitors and investors in the tourism industry to Region 10.

Tourism Development Strategy

In 1993, a detailed community survey of Revelstoke was conducted and a Vision Statement prepared. The Vision Statement, which provided direction and a statement of community values, is being used to guide Revelstoke's growth and development. In 1995, this vision statement served as the basis for the development of a Community Economic Development Strategy.

As recommended in this Strategy, a Tourism Development Strategy was prepared during 1996-97, and has served to guide the development of tourism over the past 6 years. In 2002, the members of the Revelstoke Tourism Advisory Committee recommended that the strategy should be revised to better reflect changing conditions in the local tourism industry. It was decided that revisions to the Tourism Development Strategy could be carried out 'in house' by the local Community Economic Development Department, and that the Revelstoke Tourism Advisory Committee would act as the Steering Committee for the development of the revised Tourism Development Strategy.

During 2000, as part of the development of a new Revelstoke Community Development Strategic Action Plan, an extensive community survey was undertaken to determine the priorities and concerns of Revelstoke residents. Over 68% of those surveyed identified tourism and hospitality as the highest priority sector of the economy for the community to develop. This was by far the most important sector for development identified by the community.

The revision to the Revelstoke Tourism Development Strategy was undertaken during 2002-03. The Revelstoke Tourism Advisory Committee acted as the steering committee for the project. During this time, Revelstoke had undertaken an initiative to develop a strategy to determine how best to market the community to outside investors. As part of this initiative, external consultants reviewed the state of the local economy and met with several business and civic leaders to determine community economic priorities and the most effective ways of promoting the community to international investors. The consultants recommended a focus on tourism development as the best way of attracting investors and of improving the local economy. It was decided to utilize the same consulting team to interview local tourism operators to obtain their input regarding the state of the Revelstoke tourism industry. This information (included in Appendix I) was used to assist in determining tourism priorities for the next five year period.

Objectives

The overall goal of this study is to prepare a tourism strategy that provides the community of Revelstoke with clear direction relative to the development of the community's tourism industry for the period 2003 to 2008. The specific objectives of this project include preparing a tourism development strategy which supports the following:

- Achievement of a sustainable economy in keeping with the community's Vision Statement;
- Promotion of tourism growth and development to ensure economic stability;
- Enhancement of the growing tourism and outdoor recreation sector; and,
- Diversification of the local economy and creation of job opportunities.

Study Process

The steering committee felt that the existing (1997) strategy provided a solid base. The intent of the revised strategy project was to update the existing strategy i.e. identify what has been accomplished, what still needs to be done, and establish priorities for the next 5 years.

The following activities were carried out:

1. Update baseline data (including a review of strengths and weaknesses)
2. Identify gaps/ review tourism strategies from other communities
3. Consultation with the tourism industry
4. Compile information/ identify priorities
5. Prepare draft strategy/ circulate for comment
6. Prepare final strategy.

The Development Strategy For Ecotourism in Wolong

Wolong Natural Reserve (WNR), known as a shining pearl in the southwest China, is the largest national-level natural reserve specializing in protecting giant pandas and natural ecological system.

With respect to protection and development, active efforts were made in the 1990s but failed. It was widely acknowledged that tourism should be given the top priority for the development and protection of WNR. Therefore it is of great necessity to reconsider the tourism development strategy so as to make it more efficient and more compliant with market rules.

Advantages in Resources & Marketing Orientation

Famed as the "Hometown of the Giant Panda" and with a total area of 2000 km2, WNR is located in the Aba Tibetan and Qiang Nationalities Autonomous Prefecture, and is just 120 km from Chengdu.

Advantages in Resources

Nature has richly endowed in tourism resources, including natural resources such as wild animals and plants, forests, mountains, lakes and pleasant weather conditions. WNR boasts abundant cultural resources from the religious traditions of Taoism & Buddhism, customs of Tibetan and Qiang nationality and local house styles. WNR accommodates over 100 Pandas in the wild, 10% of the total wild population, and 64 Pandas in its breeding centre. Moreover, WNR has a complicated land ecology system with 7 vertical ecology system belts resulting in tremondous biological diversity. There are 1989 higher plants varieties and 450 kinds of vertibra, of which 57 under key state protection. WNR has a world-class panda protection research centre, the only-one panda museum, and the largest trial park for training animals back to the wild. Wild animals and rare birds can be easily observed in various places within WNR. Flocks of blue sheep and Takins in Yinlonggu, thousands of swifts in Guanyingya and rare birds including the Tibetan Eared Pheasant, blood pheasants and Chinese Monals in Pengsheng Gaur Valley can all be seen in WNR. It has the largest primitive Davidia forest in China and two highland grasslands, Huangcaoping and Niupingzhi.

Market Orientation

The development of tourism in WNR should be aimed at an inter-national, high-quality ecology tours oriented to domestic and foreign markets, featuring by giant pandas and the beautiful scenery of their natural habitats.

Products Patterns & Strategic Targets

Stress will be laid on the following four tour product patterns. 1. Forest holiday-making. With comfortable weather conditions, fresh air, and sufficient sunshine and, tour products such as forest recuperation, travels, conference tours, and health-making tours can be developed. Villas and hotels for holiday-seekers can be constructed accordingly. 2. Unique eco-tour. Its waters, large areas of virgin forests, wild animals, numerous snow-capped mountains and waterfalls are extremely suitable for eco-tours. 3. Panda image products. The image resources of pandas should be turned into actual resources by constructing a panda ecology valley where people can go directly to see pandas in the wild. This would allow WNR to produce tour souvenirs for tourists and videos of the giant pandas for tourists. 4. Ethnic culture products.

Generally, the development of tourism in WNR will concentrate on creating a world-class ecology tour attraction and China's national park by 2005; bidding for world heritage, serving as a model for sustainable development among national reserves and world natural heritages, and enjoying an important position among tour sites in Sichuan as well as in China.

Principles & Measures for Development

The following principles should be observed in the tourism development of WNR: 1. Protection of unique and irreplacable resources; 2. Market-oriented, sustainable development; Harmonious co-existence between humans and nature. Based on the ideas and development principles above, and practical experiences in developing eco-tour sites at home and abroad, the development of WNR must follow the principle of "Tour inside, lodge outside". A "For-ecology Moving-out" Project will be implemented, that will move all residents in Wolong Township to Gengda Township, merging Gengda and Wolong Township to create a new township with strong ethnic flavours so as to make it a reception centre for tourists. An ecology protection system that is much stricter than other reserve areas should be established and implemented in order to have ecology-friendly protection regulations.

Operation & Management Measures

The reserve should be strictly administered in accordance with the management rules of national park and natural heritage regulations. A new method of "Separation of Rights" will be introduced, namely separating the rights of ownership, management and operation. The ideas above have been included in the just-completed WNR General Plan of Ecotourism. By now the preparatory works for merchant-invitations and project-bidding have already been started. We firmly believe that in near future China's national Yellow Stone Park or a World-Class Eco-tour Attraction will emerge in southwest China

2008 Economic Development Strategies-Agritourism Industry

With New Jersey farmers facing rising costs and stagnant commodity prices, agri-tourism offers an important opportunity to generate additional farm income and keep farms economically viable. Agri-tourism presents opportunities for New Jersey growers seeking to add value to their crops and/or capture more of the market price of their products by directly accessing consumers. Many residents consider agriculture a novelty and something to be explored and enjoyed. They desire to share the agricultural experience while increasing farm income at the same time. New Jersey's agri-tourism industry provides for a great introduction to the agriculture of the Garden State. The educational and economic contributions of agri-tourism to the state's agricultural economy are many.

A National Agricultural Statistics Survey (NASS) study conducted this year determined that the economic impact of agri-tourism upon New Jersey's economy was $91 million in 2006. This quantitative information confirms the qualitative recommendations of a 2005 Rutgers University study that examined farmers' and farm leaders' perceptions of the opportunities and challenges associated with agri-tourism.

There are other states that have comprehensive agri-tourism programs and these will be studied as work moves forward to more closely cooperate with the various agencies that share a common interest in promoting tourism in New Jersey.

A new interactive, GIS-based, agri-tourism industry website, "visitnjfarms.org", allows for easy consumer mapping based on products, services and location, within a specified town or county, or within a specified driving radius of a user-defined beginning point. It also allows farmers password access to the site to provide updates to their own listing. To assist in the development of the agri-tourism industry, the Department will be focusing on three major objectives: developing strategic partnerships, consumer promotion and industry education.

Develop Strategic Partners

Strategy – Continue to support the New Jersey Agri-Tourism Industry Advisory Council in their charge to develop, support, and market this sector of the agricultural community.

Strategy – Continue working with the N.J. Office of Travel & Tourism (T&T) to develop and market agri-tourism. Develop three agri-tourism based travel tours for each of the state's six tourism regions. Encourage T&T to integrate an agri-tourism press familiarization tour into their work. These tours acquaint the regional travel and tourism media with New Jersey agri-tourism. Encourage T&T to incorporate agri-tourism research into their established travel industry research program. Market agri-tourism to the travel and tourism trade through participation in the annual Governor's Conference on Tourism, cooperative advertising, and other industry opportunities.

Strategy –Publicize the National Agricultural Statistics Survey (NASS) study that assessed the economic impact of agri-tourism upon New Jersey's economy.

Consumer Promotion

Strategy – Produce and distribute an inexpensive agri-tourism brochure with industry websites and contact information. This brochure would promote seasonal events, special attractions, and direct farm marketing opportunities. Create and disseminate regular press releases promoting the agri-tourism industry and related websites. Work to expand the promotion of the agricultural fairs in New Jersey.

Strategy – Continue to develop and promote the "visitnjfarms.org " website.

Industry Education

Strategy-Coordinate an Agri-Tourism symposium to address common opportunities and challenges and to provide some basic tourism and hospitality industry training. Work with Rutgers Cooperative Extension to develop and implement this training.

Strategy-Conduct tourism industry outreach activities for agri-tourism operators. Promote listings in the N.J. Office of Travel & Tourism's "Calendar of Events". Promote participation in "The 2007 New Jersey Governor's Conference on Tourism". Promote the use of the "Tourism Cooperative Grant Program" to organizations representing various facets of the New Jersey's agri-tourism industry.

Strategy – Continue to review, comment, and support work towards the adoption of agri-tourism Agricultural Management Practices (AMP's) as proposed by the State Agriculture Development Committee. Compliance with the agri-tourism AMP's will aid grower protection under the Right to Farm Act.

The success of tourism in Cambodia depends in Fart on the country's ability to develop a knowledgeable and skilled work force. Meeting the wide range of education and training needs must therefore be seen as essential for d l sectors of the industry. Failure to cmbrace all of the training issues will result in an imbalance within the travel product. Visitor satisfaction can diminish in a number of ways, and destinations that fail to recognize and address the needs and expectations of their tourists place the tourism industry at risk.

There are a number of different dimensions in beginning to understand a human resource development slrategy. It cannot be assumed that classrooms are the only settings for education aild training but rather that training and education can occur in a number of different ways. Given new technology and means of delivery, significant number of Cambodians can develop new skills and knowledge that are essential in ensuring the quality of the countrys tourism industry. Thcrc arc a number of new providers in the country that have shown entrepreneurial skills in beginning to address some of the important training and education needs in tourism. It is essential that the public and private sectors come together and the research work behind the strategy clearly recognizes the importance of this partnership. The docuinent is divided into three parts: An assessment of public sector training and education needs.

The Ministry of Tourism

In assessing the training needs for each of the departments, there appears to be overlap in responsibilities. In many cases the tasks within a particular department would logically be the responsibility of other departments within the Ministry of 'Tourism. In some instances, the responsibility would be that or other government ministries where the appropriate expertise would be more readily available.

As of October 2000, the registered number of staff at MOT based in Phnoin Penh is approximately 450. It is believed that 30%-40% of the registered employees are actually active. This is derived from interviews as well as advice from consultants assigned to M01. Thc percentage of active staff to registered staff will serve as basic data necessary for determining the scale of staff training and capacity to perform daily duties. In other words we arc not dealing with 450 staff members who require training but rather a much sinaller subset that actually are working within the Ministry.

A number of staff have participated in overseas training, a high percentage being university graduates which reflects the practice of' donors to impose requirements for overseas training such as the need to possess a University degree or equivalent qualifications, three years of' employment in a related field and language competener; (English) before training is provided. While there has been a satisfactory level of international training there has not been any formal evaluation from the point view 01' quality and relevance of that training. It is recommended that all international training exercises require baronial report both of the individual as well as of the individual supervisor.

Domestic Training

Domestic training carried out in the past five years can be categorized as "introductory training the training for tour guides", "basic training" (tourism development and management) "skill training" for MOT staff, and "hospitality training related to tourism awareness".

The majority *of* the training was related to % wiliness". Though this can appraised from the viewpoint of broadening the tourism base one cannot help but say that this activity only covers a small part of the training and education gap. There is no evidence that a needs survey was conducted before deciding on the content, hereby indicating that the is no assurance that the desirable level of training was necessarily provided.

Mot and other Ministries' Training Needs

Through a series of questionnaires and several meetings has identified a number of training requirements that need to be met if the government bureaucracy in Cambodia is to meet the country's tourism objectives. However, until staff is paid a living wage much of the training will not necessarily! increase the capacity of staff given their need to seek additional forms of livelihood.

A possible solution might be in job sharing where two persons share the responsibility for specific objectives and outputs. The working day could be split into two time units, with a handover period, e.g., 7.30 to 12.30 and 12.00, 17.00 hours. Staff would then be officially free to undertake secondary employment. This strategy relieves office space increases motivation, and allows employees to supplement their income until such time as the Government is in the position to enhance the Fasic wages of civil servants.

Ministry of Tourism

Introduction to Basic Tourism Planning and Development Concepts

There is an urgent need for staff at all levels to understand what is meant by 'tourism'; to appreciate that it is basically the sale of a shared experience, based on physical comfort, providing a visual experience and a service component. The expectations of the tourists need to be clearly understood, in order to create a positive growth environment. Within this context the Ministry can then embrace its responsibility to provide guidance and support to a growing industry.

Basic General Skills

The following training needs have been identified. Private sector training organizations offer courses covering all of' these topics. Selected staff can be enrolled on an individual basis, or group rates can be negotiated for larger numbers.--

* Language skills-Basic, Intermediate and Advanced
* Report writing
* Keyboard skills
* Word processing
* Computer literacy
* Numeracy skills
* Basic accounting
* Database management
* Stock control

Statistical Analysis: In the report on the development of an economic base study for Cambodia carried out by the need for such training is well illustrated and discussed. A basic introduction to economic analysis should be included.

When the tourism law is enacted there will be an urgent need to train inspectors in a wide range of technical and jurisdictional issues if they arc to be effective in carrying out their important tasks.

Basics of Small and Medium-Sized Enterprise Creation

Staff must begin to understand how to support small and medium-sized enterprises if poverty reduction is to occur. It is important that staff move from the rhetoric that is now becoming common about the importance of small and medium-sized enterprises to actually beginning to understand the dynamics behind the creation of such initiatives.

Training Needs for MOT and Other It event Ministries

Information Officers

It is evident that the staff of various ministries interacting with tourists needs assistance to develop its tourist information services. Information should include communication and courtesy skills, care and presentation of information desks, collection and filing of' information display of promotional materials, etc. Interpretation, design of exhibits and publications and the development of multimedia presentations also need to be trained. This will have to be at various levels and directed at specific staff.

Marketing and Promotion

Staff should be exposed to the basics of market research and promotion in order to allow them to participate effectively in the research process and to interact with marketing and promotion professionals. There should be no attempt to train a large number of skilled people but it is clear that market research skills are an important need in Cambodia. Relevant Ministries: Ministry of Tourism. Ministry of Cultural and Fine Arts and Ministry of Environment. Managing Service Excellence in the Cambodian Tourism Industry Knowledgeable travellers are demanding the best quality the tourism industry can provide. A competitive hospitality or tourism organization or business requires employees who (a> arc committed to exceeding industry standards for quality service. (b) can perform effectively in a multicultural environment. and (c) can contribute creatively to addressing service challenges in the work place. Consistent, predictable service quality translates into customer satisfaction and increased revenues from positive referrals to potential customers and repeats visits. Quality service training can also heighten employment satisfaction and positively influence employee retention.

The Management of Ecotourism

Such a course would allow the participants to understand the basic elements of ecotourism, evaluate market trends, assess the? potential of individual and group ecotourist speciality markets use green guidelines for operating a successful ecotourism business, analyze and address the special needs of ecotourists and local communities, establish an ecotourism planning process at the local and regional levels, develop trip circuits and travel packages that are safe and offer a wide variety of experiences and understand the vital role of interpretation and education in adding value.

Ecolodge Development

Such a course would allow the participants to assess the market demand for ecolodge types and the experiences they provide, estimate realistic cost projections/ revenue potential and develop pricing strategies, and understand how to find the best locations and evaluate site development opportunities and constraints.

Coastal & Marine Ecotourism

Such a course would allow the participant to integrate coastal zone management and mariners conservation into a sustainable tour ism development strategy identify the special characteristics of marine ecotourists, use innovative resource planning techniques and coastal zone management best practices, establish zoning and visitor tracking methods, educate visitors and staff about low-impact forms of recreation, monitor and assess more accurately the long-term effects of tourism on local resources and increase government's commitment in marine park protection and effective coastal management.

Historical Site Management

Observation of activities within the Angkor Wat complex would indicate that site management would need to be urgently improved. While the present ad-hoc arrangements may have been acceptable for love volume traffic, there is an urgent need for staff to be trained to deal with ever larger number of visitor numbers.

Project Management

Staff must be exposed to leading-edge project management skills and knowledge areas. It is becoming increasingly important, as transparency and good governance are required that team leaders and managers understand how to manage large-scale projects in a financially responsible manner. There is increasing concern within the donor community about the level of project management in Cambodia. It is clear that this is age skill and knowledge area that will be urgently required as donors and others become more demanding.

Poverty Reduction through Tourism

As we discover more and more about the role that sustainable tourism can play in alleviating poverty, staff must be provided with the opportunity of developing their skills and knowledge in poverty reduction initiatives. The training should range from simple awareness raising to sophisticated training for small numbers in developing policies and programs designed to deal with the poverty issue in a comprehensive manner. Relevant Ministries: All ministries dealing with tourism.

Recommendations for Travelling and Education For the Private Sector

The Private Sector is made up of a number of different organizations and activities as illustrated by Figure 4. The challenge is to ensure. That the relevant actors are trained and educated to support the overall tourism development and management process. From the beginning it is important to stress that the Ministry of Tourism is only one of many government actors responsible for delivering:! quality tourism product. There are therefore a series of other ministries that require capacity building.

The assessment used the following list of private sector occupational activities as a means of organizing its work:

* Adventured Outdoor Tourism Guide
* Advertising Manager/Assistant
* Amusement Park Employee
* Amusement Park
* Operation/Management
* Bartender
* Beverage Services Manager
* Campground Operator
* Casino Dealer
* Casino Slot Attendant
* Catering Manager
* Director of Salcs and Marketing
* Door Staff
* Food & Beverage Manager
* Food Sr. Beverage Server
* Food Service Counter Attendant
* Front Desk Agent
* Golf Club Manager
* Guest Services Attendant
* Housekeeping Room Attendant

* Human Resource Management
* Hunting Guide
* Kitchen Helper
* Leisure Centre Manager/Assistant
* Line Cook
* Marketing Manager/Assistant
* Promotion Manager/Assistant
* Reservations Sales Agent
* Retail First level Manager
* Retail Sales Associate
* Sales Manager
* Small Business Owner/Operator
* Special Events Coordinator
* Special Events Manager
* Taxicab Driver
* Tour Bus/Vaii Driver
* Tour Director
* 'Tour Guide
* Tour Operator
* Tourism Small Business Owner
* Tourism Trainer
* 'Travel Counsellor
* Wine Service

Survey of Training Needs In 'the Cambodian Travel and Tourism Sector

In order to better understand the needs of the travel and tourism sector several initiatives were taken. In addition to the significant number of interviews and meetings with many members of the tourism industry, the project worked with Rege: it College in Thnoni Penh in a study that was intended to provide a snapshot of the current human resource capacity in the travel and tourism industry. This included not only the hospitality sector, but also related industries of' international and domestic travel services and other support services.

The key objectives were to provide a clear and relevant overview of the current level of skills among personnel working in the hospitality and travel industry and, by analysis of current recruitment practices, human resource and training policies, to identify clear areas where a skills gap exists. In addition the study aimed to assess the commitment and capacity of owners. Managers and currently existing training institutions 10 address these questions. To achieve these objectives. Primary data was collected from a Closs section of accommodation services restaurant and catering services, and travel and tour operators. Secondary data was provided by the hospitality. Travel and tourism sectors, the Ministry of Tourism and Ministry of Education. 'The project team wishes to thank Regent College for its cooperation and professionalism in completing the survey.

Methodology

Due to the necessarily limited nature of the time and financial resources available to carry out a survey. Three key sites were selected as representing the current focus of tourism activity in Cambodia. These were: Phnom Penh, the capital city and principal port of entry for the Kingdom. Despite a significant decrease of growth in arrivals, a< a result of the government's Open Skies policy, 56.75% of all visitors to Cambodia in 2000 still arrived through Pochentong International Airport.

Siem Reap, home of Angkor Wat and the principal centre for tourism development. In 3,000, 18.66% of all visitors to the kingdom arrived through Siem Reap Airport. a figure that has shown an enormous increase in the year to date, with a 110.98% rise in the first quarter alone.

Sihanoukville (formerly Kampong Som), Cambodia's principal seaside resort town located 230km south of Phnom Penh. one of four international border checkpoints and a popular destination for domestic holidaymakers.

Primary research in each of these locales consisted of questionnaires, scheduled interviews and, in the case of Phnom

Penh, follow-up felcus group discussions (FGD's). Potential respondents were drawn from PADECO's comprehensive listings of hotels, guesthouses, restaurants and travel and tour operators. PA1 IECO's categories were further subdivided based on considerations of price.

Facilities, site, ownership and location. Subsets in each locale were identified using these four criteria, md from these subsets a random sample was made, proportionate to the size/ number of each location. A total of one hundred respondents were selected across the three locations.

Questionnaires focused on current recruitment and HR policy, the current educational and skill levels of management and staff, recent experience of, or participation in internal or externally conducted training, management commitment to staff development perceived constraints or obstacles to the provision of training and the prioritization of specific skills for enhancement or development. In addition to the quantitative data obtained, the questionnaires contained a qualitative component in the form of brief interviews based on a set of prospected questions.

'The questionnaires were administered in face-to-face interviews with owners or managers of hotels, restaurants or travel and tour operators. Questionnaires were available in English or Khmer as required and each interview team consisted of one native speaker and one Khmer interviewer to minimize problems of comprehension. Secondary information sources consisted primarily of the Ministry of Tourism Statistical Report for 7000. The 1999 MPDF report on Developing SMEs in the Tourism Industry and the 1996 National Human Resource Strategy developed by WTO/UNDP.

Immediately following completion of the formal questionnaires, respondents were invited to colour issues which had atisen in the course of the interviews in an informal setting, and to provide a more personalized insight into the topics covered.

Following completion of all primary data collection, two focus group discussions were conducted to further explore the issues raised by the study, involving respondents from the training and education field, and owners and mangers from the private sector. 'This report provides information on the most important findings.

Findings

Recruitment Policy

It was discovered across each of the sample groups (hotels, guesthouses, restaurants, travel and tour operators) that recruitment in the main depended on either the employment of relatives of owners or managers or on word-of-mouth from current staff as can be seen. A clear majority 01' all companies interviewed expressed a preference for this lorni of internal recruitment, usually citing simple issues of trust as the principal criteria. Outweighing other considerations of specific skills or suitability. Although this was true for all groups and in each location, it was particularly marked in the restaurant sector and in Category 2 and Category 3 hotels. While newspaper advertising, usually in Reaksmey Kampuchea was the second most popular form of locating new staff this was still relatively minor.

At the opposite end of the scale as predicted there was a reluctance to consider staff with more than basic. Qualifications due to the necessarily low wages paid and the. Perception that better qualified staff would either seek higher salaries or would not remain in place long. Attitudes Towards investment in Training One of the recurring concerns stated when discussing recruitment or training was the impression that investment in training or in recruitment based on merit or achievement was undesirable due to the mobility of employees. Repeatedly owners and managers stressed that if staff were not family members, or were trained to higher standards, they would either leave.

For better employment or would establish their own business in competition. Indeed, when asked the most common reason for staff changes it is true that 40% were due to employees finding better positions, but when asked about staff turnover. The results showed a relatively high degree of stability with 72% of companies securing a minimum of six months' employment from staff: and almost 62% retaining staff for over a year. Given the seasonal nature of the industry, and the rate of hotel and restaurant development in Phnom Penh and Sictn Keap, this suggests that even in those businesses not employing family members. The situation is less volatile than one would expect.

Following on from the above data, the questionnaire then focused on what training was provided to staff, either internally or externally following recruitment. Respondents were questioned about specific positions to provide a detailed insight into the relative importance placed on training of management, front-line and back-office staff.

In the case of hotels and guesthouses, those employed in management or supervisory positions ordinarily received little more than orientation. Primarily due to being perceived as already qualified or experiment. Only *5%* of respondents offered a structured training plan For these positions and less than *90/0* of respondents sought outside training for management or supervisory staff.

In the case of front-of-house staff results were broadly similar with again only *5%* of companies having a structured training programme, relying instead on the previous experience of new staff members or limited in-service training to achieve the results required.

Cost of Training

Respondents were questioned regarding a range of options to assist with the cost of training.

An earlier question had established that the level of fees most respondents willing to sponsor training were prepared to pay was in the US$20-50 range, based on an average ten-week parttime course of 40 hours.

Preferred Training Providers

Another key question concerned the preferred training provider should external training be required. Interestingly, in Siem Reap and Phnoin Penh a clear majority preferred private sector providers to a Ministry-run training institution, with 48.6% in favour of a private institution against 37.5% in favour of a Ministry Training Centre. Most respondents were very receptive to the ideas of the Ministry adopting a {supervisory and licensing role rather than a direct training role.

It is clear from the bulk of respondents surveyed that while skills levels remain 10\+ across the tourism industry. Training represents a low priority for most owners and managers, whether of medium sized hotels. Small guest houses, restaurants aimed at the tourist market or family-run travel and tour operators. While a few companies interviewed showed an impressive commitment to training and staff development, as well as a keen awareness of the areas where i improvement was most needed. These were clearly exceptions. Of course significant variations exist between the three locales, with a sense of despondency to be found among some owners in Phnom Penh and Sihanoukville, compared to the bullish mood found in Siem Reap. At several of the mid-range hotels in Phnoin Penh owners or managers bemoaned low levels of occupancy and commented that their income and staff levels were actually lower now than four years ago.

Some other hotels quite openly discussed the level and extent of their financial losses. Although few hotels have declared bankruptcy in the last year (three in Phnom Penh in 2000) it seems that many of the interviewers encountered businesses in Phnom Penh and Sihanoukville with few positive signs of growth. In Sihanoukville, the situation is acute with a clear oversupply to rooms in the $10-25 range. The inexperience of many hotel and restaurant owners is apparent firm the moment of arrival, with little attention paid to customer service cleanliness or presentation. The vulnerability of many smaller operators to better-organized or better-fiinded competitors is also evident.

While this is true in all countries in such a small and concentrated area it is surprising to be able to go from a clean, modern hotel with facilities such as a swimming pool tennis courts, restaurants, hairdresser etc. to a hotel with extremely basic room facilities, no additional facilities a very poor standard of cleanliness and customer service, and to be offered the same rate (lJS$30) at both. It is clear that managers and staff of such hotels could benefit from training in the expectations of being tourists regarding decor.

Furnishings etc, as well as service considerations, but there is little awareness of the importance of these issues. In Sicm Reap the contrast with Sihanoukville is obviously striking. Whereas Sihanoukvillc in low season is a quiet, almost moribund setting, with little activity evident on the streets and rows of empty or sparsely populated restaurants, hotels and bars, Siem Reap continues to display vibrant signs of life. More than one business commented that low season now is similar to high season in previous years.

While this is clearly cause for optimism, in the case of some of the respondents interviewed this clearly leads to a sense of complacency in that it is clear that tourist numbers arc growing at a rate unprecedented in the history of the town and that seasonally at least business is booming with little effort necessary on their part. As has been noted elsewhere, Siem Reap is not a budget location. Prices are cospensive compared with neighbouring countries while the quality of service remains low. Consideration of this among owners arid managers however is limited.

Correspondingly while there was a greater proportion of owners and managers who expressed a commitment to training, particularly in languages and improved customer service., there were many more who clearly felt that business was proceeding well enough without the additional expense of training staff. As stated in the MPIIE' report from 1999. "many managers have a short term vision in conducting their business and are not willing to enlist in improving the quality of their services and facilities."

Perhaps the most significant findings of the surveyor that despite the fluctuating fortunes of recent years, the majority of owners and mangers persist in a short-term view of tourism development, lacking the business experience and vision to consider the impact that future market changes could have on their businesses.

Issues of quality are seldom addressed or wen considered, and the result is that trained stair is perceived as a luxury rather than a necessity. Perhaps due to inexperience, the connection between training, education and productivity is not often made. In line with a recent study by Merrill Lynch showing that companies employing a work force with a 10% higher than average educational attainment level enjoyed an 86% higher-than-average productivity, the message that training pays off is one that must be stressed if the industry is to embrac: any future proposals.

In line with this, it seems clear that left to their own devices few businesses are likely to take a proactive approach to training.

Existing Training Programs

Training and education is provided at various levels ranging from certificates diplomas, and Bachelor and Master degree programs. The Royal University of Phnom Penh currently offers a Masters program in Tourism Development, while the National Institute of Management and four other institutions offer undergraduate studies 4 in tourism. Also several private schools provide technical training. Approximately I OC students per year graduated from these institutions seeking tourism related employment in both the public and private sectors. However, the demand for people with technician training is very high making technical education and training a major issue.

As indicated above there are several institutions. Providing tourism education and training. Given the lack of national standards there is a concern about the quality of students/ people who are trained from these tourism providers. This is due to several reasons. Lack of cooperation among tourism equation providers including government. NGOs, private sector and domestic and international institutes. Teaching staff that does not have the necessary qualifications and experience. Inadequate resources and materials of villous kinds to assist students in their classroom as well as private study.

The private sector teaching establishments are keel to develop programs specifically for the tourism industry. While most of these institutions would favour topics which are an extension of their existing teaching fields, i.e.. hotel front office and tour guiding Techniques, some have already investigated the possibility of working in partnership with hotel operators to provide practical training venues for the training of lousemaids and waiting staff.

Most employers would be happy to see operational standards improve, arid would contribute more to in-house training if they had the ability. Most operators experience problems recruiting staff competent at basic skills level, let alone find trainers capable of upgrading the skills of others.

With the exception of the lop hotels, few have ever carried out ii training needs analysis, mainly because they themselves are unable to define desirable standards of performance or to relate these to guest expectation.

Any further developments in in-house training by the private sector will be dependent in part on the availability of training materials and the opportunity for their heads of department to attend a skills under relationship techniques workshop.

Defining Training and Education Needs

Developing a learning experience is at times a complex process that requires the participation of a number of individuals. This short chapter attempts to identify some of the major steps and issues to be considered when designing a learning experience. It is not designed to replace the need for trained and experienced course designers. Rather it is aimed at identifying the nature of the issues and the process that are normally followed in course design and delivery. There is certainly no one route to the development of a course or learning experience and no magic formulas to rely.

Very often after an idea for a course has been identified an expert is hired to deliver a course without any planning occurring. While this may be cost-efficient it is not effective in actually meeting the needs that will have been identified through the research process. At a possible process for designing a learning experience. ?'he course designer should ideally be somebody with a sound knowledge of adult education and preferably with a good grasp of the subject material. In many cases it is message to combine the skill of the educator with the subject specialist. When we refer to the term course designer it can either be an individual or in some cases a group of people. Increasingly with the introduction of interactive information technology there is a need to have a specialist in this area as part of the design process.

Is important that the designers start off with an pen mind on how best to meet the need identified. 'Too often it is an automatic assumption that the only way to train people is to develop a course or learning experience in the standard classroom fashion. Delivering knowledge in a classroom may at times be the least efficient and effective way of attempting to raise the knowledge and skills of a group of participants from the tourism industry. With our increased knowledge of how people learn it is becoming increasingly clear that the standard classroom experience may in fact be the least effective way of imparting knowledge and skills. In this short discussion the term course could mean a number of different types of learning experiences that will be discussed later in this chapter. The following steps can be followed in determining the nature of learning experience.

Identification of the Training or Education Need

The need for a particular skill or knowledge to be developed into a course can come from a number of sources. In the case of Cambodia a staff person of the Ministry of 'Tourism in his or her work could observe the need for knowledge and skills to be developed and then transmitted to a particular group responsible for particular tourism planning or development issues. The need can come from a community group seeking help in addressing issues in their community or a group of professionals could collectively define a gap in their training or knowledge set. 'The need could also come from an overall human resource development strategy such as the one that has been developed for Cambodia. Whatever the source of the need identification it is important to start with clear identification of the need and the establishment of the priority of that particular need.

Defining Capacities and Needs

Depending on the nature of the identification process there then must be a clear definition of the actual need. This requires that the eventual provider or sponsor carry out a careful research process in order to determine the actual dimensions of the training need. Too often a wry general concept is quickly turned into a course that never meets the actual needs of the participants. Normally within the course development process the designers will use existing data from a human resource development research process or at times must carry out their own investigation. Depending on budget and the complexity of task thc following sources may be consulted: Representatives from within the particular sector where the need has been identified. People actually carrying out the task. Employers in the particular sector identified as requiring training. The providers of training to determine their views on the need itself and the actual learning experience. Consultations with institutions or organizations offering similar types of courses either in Cambodia or elsewhere in the world. In order to systematically collect information the designer can employ a range of techniques including questionnaires, surveys and focus groups. It must be remembered that the survey process simply collects information and cannot replace the need for the skill and judgment of the course designer. The course designer will bring to the process the knowledge of how best to meet the needs of a particular group given a set of realities.

This process should allow the designers to identify the following factors within the overall course design process:

The nature of the audience (level of education nature of their experience, language skills, previous training opportunities etc.) 'The number of people who could be trained given the opportunity. (It is important in this case to define not only the existing number of potential participants but the anticipated demand for a learning experience in the future. In some instances there is a significant pent-up demand that must be met for that need only to find that after that demand has been met there is little potential for the ongoing delivery of the course experience.)

The level of training needs to be addressed which can range everywhere from the imparting of basic awareness creation to establishing a sound basic skill or knowledge set to professional development experiences.

The length of the course must be determined based on the course objectives and the length of time participants will be in a position to spend in the learning experience. The nature of the certification is certainly always an important issue and in some cases it may be determined that the particular skill or knowledge must be met within the context of a group of courses that can take the form of a certificate, diploma or in some cases a university degree. The location of the people requiring the training and their ability to travel is especially important. Do they exist in one central location or are they in fact scattered over the entire country? 'This issue becomes particular important from a financial perspective.

Assessing the Interest and Capacity of Providers

Depending on the nature of course determined by Step 2 it is important to then work with providers to *sec* how the course can be delivered. I f the course is to be complicate, subsidized then this step becomes less important but more open than not the delivery process depends on sonic form of market response. Is important that discussions he held on: The cost of' delivering such a Earning experience. It is important to remember that the course development process has to be factored into the eventual course delivery fees unless it is subsidixt.

The capacity of the local or national providers to deliver the course must be determined. In other words do they have the experience and the trained personnel to deliver the course experience? Does the institution have the necessary reputation to enable the participants to obtain a job or for advancement in an agreement once the learning experience has been completed. The sustainability of the provider *must* be assessed especially if 'an ongoing set of courses is being contemplate.

Determining Learning Objectives

At this point the course can be more clearly understood and the factors discussed earlier determined. It is particularly important at this point that a series of course objectives for the Incurring experience be determined and agreed to by the relevant stakeholders. In effect these objectives now become the guiding principle for the detailed course development process.

Detailed Course Learning Design

Is not possible within this document to describe the detailed design process but as identified, there are number of issues to be considered:. This includes the following factors: Hie identification of instructors and facilitates and whether they themselves require training either in the from to' subject specific development or in training methods. There are times when there are people whiting the industry who may have the necessary knowledge but not the ability to treatment that knowledge in a professional and effective way.

'The nature of the subject material and the lacks to be delivered should then be identified in sufficient detail that a course instructor can deliver the required objectives.

It should be determined whether any form of prerequisite is necessary for the learning experience. This can he as basic as language skills or can be more complex requiring a participant to have participated in one or more previous courses. The delivery methods arc then carefully identified and as suggested in figure there are a series of ways of delivery methods available always renumbering that the classroom is but one specific response domestic and out of country delivery methods include:

Developing the Course Package

'The course package that includes the information from the steps described above can then be produced. In the ideal situation it is then possible to select the instructor and/or facilitator based on the material that is produced. This material would include such things as the detailed course objectives, the learning sequences. The nature of the group work to be carried out: books: video or CDs, the evaluation methods to be used and a well-designed course evaluation technique.

Evaluating and Monitoring the Learning Experience

There must be an ongoing process of assessment both while the course is being delivered and certainly once the experience has been completed. It is not sufficient to rely on an evaluation form that is often hastily completed at the end of the course. If one is truly interested in understanding the effectiveness of a learning experience the respondents. Their employers, fellow employees and most importantly in the tourism industry customers should be carefully surveyed in order to determine whether the course objectives have been met. This information of course is important in terms of redesigning or reformatting the nest offering of the course experience.

In a world that is quickly changing. It is often necessary to update material on a regular basis and to adapt delivery methods to new and more accessible technology.

Major Recommendations and Conclusions

Cambodia is faced with a number of significant human resource development challenges. As an emerging economy there are a number of demands placed on the country to meet a series of needs necessary to allow the country to achieve its full potential. It is very important that national authorities recognize the need to place a high-priority on human resource development at all levels. There is a need to ensued that children in schools are made aware of tourism as an activity and its role in the national society, there must be clear information available on opportunities in all classes of tourism activity, vocational schools must provide opportunities for obtaining basic skills especially in the hospitality industry graduate level programs must conform to international standards and there is an extreme urgency for professional developments and skills and knowledge development for those already working in the industry.

Faced with this challenge the country must seriously address its human resource needs in the tourism industry given its importance in the overall development of the society. It is important to recognize that training and education must be available to all sectors of the society and in particular the poor and women who,) have an opportunity of benefiting from tourism activity if they have the necessary skills and knowledge. It is clear that human resource development is an essential element in an overall poverty reduction strategy related to tourism.

As discussed earlier in this document the role fought Ministry of tourism and in particular the 'Training and Education Department is crucial in helping to ensure consistent human resource not be to act as a provider but to contribute advice and direction on crucial issues within the overall tourism planning and development process.

This will require that the Ministry staff is trained in human resource development in order to measure that needs and requirements can be professionally identified and that the Ministry staff can effectively work with the range of public and private sector providers that now exis in Cambodia.

It is also important that Ministry staff is in a position to design funding proposals that will meet international standards as they relate to human resource development. The Ministry is in a unique position given its presence in all parts of the country to be arvare of problems within all sectors of the tourism industry. Through its human resource development staff it can identify specific needs and work with the essential providers in meetings kill and knowledge gaps.

Cambodian Tourism Human Resource Development Commission

Recognizing the challenges identified in this strategy it is recommended that a public/private Cambodia Tourism Human Resource Development Commission be created that would be responsible for both needs assessment as well as helping to bring together the necessary public and private resources to meet the significant tourism capacity building requirements 01' the country. The Commission would be made up of representatives from the tourism industry, the Ministry 01 'Tourism and other government ministries.

It is recommended that the Commission be made up of equal numbers of public and private numbers. Private sector participants would be representatives of various groups including the hotel industry, the restaurant sector, travel companies and the tour and travel areas of activity. Training institutes and universities would have both public as well as private representatives. It is further recommended that in addition to the Ministry of 'Tourism the Ministry of Education.

The Ministry of Culture and Fine Arts and the Ministry of the Environment have membership on the Commission. The Commission would also be responsible for establishing national standards for all occupational groups. In addition, the Commission would be responsible for working with colleges and universities in designing degree programs that meet international standards. The Commission would be established in such a way that it would monitor various educational programs and on a regular basis assess these programs using both Cambodian as well as international experts to ensure that Cambodians have access to international level training and education that is adapted to the Cambodian contest.

The Ministry of 'Tourism would act as the secretariat for the Commission and provide all necessary administrative support in order to ensure the effective functioning of the Commission. It is recommended that a task force be established immediately made up of representatives from the essential sectors to further define the nature of the Commission. The approach used by the Canadian government could serve as a useful model for development.

Establishing Professional Associations

There is a need to further encourage the private sector to from and support professional associations. i.e., hotels and restaurants, tour operators and tour guides. Such associations can then speak with one voice to influence the content of training programs and to moderate the examination and testing procedures. In addition, professional associations can present specialist workshops on a cost-sharing basis by bringing in experts to meet specific objectives.

Conclusions

The Human Resource Development Strategy for Cambodia outlines the principal needs thing the country as it attempts to use tourism as a major tool of societal development. It is essential that the needs identified for the public sector be seen as priority areas for action.

Unless there are trained government employees working in various areas of cultural and natural resource development and protection with a sound understanding of market issues there is a distinct possibility that the important opportunities facing tourism in Cambodia will be lost.

Given the very rapid growth of the hospitality sector there are significant needs to he fulfilled to help position Cambodia as an international destination. It is of concern that the private sector appears place a high priority on training and education and the Ministry of Tourism along with other sectors of the industry must establish a climate were training and education is seen as essential as Canibodia continues to enjoy significant tourism growth. It is clear that without further opportunities achieving international status will be impossible. However, given the realities of the private sector it is important that be Commission adopts innovative techniques for delivering skill and knowledge development. It is stressed that innovative techniques are used to meet the market realities.

5

Financial Strategies for Hospitality Sector

Introduction

Although the travel and tourism industry covers a diversity of different organizations, including tour operators, airlines, hotels and travel agencies, financial management is important to all of them. Financial management is that part of the total management function concerned with the effective and efficient raising and use of funds.

Finance, like physical resources, has a large number of competing uses, is scarce but can be obtained at a price, and is bought and sold in markets. Financial management is concerned with managing this scarce resource so as to ensure that:

- Finance is obtained at the least possible cost and
- Finance is used in the most profitable ways.

The Scope of Financial Management

Financial management can be seen as a function of management concerned with managing the financial aspects of a company's activities, just as the marketing function and personnel functions, for instance, are concerned with the managing of products and the managing of people, respectively. Financial management encompasses a broad range of activities including :

- Financial planning, control and reporting;
- Budgeting;

- Treasury management.

Of these, this chapter will focus specifically on treasury management, as this area of financial management has a considerable significance for most companies operating in the international travel and tourism industry.

Treasury Management

Over the last two decades, increasing attention has been paid to the Treasury aspect of financial management. It has become a specialist aspect of financial management with a professional body, The Association of Corporate Treasurey, founded in 1979.

The increasing internationalization of business and the extreme volatility of exchange rates (following the breakdown of the previous fixed rate regime in the early 1970s), together with volatility of interest rates, has forced many businesses to concentrate resources and attention on this aspect of their business. Since travel and tourism is the most international of business, treasury management is of particular importance.

Treasury management is concerned with the management of a company's cash so as to ensure:

- The right amount of cash is available;
- In the right place;
- In the right currency;
- At the right time.

In managing the company's cash in such a way, Treasury management is about minimizing risks, (such as minimizing exposure to movements in foreign exchange and interest rates and minimizing the financing costs of the business), and maximizing returns, specifically, maximizing the returns on surplus funds. Since maximizing the returns entails taking risks, decisions have to be made which require compromising some degree of profitability in return for a reduction in risks.

The Role of Treasurer

The role of treasurer or treasury manager is still developing but, in broad terms, it can include any corporate activities or services directly associated with banking and the financial and currency markets. Indeed, many companies (and most in travel and tourism) may not have a treasurer or a treasury department as such. The responsibilities may be split across several departments or operations, or carried out by outside financial institutions or consultants.

In most cases, however, whether treasury management is centralized or decentralized, is carried out internally or is delegated to outsiders, some degree of management of cash activities takes place and overall responsibility is vested in one person, if not the treasurer, the financial director.

Arguably, this area of management is poorly understood and managed by many travel and tourism companies, particularly small and medium sized enterprises.

The Relevance of Treasury Management to Travel and Tourism

The importance of treasury management can be attributed to two particular factors that affect the industry:

Managing Foreign Exchange

The industry operates internationally producing international flows of funds in various currencies. Tour operators and airlines typically have a very large exposure to movements in foreign exchange rates, almost certainly far larger than for most companies of a similar size engaged in other areas of the economy, for instance, manufacturing companies. The very purpose of these companies implies that they are international in their activities, thereby leaving them exposed to international risks associated with foreign exchange transactions.

So for instance,

(a) a French airline may:

- sell tickets in many currencies
- buy its fuel and aircraft in US dollars
- pay most of its staff and report its profits in French francs (or euros).

(b) similarly, a British outbound tour operator may:

- receive most of its income in sterling
- buy aircraft fuel and pay leasing costs in US dollars

- pay its staff in sterling
- pay its hoteliers and other suppliers in various currencies, including euros and US dollars.

Cash Management

The industry is highly seasonal, which usually leads to a highly seasonal pattern of cash flow. At certain times of the year, companies may have large cash balances and, at other times of the year, many companies need to borrow money in order to maintain payments to suppliers (creditors). The industry is also cyclical in nature, in that cash flows are very responsive to changes in the general level of economic activity.

In terms of cash management, tour operators and travel agents are typically low margin business, deriving important parts of their income not from operating profits (through the selling of holidays), but from interest income derived from investing cash surpluses they may be holding at certain times of the year.

So, for instance, a British tour operator may:

- receive revenue from customers before the company has to pay its suppliers
- invest this revenue to produce interest income
- view the interest income derived as a major source of the company's profitability.

We will now look in greater detail at these two important aspects of treasury management.

Foreign Exchange Management

The profitability of any company that trades internationally is affected by changes in foreign exchange rates. As Lockwood (1989) states:

> *As a large part of the travel and tourist industry is concerned with persuading and assisting people to cross national boundaries and thus to buy goods and services priced in a foreign currency, the identification and management of exchange rate exposures is vital to the profitable operation of a travel and tourist business.*

Thus, foreign exchange management is very significant for many travel and tourism businesses. The lack of stability caused by the continual changes in exchange rates between currencies creates uncertainty. Specifically, uncertainty is created as to:

- what foreign income will be worth when it is received
- what payments will cost when they have to be made, and also
- what the value of foreign assets and liabilities might be in the future.

The overall foreign exchange position of a company may be complicated as illustrated by the position of British Airways. The British Airways Annual Report and Accounts for 1998-99 states that:

> *The group does business in approximately 140 foreign currencies, which account for approximately 60% of Group Revenue and approximately 40% of operating expenses. The Group generates a surplus in most of these currencies (i.e. revenue are greater than costs). The principal exceptions are the US dollars and the pound Sterling in which the Group has a deficit arising from capital expenditure and the payment of some leasing costs, together with expenditure on fuel, which is payable in US dollars and the majority of staff costs, central overheads and other leasing costs, which are payable in pounds Sterling.*

British Airways, consequently, has a highly complex foreign exchange position, but it is imperative to the profitability of such a company that this exposure to foreign exchange rate movements is recognized and managed appropriately.

In all cases, risk attributed to foreign exchange rate movements arises out of uncertainty about the future exchange rate between two currencies. This risk would be minimized if it were possible to predict future rate movements. Unfortunately, however, it is not possible to do so with any degree of accuracy and for a company to try to do so can be financially dangerous. Therefore, given that foreign exchange rates cannot be predicted, another option might be to pass on to the customer the effects of any adverse movements in exchange rates and, hence, the company would incur no impact. In most cases, however, the highly competitive nature of the travel and tourism business prevents higher costs being passed on to the customer in this way. For instance, if Spain as a destination increased in price as a result of an appreciation of the Spanish peseta or euro, (making Spanish hotel costs more expensive to foreign customers), over time customers might switch to say Turkey as a cheaper alternative.

Furthermore, because many tour operators now have to 'no surcharge guarantees' it effectively means that increased costs resulting from adverse foreign exchange rate movements cannot be passed on to the customer. At the same time, even if 'no surcharge guarantees' are given, passing on increased costs can be difficult, as the Association of British Travel Agents (ABTA) Code of Conduct requires members to absorb unforeseen costs up to 2 per cent of the original holiday cost. Similarly, although the European community Package Travel Directive allows tour operators to impose surcharges to pass on the increased costs arising from adverse movements in currency (or fuel) rates, the directive stipulates that a maximum surcharge of 10 per cent can be levied, with any increase over and above this level having to be absorbed by the operator.

Clearly, then, it is prudent to manage these risks, although it is common in the industry for the risks to be ignored, especially by smaller companies. We can identify three different types of foreign exchange risk or exposure a company may be faced with.

Transaction Exposure

Transaction exposure arises 'because the cost or proceeds (in home currency) of settlement of a future payment or receipt denominated in another currency may vary due to changes to exchange rates'.

Transaction exposure relates to the foreign exchange exposure where contracts have already been entered into. When a company has counteracted to receive or pay an amount of money in a foreign currency at some time in the future, a risk is incurred. The specific task is that adverse exchange rate movements between now and the time of the eventual cash receipt/payment which will increase the amount to be paid out or decrease the amount to be received.

For example, a UK tour operator selling holidays to America would receive its income in pounds Sterling, but has to make payments to hoteliers and other suppliers in US dollars. In order to make the payments, the company would at some stage have to convert sterling into US dollars. This would entail a risk that the US dollar might rise in value (appreciate) against sterling, thereby making the payments more expensive in sterling terms. Assume, for instance, the company had costed its hotel beds in its American programme at a rate of $1.70 to the pound (i.e. 1 pound buys 1.70 US dollars), and that the total cost to purchase the required bed spaces was $1,700,000. The cost in sterling to the company would be $1,700,000/1.70 = £ 1,000,000. Now if the rate subsequently fell to $1.60, the cost would increase to $1,700,000/1.60 = £1,062,500.

Translation Exposure

Buckley states that 'translation exposure arises in the consolidation of assets, liabilities and profits denominated in foreign currency in the process of preparing consolidated account'. The concept is also known as *accounting exposure.*

For example, if a UK hotel company purchases a hotel in Australia, it acquires an asset priced in Australian dollars. Each year, when the balance sheet of the business is prepared, the value of the hotel would be translated into sterling at the prevailing rate on the balance sheet date. The hotel might therefore be worth less in sterling terms as shown in the balance sheet of the company.

In general, the management of translation exposure receives less active management attention than the management of transaction exposure. It might be argued that such an exposure is not a real exposure, since the asset itself remains unchanged; that is, the company still owns the same hotel. However, if at any time the company wishes to sell the hotel and want to realize its value through the repatriation of the proceeds to the host country, then the revenue received will be affected by the prevailing exchange rate. Therefore, to give a true and fair picture of the current value of assets and liabilities, it is necessary for them to be revalued in the balance sheet of a company.

Consequently, under UK accounting convention (Statement of Standard Accounting Procedure 20), translation exposure is seen as a potential risk that might be incurred and is reported through a movement in reserves on the balance sheet. All foreign assets and liabilities are translated into domestic currency at the rate of exchange ruling on the balance sheet date (the *Closing Rate Method*) or the average rate throughout the year (the *Average Rate Method*).

Economic Exposure

Economic exposure (sometimes referred to as political exposure) arise from the effect of adverse exchange rates movements in future cash flows where no contractual arrangement to receive or pay money has yet been made. This kind of exposure is longer term in nature and often difficult to quantify exactly and forecast accurately.

For instance, suppose a specialist tour operator operates most of their programme to one country, such as The Gambia, then the company will have an economic exposure to that country and its currency. In some cases, the political and economic circumstances are very uncertain and if, for example, the government should be replaced in a violent way, (as occurred in The Gambia in 1994), customers will be reluctant to book holidays to that country, thereby severely limiting the revenues of the specialist tour operator.

Another example of such a risk might relate to the effect that relative exchange rate changes have on demand. For instance , if the value of the euro appreciates versus sterling whereas the value of the Turkish lira falls, it may well lead over time to reduction of demand for Greek holidays among British customers and an increase in demand for competing Turkish holidays. Consequently, a company selling Greek holidays would suffer a fall in revenues.

Thus, movements in foreign exchange rates lead to a number of different problems or exposures for travel and tourism companies. These exposures can be dealt with in a number of ways, the most obvious way being to avoid the exposures altogether, either by trading in domestic markets only or by passing the exposure over to suppliers or customers. However, these alternatives are seldom possible in international travel and tourism and so other management methods have to be employed in order to reduce the risks.

The Management of Transaction Exposure

The first step in managing transaction exposure is to identify the magnitude and the timing of the risks involved. An exposure occurs as soon as the commitment to buy or sell in a foreign currency is taken and a company needs to build up and overall picture of these commitments in order to work out total transaction exposure. This information can then be presented on an exposure summary.

To demonstrate how we can show the risk and how that risk can then be managed, we will consider a simple example using a fictitious UK tour operator, Stateside Travel. The major part of the business of Stateside Travel is selling package holidays to the USA to British customers. The operator also has a smaller operation selling British holidays in America. This produces both payments and receipts in US dollars. Table 1 shows a summary of Stateside's total transaction exposure for US dollars. A similar table would be produced for each currency for which an exposure exists.

Table 1 : Stateside Travel—US $ transaction exposure ($000's)

	Mar	*Apr*	*May*	*Jun*	*Jul*	*Aug*	*Sept*	*Total*
Payments	(600)	(900)	(1100)	(1250)	(1350)	(1500)	(900)	(7600)
Receipts	50	100	100	(150	200	250	50	900
Net Cash Flow	(550)	(800)	(1000)	(1100)	(1150)	(1250)	(850)	(6700)
Cover	300	600	800	(900)	950	1000	700	5250
% Cover	55	75	80	82	83	80	82	78
Net Exposure	(250)	(200)	(200)	(200)	(200)	(250)	(150)	(1450)

In this example, Stateside has a large amount of US dollar payments (because it has to pay its American suppliers) than receipts. These payments, therefore, have to be met using funds from elsewhere. In other words, the company has at some time to purchase US dollars with sterling and thus has US dollar exposure.

There are a number of methods that could be used to manage such an exposure. These include:

Matching (sometimes termed 'netting')

The company could develop an American source of income to offset against the payment. That is, it could use US receipts to directly make US payments. The company could do this by developing its American sales of UK holidays, the effect of which would be to equalize receipts and payments, payments being made from the money derived from receipts. Since in such a case no foreign exchange purchases would be necessary, the company can be said to have covered its exposure. However, such a position is difficult for a company to achieve, at least in the short term, because different products grow at different rates.

Forward Foreign Exchange Contracts

A forward foreign exchange contract allows a company to:

- Arrange to enter into a binding contract with a bank.
- To buy or sell at a specific future date, an agreed amount of a foreign currency.
- At a rate of exchange that is determined 'now', that is, when the forward contract is made.
- The rate agreed will be linked to the current or spot exchange rate, with an adjustment made (the premium or discount) for forward value.

Forward contracts allow a company that knows it will have to buy or sell a foreign currency at a date in the future to make the purchase or sale at a predetermined rate of exchange. The company will, therefore, know in advance either how much local currency it is likely to receive (If it is selling foreign currency from the bank), or how much local currency it must pay (if it is buying foreign currency from the bank). The contract is entered into now for an agreed date in the future (the maturity date) at which time the currencies are actually exchanged. Note the premium or discount is added or deducted from the spot rate and represents an adjustment for the interest rate differential between the two currencies.

Taking out forward cover by means of forward foreign exchange contracts is by far the most common method of covering known transaction exposures. There are, however, costs involved with forward contracts. In some cases, banks demand collateral of up to 20 per cent of turnover in order to agree to transact forward contracts with smaller companies. Also, if the foreign currency is trading at a premium to the home currency, it makes it more expensive to buy in the future than the current prevailing spot rate. However, the fact that foreign costs and receipts are known exactly in advance is an important benefit in that uncertainty is removed.

Furthermore, knowing in advance the costs of foreign currency purchases or the revenues to be received as a result of foreign currency sales can allow a company to put these details into its calculations when formulating brochure prices. The company, therefore, protects itself against the risk of adverse currency movements between the time it makes the forward contract and the time the foreign currency actually needs to be delivered or received at some future date.

This can be illustrated by referring again to the Stateside example. At the start of the season, Stateside has estimated that in June, for instance, payments exceed receipts by $1.1 million. That is, there is a net exposure of this amount in June. There are three ways in which this shortfall can be met:

(i) The company could purchase the necessary US dollars now and retain them on deposit earning interest until required. This necessitates the immediate availability of sterling to pay for the US dollars and ties the money up in a foreign currency until it is needed.

(ii) The company could leave the transaction until the US dollars are required in June. This would, however, leave the company open to the risk of an adverse movement in exchange rates. If, for instance, the US$/£ rate is now $1.75 (in late February when the forecast cash flow was drawn up) and this rate it is assumed is maintained until June, the US dollars would cost the company 1,100,000/1.75 = £628,571. If, however, the rate between US dollars and sterling fluctuates, so the rate had moved to say $1.55 (quite possible in the timescale), the US dollars would cost 1,100,000/1.55 = £709,677, that is, an additional cost of £81,106. In an industry such as travel and tourism, where 10 per cent profit margins are commonplace, an adverse rate movement such as that outlined above of some 13 per cent could completely eradicate all profits.

(iii) The company could arrange a forward foreign exchange contract with a bank. The bank would, for instance, arrange to sell US dollars to the company at US$/£1.74 on 1st June. This transaction would cost US $ 1,100,000/1.74 = £632,184, that is, £3,613 more than if the current or spot exchange rate had been applied. However, in this case the company would have paid for the certainty that, whatever the prevailing rate might be on 1st June, it could nevertheless purchase its requirements at the agreed rate and that no funds need to be transferred until that date.

Forward cover is, however, an acceptable means of covering exposure only where there is a reasonable degree of certainty as to the size and timing of foreign currency receipts and payments. Nevertheless, it is usually taken out on the basis of forecasts which will almost certainly turn out to be wrong (especially given the volatility of travel and tourism demand). Therefore, in order to deal with this problem and to introduce a degree of flexibility, other ways have been developed to cover foreign exchange exposure, most notably foreign currency options.

Foreign Currency Options

A foreign currency option can be described as a method by which the buyer has the right, but is not obliged, to buy or sell a certain quantity of a currency at a specified rate of exchange *(the exercise price)* within a certain limited time or at the end of that period. Thus, the primary difference between a currency option and a forward contract is the absence of the obligation to buy or sell the currency once the option contract is entered into. This facility gives the contract a greater degree of flexibility, since if cash flows fail to materialize, then the contract can be allowed to lapse without being exercised; that is, no currency is exchanged. Additionally, if rates move in a favourable direction, then the contract can also be allowed to lapse. The company can take advantage of the favourable rate through the purchase of the currency needed at the time it is required.

The increased flexibility of foreign currency options also makes them more expensive than forward contracts but, in industries such as travel and tourism that often have highly volatile and unpredictable cash flows, the increased flexibility may be highly desirable for atleast a part of the cover taken out.

In the Stateside example, the cover taken out (whether in the form of forward contracts or options), is shown. The difference between the net cash flow and the cover represents the proportion of the cash flow remaining at risk from exchange rate movements. For instance, in the example, Stateside needs to pay $1,100,000 in June of which $900,000,or 82 per cent, has been purchased (forward contracts and options), leaving $200,000 at risk from adverse currency movements.

The meaning of the risks arising from transaction exposure, often referred to as *hedging* the risk, can be illustrated by looking at the approach of two companies, British Airways and Thomson.

The Management of Translation Exposure

Translation exposures are different to transaction exposures in that they represent potential changes in the profitability of a company. Only when assets are sold or when liabilities are settled do these risks directly affect profitability. However, translation exposure can lead to very large changes in the size of a company's reserves and so most companies attempt to manage the total size of their translation exposure in some way.

The most common method of managing translation risks is by *matching* currency assets and liabilities, so that a company has equal amounts of assets and liabilities denominated in a particular foreign currency. As a result, the assets and liabilities are translated at the same rate and, consequently, the effects of a revaluation of assets and liabilities offset each other. If, for example, Hilton decided to build a hotel in Germany (an asset) the company, might may finance it by borrowing in local currency, namely euros. The euros borrowing, which would be a liability on the balance sheet, would be translated into pounds sterling for the accounts at the same rate as the hotel. Consequently, an increase or decrease in the viable of the hotel is offset by a corresponding increase or decrease in the value of borrowings. Also, the stream of earnings from the hotel can be use to repay the interest on the loan.

Another method of managing translation exposure could be through the use of forward contracts. The method of management is often viewed as being inappropriate, since contracts have to taken out for a specified period of time, (the maturity of the contract), whereas the assets or liability that is to be covered by the contract may have no known maturity date. That is, it is not known when the asset will be sold or the liability will be settled, and the risk realised.

The Management of Economic/Political Exposure

Since economic or political exposure is difficult to measure and forecast, it is also difficult to manage effectively. Such risk can, of course, be avoided entirely if a company declines to trade internationally, but this is rarely an option in travel and tourism.

The main method of managing the risk that can be employed is through diversifying the product and, thus, spreading the potential risks. A company will normally seek to have a balanced portfolio of products that cover different countries and currencies diversifying products in such a way lessens exposure to any one country or currency. If, for instance, in the case of a company that sold holidays to Croatia, the company also sold holidays to other parts of the Mediterranean, only part of the business would be affected if hostilities were to break out in Croatia.

In managing the economic risks, British Airways Annual Report and Accounts states that exchange rates can affect demand for services, especially form lesisure travellers whose decision whether and where to travel may alter a result of exchange rate movements. While it is not possible to quantify this effect, British Airways does monitor exchange rate movements in an attempt to antipate likely changes in the pattern of demand'.

Foreign Exchange Risk Management Strategies

Different companies implement very different strategies for dealing with the various risks described. The reasons for these differences on how to manage the risks stem, fundamentally, from management attitudes to taking risk. Some company managers as *risk averse* in their attitudes to taking risks, in that they will attempt to cover all foreign exchange exposure, Conversely, other managers may accept risks, duty to either a lack of understanding or to a readiness to speculate in the hope of gaining increased profitability from favourable foreign exchange rate movements.

Three strategic options can be considered by management in relation to taking our cover against foreign exchange exposure:

Doing Nothing

A firm my be unaware of the risks or the opportunities for reducing the risks. This may well be the case, for instance, with small tour operators who may worry about the operational aspects of the business to the exclusion of the financial risks. Attentively, the firm may take the view that exchange rates will remain unchanged or move in its favour. Effectively, such a firm would be said to be speculating.

Covering Everything

This is the only way to avoid all risk, but the total costs involved in terms of commissions to banks, premiums and collateral may be substantial. However, once the cover has been taken out, and the costs are known, they can then be included as part of the calculation for working out holidays costs.

Selectively Cover

By hedging only a proportion of the total risk, total costs can be reduced, for example, 70 per cent of transaction exposure. This strategy, covers the majority of the risk whilst leaving some room to benefit from favourable exchange rate movements should they occur. It also allows for errors in forecasting.

Cash Management

Travel and tourism companies make profits from their operations, such as selling accommodation, holidays, airline tickets and so on. However, they also drive substantial revenue from investing the cash that they receive from their customers. Indeed, in some cases, it represents the major source of income to companies in the industry. Cash management is concerned with the investing of cash surpluses and financing of cash shortages. During the course of trading, companies often generate *surplus* cash for which there is no current requirement. This cash surplus can be invested in order to obtain income in the form of interest receivable. At other times, however, even the most successful of companies may encounter periods of cash shortage during which cash has to borrowed and interest paid. The task of a *cash management* is to manage the cash in such a way so as to maximise the amount of interest receivable and minimise the amount of interest payable.

All companies have a need to hold cash or have the ability to borrow cash. Cash is used to pay creditors (suppliers) which for a tour operator, for instance, might include airlines, hotels, ground handing agents, and travel agents. This cash expenditure is used to provide a service, such as a holiday, to coustomers.

The Importance of Cash Management in Travel and Tourism

An important feature of travel and tourism products is that, usually, a full cash payment is received for the product before it is provided. For instance, the holiday business generates substantial positive cash flows as passengers traditionally pay in advance, while the holiday companies themselves pay their suppliers in arrears. This is in sharp contrast to other sectors of industry, such as manufacturing, where the product normally has to produced before it is sold to the customer and cash is received by the company. This feature of travel and tourism has a highly significant effect on company cash flows. Cash management is, consequently, one of the most important aspects of financial management in many travel and tourism businesses, with many companies within the sector holding large amounts of surplus cash for periods of the year. The income earned on these surplus cash balances is important. Indeed, in a business where trading margins are often low (or even negative), interest income is often a vital source of income. Taking the Airtours Group (which includes Airtours Tour Operations, Going Places travel agencies and the airline Airtours International) as an example, profit figures reveal substantial interest income even over a period of relatively low interest rates (Table 2).

Table 2 : Airtours profits (£mn), 1999 and 2000.

	2000	*1999*
Profit from operations	38.0	125.9
Bank Interest receivable	38.2	40.7
Operating profit and interest receivable	76.2	166.6

Source : Airtours plc Annual Report and Accounts.

Table 2 illustrates the significance of interest income and, hence of cash management to a company such as Airtours. In both years, interest income was highly important to overall group profitability (although interest expenses were also incurred on loans and lease agreements). In 1999 and 2000, the group had significant amounts of cash and bank deposits amounting to £554.2m and £793.3m respectively.

The pattern of earnings demonstrated by Airtours is repeated throughout the travel and tourism industry. Hence, the importance of, in effect, 'making money out of money', as well as from the operations of the business, should not be under- estimated. David Crossland, Airtours Chairman, speaking on the publication of his company's 1992 results in January 1993, gave an indication of the significance of this area of management to his company. There is, says Crossland (1993).

> *a degree of seasonality to this cash flow, but even at its lowest point in February 1992. Airtours' net cash balance did not fall below 65 million. Effective cash management is therefore a very important part of managing the business.*

Seasonality of Cash Flow

Travel and tourism has one of the most highly seasonal patterns of demand for any product or service, with less variation than the demand for Christmas cards or air conditioners, but more than nearly all high value individual purchases. This seasonality is largely due to climate, but is also related to factors such as school holidays, festivals and historic travel patterns.

Seasonality of demand for the product leads to a highly seasonal pattern of cash inflows and outflows. Consequently, at some times of the year, companies often have large surplus cash balances to invest whilst, at other time only small amounts of cash may be available to invest or it may even be necessary to borrow in order to meet cash requirements. If we take, as an example, a typically UK tour operator selling mass-market package holidays largely to Europe, the company is greatly affected by the seasonality of the product which directly affects its cash management. Such an operator may have a number of operating characteristics:

- The bulk of holidays sold would be summer sun with the season lasting from April to September, but with the peak months being July and August during school holidays.
- Summer sun holidays are typically booked in there distinct periods:

  the early booking period starting in August or September, when a significant number of people book. This applies especially to families, and these who are tied to taking holidays between certain dates, or are trying to take advantage of particular offers such as 'free child places', or low deposits.

  the post Christmas period form January to March which is usually the large *booking* period, and during which customers may be targeted with a second edition of brochure.

  the late booking period, from April onwards, which become increasingly *significant* in recent years, and may be a time of intense competition as operators try to sell remaining capacity and vary prices in order to do so.
- Many tour operators have attempted to widen their range of activities, and reduce the effects of seasonality, by, for instance, introducing winter sun and skiing programmes. The winter sun season normally lasts from October to April, whilst the skiing season normally lasts from December to April with peaks in February and at Easter. In most cases, the combined size of these programmes is far smaller than the summer programme, representing perhaps 25 per cent of the summer programme in terms of receipts. Booking for the winter sun and skiing programmes are taken throughout the summer and autumn, but the winter ski programme in particular is subject to a great deal of late booking in late autumn and early winter as customers wait to see what snow conditions are likely for the season.
- The tour operator will have a number of seasonal costs such as airline fuel, staff working at resorts, and accommodation charges. However, the tour operator will also have a high level of costs that have to be met

throughout the year, such as the costs of head office staff, aircraft, and computer facilities.

The characteristics of the tour operating business outlined above have certain implications for cash management. Cash builds up and declines in a seasonal way and, therefore, the cash position of a typical tour operator will vary greatly over the course of a normal years

The cash flow profile shown in Figure 7.4 is, perhaps, typical of a mass tour operator in a normal year. It shows that during certain times of the year, particularly the first five months of the calendar year, large surplus cash balances are free to be invested until the cash is needed to pay bills during the summer season and for the remainder of the year. The size and timing of the cash balances and the interest to be earned from the invested balances will vary from year to year, since the profile of bookings and level of interest rates also vary from year to year.

The period of greatest risk for many travel and tourism companies, however, usually comes in the autumn and winter. Cash balances have been run down as seasonal payments have been made during the preceding summer season and the bulk of bookings for the subsequent season have yet to be made. The position is often exacerbated by companies offering favourable payments terms to customers whereby a low initial deposit is required and, as a result, companies often have to rely on bank support to help them through this period. The problem may be compounded, however, if the early summer booking period for the forthcoming season and winter ski and sun bookings are poor and post Christmas bookings are delayed.

In a case where a bank (or other party) fails to lend the necessary support, insolvency is the inevitable result. Insolvency, (the inability to pay bills as they become due), has often befallen companies in this sector when revenue from expected bookings has failed to materialise. When a company reaches an insolvent position, it normally leads to the company's failure and liquidation. A company can sometimes survive for many years without making profits or making very low levels of profit but, if they run out of cash, it is difficult for them to survive become employees and creditors must be paid. Many travel and tourism companies routinely rely on banks to provide short term finance for a part of the year, but it is when these negative case balances are larger or more prolonged than usual and banks feel unable to provide finance that problems occur.

Cash Forecasting

An essential starting point for efficient cash management is to produce cash flow forecasts. Cash flow needs to be carefully planned and monitored so that the necessary action can be taken when cash surpluses of deficits are indicated. The main purposes of cash flow forecasts are :

- To plan/forecast the organisation's cash shortages or cash surpluses over the forecast period.
- To monitor how actual cash inflows and outflows vary from forecast cash flow.

Detailed cash flow forecasts should, ideally, be produced for all travel and tourism businesses and these forecasts should be continually updated as and when new information becomes available. The cash flow forecast involves the calculation of future cash inflows (receipts) and cash outflows (costs), but it is usually easier for a business to forecast its costs than its revenuers.

Costs are made up of major items such as salary costs, administrative costs, accommodation costs and transportation costs. Money of these costs can be estimated in advance with some degree of accuracy since they are subject to contracts agreed before the costs are incrurred. Further more, uncertainties with regard to costs can be minimised by management actions. For instance, the costs of foreign currency and jet fuel purchases can established in advance through purchasing forward contracts. In the case of receipts, however, the forecasting process is much more difficult and usually less accurate since, ultimately, the forecast depends upon the attitudes of customers. Customers can be fickle and their attitudes are influenced by a range of factors and events, such as wars, political instability, recession, unemployment and mortgage rates. Nevertheless, despite the inherent difficulties and inaccuracies involved in forecasting, it is an important management activity and an essential pre-requistic for successful cash management.

The forecast shown indicates that, for nine months of the year, the company involved has a positive net cash balance. That is, it has a surplus of cash over and above the amount that is necessary in order to pay its bills. For the remaining three months, the company has a negative net cash balance. That is, it has a deficit of cash and must find other sources of cash in order to pay its bills as they become due. The questions posed by such a cash flow are:

- How are the cash surpluses to be invested?
- How are the cash deficits to be financed?

Principles of Investing Surpluses and Financing Deficits

It surplus cash is available, an investment decision is required. This decision will be based on a consideration of the pertinent facts :

- The size of the amounts available.
- The period for which the cash is available.
- Whether there is a possibility that the cash will be required sooner than forecast in order to make unexpected payments.
- A knowledge of the competing institution with which funds can be placed and the terms and rates that they are prepared to pay in *bidding* for the cash.

The aim of the investment should be to secure the maximum interest possible consistent with a satisfactory level of risk and the required level of liquidity (Samuels, Wikes and Brayshaw 1990). Liquidity is the ability to access the funds invested as and when required.

Similarly, a cash deficit requires a decision as to how the deficit is to be financed. The decision will also depend on the length of time financing is required, the size and certainty of the financing requirement and knowledge of the terms and rates upon which cash will be *offered*.

Investment of Cash Surpluses

Cash can be invested and deficits financed in a number of ways. As with most from of investment, returns on the investment of surplus cash will be higher if the level of risk accepted is higher, if the funds are invested for long periods and if a longer period of notice to uplift the funds is accepted. That is, the consideration of investment in detail is concerned with risk, maturity dates and liquidity.

There are many ways in which short term funds can be invested that very in relation to risk, maturity dates and liquidity. Four of these methods of investing short-term cash surpluses at relatively low levels of risk are now outlined.

Call Accounts

Call accounts are similar to personal deposit accounts and are provided by all banks. They provide flexible accounts whereby cash can be called upon, should it be needed, at short notice, such as on the same day, with one or two days' notice or sometimes with one weeks' notice. In return for the flexibility, a fairly low interest rate is applied to such accounts and the rate of interest varies in accordance with money market rate movements.

Term Deposits

All major banks takes cash on term (or time) deposits in amounts from about £50,000 upwards. A term deposit is an investment of a fixed amount of cash for a fixed period of time (i.e., there is a set maturity date for the investment) and at a dixed rate of interest. Consequently, the cash is tied up for a set period of time so that this form of investment offers a low level of liquidity and requires a good knowledge of expected future cash flows. It the cash was to be required at an earlier date, the deposit could in some circumstances be *broken* (received back earlier than the maturity date), but a penalty would be applied. The rate of interest earned on term deposits is fixed at the time the deposit is made, but is like to be substantially higher than on call accounts due to the lack of flexibility with such a deposit. Term deposits can be made for periods ranging from overnight to several years.

In addition to the large British commercial banks, there are over 400 foreign banks in the City of London that quote competitively for term deposits. Therefore, the market for such cash deposits is large and extremely active (especially in the major currencies), and it pays a company to shop around for the best rates available at the time.

The term deposit represents the primary investment method used by most Travel and Tourism businesses. Airtours, for instance, 'invests surplus funds on term deposits with mainstream banks but, as the rates decline, it has indicated that it is examining other areas of investment for these funds'.

Certificates of Deposit

A certificate of deposite (CD) is a certificate acknowledging a deposit issued by a bank. These are issued for periods ranging from three months to five years on amounts usualy over £50,000 and carry a fixed rate of interest which is likely to be at a rate similar to a term deposit of the same maturity. The main advantage of the CD over a term deposit is that it is a *negotiable* form of investment and is, consequently, more liquid. That is, if the investment needs to be realised, the CD can be sold to another party at a price agreed through negotiation. In London and other financial centres, there are large secondary markets for CDs so that buyers can usually be found if CDs need to be sold.

Commercial Paper

Large companies with good credit raings can raise short-term finance by issuing commercial paper. Only larger companies can normally raise finance in this way, but all companies can use the market to invest during the short term. Commercial paper represents a promise to pay back the investment by the company that issues the commercial paper at a fixed maturity date (typically between 7 days and three months), in return for cash deposited.

One company can invest in another's commercial paper. For instance, Thymosin might purchase Shell Oil Company commercial paper. The *instrument* is like a certificate of deposit, negotiable, so that the investment can be sold if it is no longer required, thereby providing flexibility. The market for commercial paper has grown considerably in recent years and interest rates (agreed at the time of purchase) tend to be slightly higher than those available on term deposits or CDs, reflecting a slightly higher level of risk.

Financing of Cash Deficits

At certain times of the year, many travel and tourism organisations have cash deficits which have to be financed in some way. Cash deficits can be variously financed but, before resorting to external sources for the necessary finance, there are a number of broad methods of easing temporary cash shortages that a company will probably wish to consider. Some of these measures might include the following :

Postponing Capital Expenditure

Some capital expenditure items are more important and urgent than others. It might be imprudent to postpone expenditure on fixed assets (such as new aircraft) which are needed for the growth and development of the business. It may, however, be possible to postpone some capital expenditure without serious consequences, such as the routine replacement of company cars.

Accelerating Cash Inflows which would Otherwise be Expected in Period

The most obvious way of bringing forward cash inflows would be to press debtors (customers) for earlier payment. This might be achieved, for instance, through early payment discounts or through providing commission incentives to agents to collect and pass on cash from customers at an earlier date. Such actions must, however, be seriously considered before they are taken, since they might result in some loss of goodwill with customers.

Decelerating Cash Outflows

Longer credit might be taken from suppliers, by taking longer to pay hotels, airlines and so on. The longer credit might be the result of a negotiated agreement or a decision may be taken unilaterally to take longer to pay bills. Such a policy might run a serious risk of incurring bad feeling among suppliers and make renewing contracts difficult or expensive.

Reversing Past Investment Decisions

Some assets are less crucial to a business than others, so that if severe cash flow problems occur, the option of selling off investments or property might have to be considered.

Although internal method of avoiding cash deficits may be implemented, most companies will need to obtain short-term finance from external sources at some time. This need for short-term external finance in either because they do not want to use the internal methods, on because there is still a cash shortfall after the internal methods have been exhausted. There are many methods of obtaining short-term finance for a business including short term loans, factoring, commercial pager, sale and lease-back of assets. By far the most popular form of short-term finance in the UK is provided by banks in the form of overdrafts. The overdraft has a number of characteristics:

- It is a very flexible form of finance with limits on borrowing set by negotiation.
- It given enterprises the scope to move freely within these limits and only be charged on the outstanding debit balance (although small commitment fees on undrawn balances are often charged).
- Overdrafts can generally be arranged quickly.
- The rate of interest charged normally fluctuates with market rates.
- Technically, the overdraft is 'repayable (to the bank) on demand', but usually some notice is given of repayment.

The overdraft is a very flexible and commonly used method of short term fainancing. However, the fact that the finance can be recalled on demand, or at least at short notice by banks, has often given cause for concern and sometimes has led to the insolvency of travel and tourism companies. For instance, the failure of Barclays Bank to agree to an annual overdraft facility to provide finance for the slack winter period for Exchange Travel (then the country's seventh largest travel agency group), was the event that pushed the company 'over the edge' into failure is September 1990.

Good cash management practice involves the building of a relationship between the bank and the company so that the bank fully understand the company's financing requirements. Requests for overdrafts do not then come as a surprise to the back but are seen as a normal part of the company's operations. Consequently, overdrafts are often renewed from one period to the next or agreed on a annual basis without problems.

Conclusion

This chapter has considered two aspects of financial management that are of vital importance to an international business such as travel and tourism, namely foreign exchange management and cash management. It has argued that these two areas (that are normally seen as being part of the treasury area of financial management) are vital to the well being of most travel and tourism companies. These two areas of management concern are important primarily because :

- In the case of foreign exchange management, the risks stemming from movements in foreign exchange currency rates are so large that if they are not managed in an appropriate fashion, profits derived from the operations of the business can be completely eliminated and the business as a whole placed at risk.
- In the case of cash management, the short term investing of cash balances is often a major source of income for travel and tourism companies, so that it is imperative that these balances are managed in an active way and invested at competitive market rates, thereby maximising profitability, whilst cash deficits need to be planned for and financed appropriately.

These two areas of travel and tourism management have received little attention in the travel and tourism literature, but their importance to the profitability and well being of many companies in the sector should not be underestimated.

6

Cooperation Strategies in Tourism Industry

More on Co-Operation in Tourism

Statistical support is one of the major tools needed for a better understanding of the tourism sector. The finalisation of a new Statistical Regulation in the field of tourism is in an advanced state and it is expected to enter in force in 2010. At the same time, the Commission, together with Member States and in collaboration with OECD and the World Tourism Organisation, is promoting the introduction of TSA (Tourism Satellite Account) in Member States. TSA is a statistical accounting framework in the field of tourism to measure the goods and services according to international standards of concepts, classifications and definitions, which allow valid comparisons from country to country in a consistent manner. A complete TSA contains detailed production accounts of the tourism industry and their linkages to other industries, employment, capital formation and additional nonmonetary information on tourism.

Enhancing the visibility of European tourism is another of our main goals. To draw attention to the value, diversity and shared characteristics of European tourist destinations, and to promote destinations where the economic growth objective is pursued in such a way as to ensure the social, cultural and environmental sustainability of tourism, the European Commission is running the European Destinations of Excellence (EDEN) preparatory action. Some of the main aims of such a preparatory action are enhancing visibility of the emerging European tourist destinations of excellence, especially the lesser known, and creating awareness of Europe's tourist diversity and quality. The Commission also intends highlighting the richness and diversity of European tourism through its Calypso programme, which seeks to facilitate tourism exchanges in Europe. Finally, again in the direction of cooperation with other actors of the tourism sector, and with the aim of strengthening European tourism, the Commission proposed an operational framework through the organisation of a number of events. Such events are deemed important in order to improve the interface between European tourism stakeholders. One of the measures provided are an annual European Tourism Forum, which normally brings together more than 300 leading representatives from the tourism industry, civil society, European Institutions, national and regional authorities dealing with tourism, and international organisations to discuss the challenges of the sector. Every year the Forum focuses on specific themes of interest.

E-Collaboration: A Universal Key to Solve Fierce Competition in Tourism Industry?

The development of Internet technology and the dramatic spread of its use throughout the world in the past decade brought business into a new stage, a stage known 'e-time'.

Before 'e' time, tourism industry players mainly maintained workable vertical relationships with its suppliers and their sales force (Appleman & Go 2002). The walls of each company's office were not just physical bricks; they were also the spiritual boundaries isolating the company from its horizontal neighbours who do similar business. While drivers in the business environment such as globalization, regionalization, information technology and e-commerce decreased barrier effect of brick walls (Timothy 2003). Consumers are becoming more experienced. Competition between organisations by throwing bricks to each other can no longer lead to success (Stern & Hicks 2000).

This article starts with relevant definitions of e-collaboration and the description of the change in the business environment and then analyses these motivations, advantages and the problems of e-collaboration in the tourism industry. Multinatinational enterprise (MNE) and small business/tourism organisations are tending to adapt e-collaborative strategies. Gartner (2001) predicts that 70% of firms will have a coherent e-business strategy within a year. However, this is not a universal key if being used improperly. Addressing the theories of collaboration and e-business in other industries and trying to find a way of applying them to today's tourism industry players to create and guide thriving e-collaboration strategies is the main aim of this article.

E-collaboration bridges national borders and continents. E-collaboration and collaborative systems bring geographically dispersed teams together, supporting communication, coordination and cooperation. Indeed, it has become a cornerstone of global competition (Doz & Hamel 1998; Timothy 2003). It is a logical and timely response to the quick change in the economic and IT world and split organizations into two competition divisions: one for the global market, one for the future development.

Relevant Definitions

E-Business

This field of activity is relatively young and evolving rapidly, and as such no single definition of the term has become accepted as the universal norm (Clegg *et al* 2001). E-business was initially limited to the financial transactions online. It was coined with a meaning of conducting business on the Internet by IBM back in 1997 as part of an advertising campaign. For the purposes of this essay, both business-to-business (B2B) and business-to-consumer (B2C) transactions and relationships are considered. Thus, e-business here is defined as the transaction of commercial activities on global open networks between an ever-increasing number of corporate and individual participants (Richmond *et al.* 1998).

Collaboration

According to Cambridge Advanced Learner's Dictionary (2003), collaboration means working jointly with others or together for some purpose or achieve the same thing. Words like strategic alliance, collaborative partnership, collaborative form, collaboration, partnership, and coalition are interchangeable utilized (Fyall & Spyriadis 2003). E-collaboration is an extension from the old collaboration type in e-age. It is Internet-based cooperation/collaboration with exchange of information, materials, or cash among entities (Brown & Sappenfield 2003).

The Changing of the Business Environment

Information is the "lifeblood" of tourism. Since the tourism products can not be pre-tested, the access to accurate, timely and relevant information is therefore essential to consumers. Before the spread of Internet, telephone, fax, letter and face-to-face meeting were the main communication channels between suppliers and buyers. The generation, gathering, processing, application and communication of information was time consuming (O'Connor *et al* 2002).

Consumers almost completely relied on representation and description to make an appropriate choice (Go and Pine 1995). Intermediaries played a very important role between disciplines and end-customers. Collaborations between horizontal tourism players were very rare.

While technology can act as a 'creator, enhancer, focal point and/or destroyer of the tourism experience' as O'Connor (2002 p332) indicated, the development of IT brought the business world a revolution of electronic. Business-related "dotcom" Web sites emerged all over the virtual world. A matching between buyer and seller was set up. Andy Grove, the chairman of Intel, predicted in 1999 that, within five years, all companies will be Internet companies or they will not exist.

As web-based technologies expanded, core back-office processes, including order management, procurement, logistics, financial management, and supply chain planning was incorporated (Gould 2004). The barriers and distance competitors were reduced. Information flows among the client, intermediaries and each of the suppliers involved in serving the client's needs. New relationships with customers, new relationships between competitors and suppliers and buyers, new business process, new information and communications technologies came into being and empowered employees are required.

Motivations for Collaboration

Globalization and regionalisation are emerging worldwide. This macro environment stimulates the development of IT; and the development of IT enhances the integration inversely. Hastings (1993) states that the need for 'quality, as well as the high costs and complexity of servicing global markets' is forcing organisations into collaborating with their clients, their suppliers and with their competitors in many new ways.

The power of IT allows information to be managed more effectively, and transported worldwide almost instantly (Frew and Pringle 1995). The physical boundaries between brick walls or territories can't block the information flow. Smaller countries, organisations, in particular, can benefit by gaining access to a much larger market than that in their own territories; large economic regions become available to them for sale of their goods and services (Timothy 2003). From horizontal view, market is limited, the more ratio one company occupies, the less other companies occupies. But competitors in well-matched strength always exist. It's time for antagonists to begin to use the bricks to build something useful instead of throwing bricks at one another (Stern & Hicks 2000). Collaboration offers a way to pursue business development, revenue increase, cost reductions in promotions and marketing and enhance market image and reputation (Fyall & Spyriadis 2003). A partnership of collaboration is a tailored business relationship based on mutual trust, openness, shared risk and shared rewards that yields a competitive advantage, resulting in business performance greater than would be achieved by the firms individually.

In an executive report, META pointed that by 2001/02, high-performing enterprises will recognize the value of business collaboration to achieve flexibility, speed, and agility. By 2004, more than 30% of G2000 companies will have developed a collaborative competency and will use collaborative tools to extract superior value from their collaborative efforts (Passori 2000).

Types of Collaboration

There are three types of collaboration: vertical relationships, horizontal relationships and diagonal relationships. (Fyall & Spyriadis 2003) This is a classifying according to the different structure of collaboration and could suit *International Business Research* October 2008

Vertical Relationship

Vertical relationship is the collaboration between suppliers and buyers e.g. travel operator and travel agency, travel agency and hotel. There is growing emphasis in modern supply chain literature on the importance of forming collaborative strategic partnerships with select trading partners (Kolluru & Meredith 2001). The official site of Scotland's tourism board is one example. The links to travel agencies which sales its products can be found in this website. It offers you the service of journey booking while not owning a travel agency itself.

Horizontal Relationship

Horizontal relationship is the collaboration between competing companies selling similar products or services, e.g. hotel and hotel (Bernal *et al* 2002). In tourism industry, horizontal collaboration happens more often than other two types with the spread of IT. This collaboration can be either inter-organisational which refers to licensing, franchising, sub-contracting and etc under one brand or alliance between different brands. Whichever horizontal collaboration the tourism industry players join, they are separated organisations by law. Orbitz.com, for instance, was initially started by five airlines-American, Continental, Delta, Northwest and United to serve customers better and only sell flight tickets of these five owners. To gain more "click", it encourages other airlines to sell their tickets through its website. At the same time, other airlines are seeking for multi-distribution channels to explore market. Now Orbitz's inventory has hundreds of choices of airlines for customers.

Marriott International has just signed a deal with Hotels.com. As part of the agreement, Marriott will have a direct link to the websites from its own central reservation systems. It will make its inventory of hotel rooms available to the sites.

Diagonal Relationship

Diagonal relationship is the relation where companies in different industries and sectors are working jointly. It's a dynamic structure and is growing follow closely to the other two types of e-collaboration (Brenner 2004).

Grandheritage.com can illustrate this type of collaboration. Grandheritage.com is an online hotel booking website, but it has collaboration with Currency Converter, BBC Weather, Multi Map, British Tourist Authority (a site for events & general information), British Airports Authority, London Transport, UK Genealogy (a site for tracing UK ancestry), Festivals.com (festivals and events in Europe), BITOA (The British Incoming Tour Operators Association), (suppliers of water to hotels), and (low cost car hire). The collaboration is not just limited to the vertical supplier and buyer's relationship and horizontal relationship with competitors, but extends to other industries.

The Influence of E-Collaboration

Advantages

Wider market and better competitive position. Collaborative partners share common reservation system and customer databases. In this way tourism destinations, hotels, travel agencies and etc. can access to worldwide markets despite of the territory boundaries (Fyall & Spyriadis 2003). The collaborated members can market as a whole sometimes (Teye 2000). Hospitality industry is witnessing the growth of technology-based collaboration best. An example of this is the Hilton International (UK based unit of Ladbroke Plc.) and Hilton Hotel Corporation (US based) alliance.

These companies have entered into a relationship that involves sharing customer databases throughout the world. According to Hilton, the objective of this collaboration is to grow the brand to be able to compete on a global basis. Hotels.com is another good example for global market. It is one of the fastest growing hotel booking sites on the Internet. It offers savings of up to 70% off regular hotel rates in some of the world's most popular and expensive cities.

What's more, the collaboration of the hotels guarantees traveller a room when cities are sold out. As Bruce Wolff, Marriott's senior vice president of sales and e-commerce strategy, said on Marriott's collaboration with expedia and hotel.com:' We want to ensure the travelers have access to Marriott properties no matter how they prefer to plan and book travel.'

This advantage is especially helpful to small and medium size tourism industry players. Collaboration through Internet enables them to source components and raw materials so as to widen their market and reputation (Gani 2001).

E-collaboration offers the opportunity for companies to increase the numbers of potential suppliers, and for smaller companies to reach a larger trans-national client base (Leadbetter 1999) 'Through a close collaboration between hotels, restaurants, tourism and commerce, we can cater for anyone who wants to arrange their meeting or conference in Kristianstad or the surrounding area,' says Gunnel Ahlbeck of Turism Kristianstad (2003). When cross-border collaboration and cooperation in tourism promotion are formed, the global competitive advantage is likely to increase (Timothy 2003).

Value Creation

Collaboration between competing firms may create favourable conditions for "inter-partner" learning (Dussage *et al.* 1999), allowing one firm to acquire capabilities that they lack from a partner, particularly when partners from different geographic region. Each partner will bring its product markets, technology, and experience to the collaborated group. A high-speed search and accurate results can be offered to customers with the sharing resources contributed by collaborators (O'Connor *et al* 2002). This caters for the increasing business-to-business or business-to-consumer demands for products and services with a wider resource of combination of each partner's limited resource.

What's more, value creation and its role in business network relationships is becoming an area of increasing interest (Blankenburg-Holm *et al.* 1998 in Bernal 2002) and enables firms to focus on combining internal and external resources in innovative ways.

Inventories Reduction

The closer, long-term, collaborative buyer-supplier relationships, i.e. partnerships, are enabled through seamless integration and transfer of information up and down the chain (Kolluru & Meredith 2001). Strategic SCM can lower inventory risks and costs, improve customer service and satisfaction, increase customer retention and more effective marketing. (Horvath 2000) As distributors enter the same web, data on sales and inventories are received; forecasts are much easier to be made. With the forecasting and planning ability's improvement, collaborators will get benefit to know what to do next clearly.

For example, Depkon's Hilton properties use a software application called Birch Street that manages the procurement and inventory at the property level.

It allows the properties real-time access to suppliers' inventory. The sound e-collaboration makes the hotel managers focus on the day-to-day issues more and saves the hotel 8 percent to 15 percent (Higley 2004).

Better Communication

E-collaboration enhances inter-organizational relationships. Though reduction in face-to-face contact and an increase in the opportunities for dispersed or paperless offices and people-less factories that have proved to be largely unfounded (Clegg et al 2001), e-collaboration does allow managers/staff to share information dynamically and far more quickly than previously. It enhances the gain from face to face meetings and other types of communication.

Fewer Cultural Conflicts

As more collaborations are made, defining company culture is critical, especially when companies come from different countries. The social cultural environment will impact the company. While e-collaboration is based online, whether to customers or managers, it is more virtual than physical. Communicating while not working and meeting face to face day to day. Emotion and behavior interference will be less (Stern & Hicks 2000).

Key Problems

Collaboration offers a way out of the fierce competition but it is not a universal key. Without good understanding and preparation, e-collaboration can also damage business. Not all collaboration or alliances or cooperation are successful.

America's Tribune newspaper (2003) has reported a trend of hotel operators breaking away from their franchises and going it alone without big brand backing. The following are several key problems exist in e-collaborative relationship.

Unequal Resource Commitments

Perhaps the most critical thing in collaboration is the degree to which the partners' contributions are committed and complementary (Stern & Hicks2000).

Timothy (2000) pointed that the commitment on the part of individual nations to giving up absolute control in some areas is lack, because national interests nearly always outweigh cross-national interests when he talked out the collaboration between countries. It is a common problem throughout the world where collaboration is being undertaken no matter it is a horizontal collaboration, vertical collaboration or diagonal one.

Unbalanced Management and Power

Unbalanced management and power results from unequal commitment. But no party wants to be at a disadvantage in cooperation. The unbalanced situation sometimes leads to inefficient if dealt wrong.

Different Maintenance of Quality Standards between Partners

Every tourism industry player has different internal needs for different technological and organizational systems and external needs for connectivity and shareability of messages, data, applications and processes (Stern & Hicks 2000). But once collaborated, the reputation and services of each collaborator are bounded together. One comparatively worse website or service will lead to the poor impression of the whole group to customer. And also because of the collaboration of huge database, the difficulty of maintenance is increasing (Bernel *et al* 2002).

Losing the Opportunity for a Creative Solution

Problems are sometimes unavoidable no matter what product and what life stage. When an enterprise meets conflicts or problems entering a market, it might find its own way to solve itself. E-collaboration may need certain managers to negotiate with those who have been in the market and link their websites and database to bridge the markets.

Suggestions and Conclusions

E-collaboration is a very vital strategy for tourism industry players in today's business world. Vertical and horizontal e-collaboration is more often to see in tourism industry than diagonal collaboration. But this type of e-collaboration will be a trend when vertical and horizontal collaboration have developed well. Cooperation between different industries will enhance each other and help each industry's development.

Smartly using this strategy can avoid the fierce competition between hotels, travel agencies and travel operators. As discussed above, e-collaboration can help to widen market, enhance competitive position, add value, reduce cost, bridge communication and lessen cultural conflicts. It is a great strategy more SME to compete with stronger competitors. But Zaid Ismail (2003), senior director of the National Chamber of Commerce and Industry of Malaysia (NCCIM), said though many small and medium size companies have their own websites, not all of them are aware of the benefits of e-business and fully utilize this tool. Either to small business/tourism organisations or multinational enterprise, to take successful e-collaboration strategy to compete in the global market, the following suggestions should be considered:

- Choose your partner carefully. Every enterprise should know clearly its own strengths and weaknesses before collaborating, and then smartly look for partners that can fit its wants.
- Necessary information technology. The information that an organization communicates with its supply chain partners is among the most critical of its assets. Powerful, integrated collaborative technology is the backbone of an e-collaboration (Vlachopoulou and Manthou 2003). Protection must be provided against external threats and from internal abuse (Kolluru & Meredith 2001). The data that is shared between the partners and customers engaged in these different types of relationships varies widely in its criticality, thus requiring different levels of security.
- Managing the balance of power and dependence. Normally a partner who brings differentiating contributions of a

more sustainable nature — such as a leading brand— will enjoy a more sustained influence. And the smaller partner is comparably more dependent. The dependence comes from commitments. As the commitments are irreversible, more specific commitments should be done so that every partner is very clear about its role and contribution, for example, the service standard, price, credit policy, service level performance, response time, image and etc. The trust between partners should be well set up as the basis of enduring collaborative relationships.

- Monitoring the quality. Quality is the life core in any industry. Service, price, credit policy, response time, and legal issue warranties and so on detailed things should also be considered carefully. Online service and face-to-face service should be both monitored. Keeping a sustainable good quality can enhance customer's loyalty and then raise the company's reputation.
- Hiring intelligent and empowered employees. Managing e-collaboration will be more difficult than traditional management activities, as the systems become potentially more complex, more tightly coupled, and increasingly involve complex interrelations between people, organizations and technology (Timothy 2003). Companies need more than just good technology to make the most of the Internet (Cairncross 2000).

Evaluation can also not be forgotten while using e-collaboration strategy. Individually, jointly and publicly evaluation all are important to keep the process on its way to success.

This paper addresses the relevant theories on e-business and internet to the specific tourism industry. But as time and resources are limited, no particular case study is offered to support the researcher's ideas. E-trading is the industry witnesses the technology information development first and reacts first. The theories and practice in this industry can be studied more to contribute to tourism. A further research of comparing and analysing the similarities and differences between these two industries, especially the e-market place and online travel agencies can be carried out. What's more, the research of the trend of diagonal e-collaboration in tourism industry is also worth researching.

Interorganisational Collaboration in Tourism

Collaboration between organisations involved in the tourism industry is a widely established practice. Many of the benefits of such participation have been widely reported. For example, organisations have been known to co-ordinate their activities to cope with the turbulence and complexity of their environments, to solve environmentally-related problems, and to enhance sustainable development. Forming such relations, however, is not a simple process.

Frequently, difficulties are confronted. These difficulties derive from the complexity of the 'industry' for it actually involves a collection of businesses, from different sectors, all marketing travel-related services (Leiper, 1990). These tourism organisations, while diverse, are interdependent. This means that any developments or changes in one industry or firm will, in turn, affect another to a greater or lesser degree. To clearly understand the characteristics of this industry, Leiper (1979) suggested that we should view it as a system. This conceptualisation is laudable as it captures the highly interdependent nature of organisational relationships in tourism. Implicit in this systems explanation is the need for close organisational coordination if tourism activities are to succeed. Leiper (1979: 404) explains:

The behavioural element, (1) tourists, are represented leaving (2) generating regions, travelling to and staying in (3) destinations, and returning home. The tourist industry element is represented within all three (4) geographic elements. Also symbolic is the representation of part of the tourist element outside the (5) industrial element, signifying the partially industrialised characteristics of the process.

Propositions about Collaboration Environmental Forces

Growth in Tourism

Collaborative marketing was developed to take advantage of growth opportunities and in an attempt to gain sufficient return on investment for stakeholders in tourism development.

Demand Uncertainty

Any problem domain, such as demand uncertainty, of concern to all stakeholders that cannot be satisfactorily managed by a single organisation, will lead to the formation of collaborative marketing.

Growth of Tourism Organisations

The growth of any tourism organisations or associations will facilitate the development and/or initiation of larger-scale collaborations in tourism destination marketing.

Motives

Perceived Benefits : Collaboration will not occur unless two conditions are satisfied: (a) stakeholders share at least one common interest in relation to the proposed collaboration and (b) they recognise the individual and mutual benefits of being involved in collaboration.

Perceived Interdependence

Collaboration in tourism destination marketing requires a recognition of the high degree of interdependence. The formation of any collaboration is enhanced by an initiator or convenor who emphasises the shared responsibility of all stakeholders as well as the potential negative effects of a lack of collaboration in marketing destinations.

Extendedness of a Relationship

Stakeholders will be motivated to collaborate by their expectation of extendedness in a future relationship.

Commitment

Collaboration will require a certain degree of commitment between a firm and its partners.

Legitimacy

An organisation's motives to gain future recognition from other stakeholders is positively related to their decision to participate in collaborative marketing activities.

Trust

Collaboration will be enhanced when stakeholders have trust

and/or confidence of the tourism association's ability to market the destination as a whole.

Conditions

Organisational Factors

Organisations with a small budget will collaborate where their budget allows them room to manoeuvre.

Problem Domain

Domain focus and domain consensus facilitate the formation of collaboration. The degree to which this occurs is related to the degree of acceptance of other's claims to specific goals and functions.

The Referent Organisation

A convenor and/or bridging organisation are required to initiate and facilitate collaboration in tourism destination marketing. The role of the convenor is to identify and bring all legitimate stakeholders to the table.

Any effort to involve all stakeholders in the development of collaborative marketing in tourism is likely be thwarted by divergent stakeholder views.

e-Tourism

e-Tourism is a subset of Travel technology with a particular focus on the tourism industry. In June 2003, the United Nations Conference on Trade and Development, UNCTAD, established a Task Force on Sustainable Tourism for Development that proposes the use of the concept of e-tourism as part of a strategy to build sustainable and locally rooted tourism industries. The e-Tourism Initiative aims to promote ICT-driven growth through a participative strategy that includes networking and competitive collaboration for the tourism sector of developing countries.

e-tourism: An Innovative Approach for the small and Medium-Sized Tourism Enterprises (Smtes) in Korea

The definitions of tourism innovation (*e.g.* product, service and technological innovations) remains unclear, with the exception maybe of the Internet. New technologies can produce an essential contribution to tourism development. For tourism businesses, the Internet offers the potential to make information and booking facilities available to large numbers of tourists at relatively low costs. It also provides a tool for communication between tourism suppliers, intermediaries, as well as end-consumers. OECD (2000) revealed that the advent of Internet-based electronic commerce offers considerable opportunities for firms to expand their customer base, enter new product markets and rationalise their business. WTO (2001) also indicated that electronic business offers SMEs the opportunity to undertake their business in new and more cost-effective ways.

According to WTO, the Internet is revolutionising the distribution of tourism information and sales. An increasing proportion of Internet users are buying on–line and tourism will gain a larger and larger share of the online commerce market. Obviously, the Internet is having a major impact as a source of information for tourism. However, the SMTEs are facing more stringent impediments to the adoption of new information technology, in particular, e-business. Part of the problem relates to the scale and affordability of information technology, as well as the facility of implementation within rapidly growing and changing organisations. In addition, new solutions configured for large, stable, and internationally-oriented firms do not fit well for small, dynamic, and locally-based tourism firms.

Despite these challenges, SMTEs with well-developed and innovative Web sites can now have "equal Internet access" to international tourism markets. This implies equal access to telecom infrastructure, as well as to marketing management and education. According to a UN report (2001), "it is not the cost of being there, on the on-line market place, which must be reckoned with, but the cost of not being there." It is certain that embracing digital communication and information technology is no longer an option, but a necessity. Thus, one of the most important characteristics of electronic commerce is the opportunity and promise it holds for SMTEs to extend their capabilities and grow.

Recent Research on e-Commerce in Tourism Industry

The study of e-commerce in the tourism industry has emerged as a 'frontier area' for information technology. The literature on e-commerce in the tourism industry was critically reviewed with a view to developing a framework suitable for this study. E-commerce is defined as the process of buying and selling or exchanging products, services and information via computer networks including the Internet. However, adoption of Information and Communication Technologies (ICT) is only part of the story. In particular, network access costs, dissemination of information on electronic commerce, training, skill development and human resources provide big challenges for smaller companies.

The difficulty in addressing issues of trust and confidence also makes SMTEs more vulnerable than large firms to problems linked to authentication/certification, data security and confidentiality and the settling of commercial disputes.

However, a SME Electronic Commerce Study done by APEC reported that "Small and medium enterprises are significant players in business-to-business electronic commerce, which constitutes more than 80 percent of all e-commerce activities. SMEs that can demonstrate their capabilities to use e-commerce will have a competitive advantage in the e-commerce marketplace." Most research suggested that government plays an important role in facilitating the use of electronic commerce for the tourism industry and in increasing their ability to reap the benefits, (*e.g.* via awareness building and training programmes). Governments in partnership with the private sector should establish a more comprehensive and consistent policy approach to the tourism industry and electronic commerce, and apply evaluation mechanisms to assess what works and does not work (UN 2001, OECD, 2000, Korea Information Society Development Institute 2000, APEC-TEL 1999).

Key Factors for Successful e-Commerce for SMTEs

Research was performed to collect the secondary data regarding e-commerce for the tourism industry. Based on those data, a questionnaire was developed to get information on the challenges and opportunities faced by the tourism industry. The survey covered e-commerce activities, benefits, barriers and key success factors. It covered essentially the Korean SMTEs. SMTEs are defined as businesses that have 300 or fewer employees or sales from USD 2 million to 20 million, depending on the characteristics of business.

Benefits of e-Commerce for SMTEs

Respondents considered that the main benefits of e-commerce for tourism enterprises are 'providing easy access to information on tourism services,' 'providing better information on tourism services,' and 'providing convenience for customers'. This result implies that respondents are less aware of many other benefits of e-commerce, such as 'creating new markets,' 'improving customer services,' 'establishing interactive relationships with customers', 'reducing operating cost', 'interacting with other business partners', and 'founding new business partners'.

Barriers of e-Commerce for SMTEs

There are a number of barriers for SMTEs in adopting e-commerce in Korea. These barriers include 'limited knowledge of available technology,' 'lack of awareness,' 'cost of initial investment,' 'lack of confidence in the benefits of e-commerce,' and 'cost of system maintenance.' These barriers also include 'shortage of skilled human resources,' and 'resistance to adoption of e-commerce.' In terms of market situation, one might also mention 'insufficient e-commerce infrastructure,' and 'small e-commerce market size'.

Factors for Successful SMTEs E-Commerce Practices

The two main factors for conducting successful e-commerce are 'security of the e-commerce system' and 'user-friendly Web interface', thus recognising that building customer trust and convenience for customers are essential to succeed. 'Top management support,' 'IT infrastructure,' and 'customer acceptance' were also considered as important factors. On the other hand, most SMTEs do not recognise the importance of 'sharing knowledge and information between SMTEs' and 'business partnerships' as e-commerce successful strategies.

Importance and Performance of SMTEs' e-Commerce

The study used Importance and Performance (IP) analysis to examine e-commerce strategies. For 'Importance' respondents indicated the importance of each of the 16 proposed factors for a successful implementation of e-commerce by SMTEs. For 'Performance,' respondents indicated how well their member economy performs regarding e-commerce, in relation to their response to 'Importance.' Four IP categories emerge from this analysis. The 'Keep up the good work' category means that both 'Importance' and 'Performance' are high. The category 'concentrated efforts' refers to 'high importance' and 'low performance' responses. The 'low priority' category refers to 'low importance' and 'low performance' responses. The 'Possible overkill' includes 'high performance' with low importance".

Keep up the Good Work

Respondents considered the following factors as important; 'Security of e-commerce,' 'User-friendly Web interface,' 'IT (Information Technology) infrastructure,' 'Level of trust between customer and company,' 'Customer acceptance.' All factors are strongly related to consumer issues such as security and user convenience. These factors were also considered as relatively well-performed.

Concentrated Efforts

The factors in this category include 'Top management support' and 'Skilled human resources'. These factors are considered as very important for implementing e-commerce but are considered as performed insufficiently. Thus, more efforts need to focus on these factors.

Low Priority

'Government support,' 'Sharing knowledge and information between SMTEs,' 'Integration with the existing corporation,' and 'Relationship with other business partners.' received low marks in importance and performance. These factors, however, are actually critical to successful e-commerce of SMTEs. This implies that managers have limited information and knowledge on e-commerce. More information should be delivered to entrepreneurs about the importance of those factors.

Possible Overkill

'Market situation' falls in the 'Possible overkill' category. According to the survey results, managers of SMTEs utilise the Internet for market analysis (may include competitor analysis) but do not consider this factor as important. Researchers believe that this result has some discrepancy with previous reports that SMEs

(Small and Medium-Sized Enterprises) usually do not use the Internet for market research.

Remainder

Three factors including 'Specific tourism products or services for e-commerce,' 'Corporation knowledge, culture, and acceptance,' and 'Internal communication' fall somewhere between 'Low Priority' and 'Possible overkill.' One factor, 'Cost of establishing and maintaining e-commerce system' is between the 'Concentrated efforts' and 'Keep up the good work' categories. These factors were assessed relatively similarly as 'low importance' and 'middle performance.'

E-Commerce Strategies for Innovation of the SMTEs

For Rayport and Jaworski (2002), e-commerce strategy should be implemented with the four critical forces: technology, capital, media, and public policy infrastructures. An infrastructure is defined as the foundation of a system. E-commerce strategies refer to these four infrastructures:

- The technology infrastructure means the technological foundation of the Internet, which enables the running of e-commerce enterprises, including the hardware of computers, servers, routers, cables, network technologies, software, and communications. Understanding technology infrastructure – and thus understanding what is and is not achievable – is essential to formulating travel and tourism's vision and strategy.
- The capital infrastructure relates to how to secure funding for an e-business and subsequently value that business.
- The media infrastructure is an important issue for all e-commerce managers because the Internet is a mass communication platform. Managers who run on line enterprises must learn to manage a staff responsible for design interface, stylistic choices, and editorial policies, and content choices associated with the new communication venue. Therefore, the e-commerce manager is now a publisher of digital content on the Web. He/she should make choices about the types of media

employed (*e.g.* print, audio, video), the nature of the media, and editorial policy, including style, content, and look-and-feel.

- Finally, all of the decisions related to technology, capital, media, and strategy are influenced by laws and regulation, that is, public policy decisions. The public policy infrastructure affects not only the specific business but also direct and indirect competitors. E-commerce managers should understand both the current laws and how the laws may affect their businesses and those around them. This paper suggests different strategies according to the e-commerce infrastructure of the business and stage of e-business development:
- Internet start-up SMTEs should adopt a business model appropriate for their own e-business objectives and environments. External service providers have great potential for them. Marketing should be done selectively. Earning a good reputation in the local market should be the top-priority. Internet start-up SMTEs can develop a strategy to access international markets directly to sell their tourism products and services.
- Established SMTEs should focus on two key strategies: 1) expanding the range of services and products and 2) upgrading their quality. They should redesign their Web sites to focus more on 'customer retention' than 'customer acquisition' to ensure quality of service. The Internet is a useful tool to reach international markets. E-partnerships between SMTEs or large firms are important. They should utilise their resource to build an e-community.

Their e-business strategies should be formulated according to their business environments. Linkage to a site of destination management organization (DMO) is critical to success. Development of an online booking system is the most important technological aspect. Various measures to overcome lack of trust and confidence of consumers should be taken, such as utilization of 'about us,' 'frequently asked questions (FAQs),' and 'call center' services.

Established SMTEs should consider e-strategy issues, including; 1) target market segments, 2) building trust and confidence of e-consumers, and 3) expanding e-commerce activities.

Implications for Tourism Policy

The role of government is very important. The key principle is that the private sector leads the market. The government should avoid creating undue obstacles to e-commerce and its aims should be to support and enforce a predictable, minimal, consistent and simple legal environment if governmental involvement is needed. Active government support to foster an entrepreneurial culture is important. Key policy agendas include; 1) improving the legal and regulatory framework, 2) moving government procurement on line, and 3) facilitating e-transformation in industry sectors.

Legal and regulatory issues should consider consumer protection, legal resource mechanisms in disputes (*e.g.* e-commerce mediation committee), intellectual property protection, and validity and enforcement of contracts. The policies cover issues such as what taxes should apply to Internet transactions, the identification and residence of users, and the problem of tax avoidance. The guidelines of international organisations such as APEC and OECD can be a basis for e-commerce laws and regulations. To support consumer trust and confidence, a programme of e-trust certification could be effective. Online government procurement and government participation in e-transformation of industry sectors should be planned and implemented in the medium-and long-term. Government support can be provided in tax reductions, monetary support, and sharing of knowledge and information between industries and research organisations.

In Korea, a pilot project aims to construct a B2B network in all key industries. The government has also implemented a 'System to Certify Venture Tourism Business,' which indirectly supports the industry. In 2001, 11 companies were selected as venture tourism businesses and can receive support and benefits. Applications for the status of venture tourism are evaluated twice a year. Most domestic software companies in Korea do not have distribution channels of their own.

Therefore, they pay a commission of almost 40% to distributors of their products. This is a major disadvantage in the competitive market. To solve this problem the government established a software cybermall. The Internet shopping mall, which opened in 1998, provides product demonstrations and the ability to purchase products electronically. The mall is linked to the sites of many vendors.

Finally, government could help the growth of e-commerce in various ways through, planning, creating the legal and regulatory framework, building capacity in information technology infrastructure, skill formation and manpower planning, and also undertaking promotional and incentive measures. The government should function as a facilitator, promoter, educator, and 'anchor tenant' for testing and pilot deployment of new applications. It is expected that OECD member countries facilitate international strategic alliances at government-to-government (G2G) and industry-to-industry (I2I) levels and help local firms to grow, regionalise and also globalise. Government can also help create markets in emerging areas at the initial stage and help remove regulatory obstacles that may impede the growth of markets and businesses. Again, the ultimate objective of the government remains the promotion of private sector initiatives in e-commerce development (Kahn, 2002).

Conclusions: Recommendations for e-Tourism Innovations

In conclusion, this paper suggests some recommendations for decision makers, entrepreneurs and practitioners in the tourism industry field, particularly for SMTEs. These recommendations are made to the Korean e-tourism market, however, they can probably apply to the tourism industries in other countries.

The government should develop a national vision, a strategic plan and policy guidelines for SMTEs e-commerce activities. The development of e-commerce strategies should involve all tourism stakeholders. The policy makers are also responsible for establishing the appropriate laws, regulations and service standards that will enable to build trust and consumer confidence.

Entrepreneurs need to adopt business models which are tailor-made for their own e-business objectives and the SMTEs environment. SMTEs can combine various e-business models. External service providers have great potential to assist SMTEs.

Stakeholders should also find ways to integrate SMTEs into industry-wide associations. This will encourage SMTEs to stop competing at the destination level, and to develop networks for mutual benefit. In line with this co-operation, they need to formulate and implement networking or strategic alliances through partnerships with other SMTEs or large firms, especially in the area of brand management, customer relationship management, and human resources management.

As regards marketing, association with e-shopping will allow SMTEs to conduct Internet-based e-commerce without bearing all the start-up costs, improvements cost, advertising and technical difficulties, which could be shared by all the merchants in the mall instead. Associations of e-shopping will provide SMTEs with the opportunity to take advantage of e-commerce systems *e.g.* interactivity, mass customisation, real time and a database of customers.

In the established stage, SMTEs may need to redesign their website to focus more on 'customer retention' than 'customer acquisition'. They should also try to develop and manage their own digital brand. Brand power is more important on line than off line because the main stage of e-business is the virtual world where consumers are more dependent on recognised brands.

Finally, both the policy makers and the entrepreneurs should work together to raise awareness of e-commerce through training and education for stakeholders, employees and consumers. E-commerce cannot be implemented without empowering and enabling tourism stakeholders to take advantage of new Internet and e-commerce technologies.

Bibliography

Bolshevism, Germy: *Coping with Tourists: European Reactions to Mass Tourism*, Oxford, Berghahn Books, 1995.

Carl H. : *Internet Distribution of European Travel and Tourism Services*, Research Centre of Bornholm, Denmark, 1999.

Carter, John: *Chandler's Travels: A Tour of the Life of Harry Chandler*, London, Quiller Press, 1985.

Clark, Mona: *Interpersonal Skills for Hospitality Managers*, London, Chapman Hill, 1995.

Cukier, J. : *Tourism Employment in Bali: Trends and Implications*, London: Thompson, 1996.

Donald E. : *Public Personnel Management: Contexts and Strategies*, Upper Saddle River, NJ: Prentice Hall, 1998.

Eberts, Marjorie: *Careers in Travel, Tourism, and Hospitality*, Lincolnwood, VGM Career Horizons, 1997.

Fesenmaier D., Klein, S. : *Information & Communication Technologies in Tourism*, Springer-Verlag, Wien-New York, 2000.

Harrison, Lyndon: *Tourism Means Jobs*, Chester, Lyndon Harrison, 1996.

Judi Radice: *Restaurant & Food Graphics*, Glen Cove, PBC International, 1994.

Kotler, Philip: *Marketing for Hospitality and Tourism*: New Jersey, Prentice-Hall, 1998.

Larkham, P J: *Building a New Heritage: Tourism, Culture & Identity in the New Europe*, London, Routledge,1994.

Lucas, Rosemary E.: *Managing Employee Relations in the Hotel and Catering Industry*, London, Cassell, 1995.

Margaret Wade: *Medieval Travellers: The Rich and Restless*, London, Hamish Hamilton, 1982.

McNicol, B.J. : *Views of Residents, Developers and Government Planners About Tourists and Tourism Resort Developments in Canmore, Alberta,* The University of Galgary, Alberta, 1996.

Medlik, S: *Management of Tourism,* The, London, Heinemann, 1975.

Murphy, P.E. : *Tourism: A Community Approach,* London: Methuen, 1985.

Peter J.: *College & University Foodservice Management Standards,* Westport, AVI Pub. Company, 1985.

Peters, M: *International Tourism,* London, Hutchinson, 1969.

Richards, G. : *Culture, Crafts and Tourism: A Vital Relationship,* Tilburg: Atlas, 1999.

Robert C.: *Cases in Hospitality Marketing and Management,* New York, John Wiley, 1997.

Rocco, M.: *An Introduction to Hospitality Today,* Orlando, Educational Institute, 1998.

Rosenzweig, J. E.: *Organisation and Management,* New York, McGraw Hill International, 1963.

Sabharwal Rajiv : *Tourism and Hospitality Management in Liberalised Era,* Pacific, Delhi, 2011.

Scottish Tourist Board: *Visitor Attractions: A Development Guide,* Edinburgh, Scottish Tourist Board, 1991.

Sharma Sunil : *Planning and Development of Tourism and Hospitality,* Rajat Pub, Delhi, 2007.

Shrivastava Atul : *Modern Hospitality and Tourism Management,* Centrum Press, Delhi, 2010.

Slinn, Judy A: *Tourism: Management of Facilities,* London, Pitman: M & E, 1993.

Stear, L. : *Design of a Curriculum for Destination Studies,* Annals of Tourism Research, 1981.

Thomas, F.: *Introduction to Management in the Hospitality Industry,* New York, Wiley, 1995.

Timothy R.: *Cases in Hospitality Management: A Critical Incident Approach,* New York, Wiley, 1995.

Index

A

Agritourism Industry, 178.
Antarctic Tourism, 98, 101, 109, 122, 127, 130.

B

Business Environment, 232.

C

Cash Management, 206, 217, 218, 219, 221, 222, 227, 228.
Co-Operation in Tourism, 229.
Cultural and Eco-tourism, 33.
Cultural Impacts, 101, 107.
Cultural Management, 112.
Cultural Tourism, 124, 125, 157, 162, 164.

D

Development Strategies, 156, 166, 167, 178.

E

E-business, 231, 239, 240, 244, 248, 249, 251, 252.
E-commerce, 230, 235, 244, 245, 246, 247, 248, 249, 250, 251, 252.
E-tourism, 243, 251.
Eco-tourism, 16, 17, 18, 19, 20, 21, 23, 25, 26, 27, 28, 29, 32, 33, 34, 35, 36, 37, 38, 39, 87, 92, 93, 97, 100, 119, 131, 136, 140, 144.
Economic Benefits, 6, 16, 17, 23, 104, 105, 109, 115, 126, 147, 152.
Economic Factors, 141.
Economic Impacts, 17, 18, 24, 50, 51, 58, 64, 103.

F

Financial Management, 17, 203, 204, 218, 228, 232.
Foreign Exchange Management, 207, 228.
Forest Management, 21, 22, 25.

G

Geotourism, 136.
Global Warming, 10, 31, 139, 140, 141, 145.
Governments, 6, 10, 11, 12, 14, 16, 20, 32, 94, 104, 114, 125, 126, 129, 140, 155, 167, 168, 245.
Green Tourism, 92, 97.

H

Human Resource, 88, 90, 98, 180, 187, 188, 196, 199, 200.

I

Industry Education, 179.
Internet Web Sites, 70.

Interorganisational Collaboration, 241.

M

Management Resources, 111.
Management Systems, 95.
Management Techniques, 109, 111, 112, 114, 116, 117, 118, 120, 121, 122, 129, 130.
Marketing Orientation, 176.
Mass Market, 125.
Ministry of Tourism, 43, 86, 91, 172, 181, 182, 184, 186, 188, 189, 202.

N

Natural Resources, 6, 10, 11, 12, 14, 16, 19, 20, 23, 32, 38, 91, 104, 107, 124, 176.
Nature Tourism, 8, 104, 118, 134, 159.

O

Ownership, 37, 43, 49, 52, 54, 55, 56, 59, 60, 61, 62, 63, 67, 75, 76, 82, 178, 189.

P

Political Exposure, 210, 216.
Poverty Aliviation, 86.
Project Management, 185.
Projects, 16, 32, 38, 46, 47, 51, 57, 90, 106, 136, 144, 145, 146, 153, 160, 185.
Property, 48, 49, 50, 52, 53, 56, 57, 59, 60, 61, 68, 72, 77, 80, 81, 141, 226, 237, 250.

S

Social Impacts, 106, 160.
Socio-economic, 41, 42, 43, 63, 80, 135, 156, 159.

T

Target Market, 169, 250.
Tourism & Environment, 36.
Tourism Development, 6, 7, 8, 9, 10, 11, 15, 16, 18, 19, 20, 21, 23, 24, 25, 26, 86, 89, 90, 124, 125, 129, 148, 153, 156, 158, 162, 172, 174, 175, 176, 177, 181, 186, 188, 193, 241, 244.
Tourism Organisations, 225, 230, 239, 241, 242.
Tourism Policy, 154, 155, 165.
Tourism Projects, 46, 90, 153, 160.
Tourism Research, 21, 179.
Tourism Sector, 2, 4, 5, 16, 43, 46, 85, 86, 87, 88, 89, 96, 136, 141, 147, 151, 158, 168, 170, 187, 229, 230, 243.
Tourist Services, 18, 21, 24, 170, 173.
Travel and Tourism, 13, 87, 140, 141, 143, 144, 179, 187, 188, 203, 204, 205, 207, 208, 210, 213, 214, 216, 217, 218, 219, 221, 222, 225, 227, 228.

□□□